The International Covenant on Civil and Political Rights
and its (First) Optional Protocol

Johann Bair

The International Covenant on Civil and Political Rights and its (First) Optional Protocol

A Short Commentary Based on Views, General Comments and Concluding Observations by the Human Rights Committee

PETER LANG
Frankfurt am Main · Berlin · Bern · Bruxelles · New York · Oxford · Wien

Bibliographic Information published by Die Deutsche Bibliothek
Die Deutsche Bibliothek lists this publication in the Deutsche Nationalbibliografie; detailed bibliographic data is available in the internet at <http://dnb.ddb.de>.

ISBN 978-3-631-54219-4
US-ISBN 978-0-8204-7754-1

Printed in Germany 1 2 3 4 5 7

www.peterlang.de

Table of Contents

INTERNATIONAL COVENANT ON CIVIL AND POLITICAL RIGHTS..... 1
PREAMBLE 1
PART I 1
ARTICLE 1 1
Article 1 (1) 2
Article 1 (2) 3
Article 1 (3) 3
PART II 4
Article 2 4
Article 2 (1) 4
Article 2 (2) 6
Article 2 (3) 6
Article 2 (3) a 7
Article 2 (3) b 8
Article 2 (3) c 8
Article 3 8
Article 4 9
Article 4 (1) 10
Article 4 (2) 11
Article 4 (3) 16
Article 5 16
Article 5 (1) 17
Article 5 (2) 17
PART III 18
Article 6 18
Article 6 (1) 19
Article 6 (2) 21
Article 6 (3) 23
Article 6 (4) 23
Article 6 (5) 24
Article 6 (6) 24
Article 7 24
Article 8 31
Article 9 33
Article 9 (1) 34
Article 9 (2) 37
Article 9 (3) 38
Article 9 (4) 41

Article 9 (5) 42
Article 10 42
Article 10 (1) 43
Article 10 (2) a 46
Article 10 (2) b 47
Article 10 (3) 47
Article 11 48
Article 12 48
Article 12 (1) 49
Article 12 (2) 50
Article 12 (3) 50
Article 12 (4) 52
Article 13 53
Article 14 55
Article 14 (1) 56
Article 14 (2) 61
Article 14 (3) 62
Article 14 (3) a 62
Article 14 (3) b 63
Article 14 (3) c 64
Article 14 (3) d 66
Article 14 (3) e 69
Article 14 (3) f 71
Article 14 (3) g 71
Article 14 (4) 72
Article 14 (5) 73
Article 14 (6) 74
Article 14 (7) 75
Article 15 75
Article 15 (1) 76
Article 15 (2) 77
Article 16 78
Article 17 78
Article 17 (1) 79
Article 17 (2) 83
Article 18 83
Article 18 (1) 85
Article 18 (2) 86
Article 18 (3) 87
Article 18 (4) 88

Article 19 89
Article 19 (1) 89
Article 19 (2) 90
Article 19 (3) 91
Article 19 (3) a 92
Article 19 (3) b 93
Article 20 95
Article 20 (1) 96
Article 20 (2) 96
Article 21 96
Article 22 97
Article 22 (1) 98
Article 22 (2) 98
Article 22 (3) 99
Article 23 99
Article 23 (1) 100
Article 23 (2) 102
Article 23 (3) 103
Article 23 (4) 103
Article 24 104
Article 24 (1) 106
Article 24 (2) 107
Article 24 (3) 108
Article 25 108
Article 25 (a) 109
Article 25 (b) 111
Article 25 (c) 114
Article 26 115
Article 27 124
PART IV (Article 28 – 45) 128
Article 40 131
PART V (Article 46 – 47) 135
PART VI (Article 48 – 53) 136
OPTIONAL PROTOCOL TO THE ICCPR 139
Preamble 139
Article 1 140
Article 2 147
Article 3 148
Article 4 149
Article 4 (1) 149

Article 4 (2) ... 149
Article 5 ... 150
Article 5 (1) ... 151
Article 5 (2) a ... 151
Article 5 (2) b ... 154
Article 6 - 14 ... 156
RULES OF PROCEDURE OF THE HUMAN RIGHTS COMMITTEE .. 159
PART I. GENERAL RULES (Rule 1 – 65) ... 159
Rule 51 ... 166
PART II. THE FUNCTIONS OF THE COMMITTEE (Rule 66 – 98) ... 169
Rule 86 ... 176
Rule 88 ... 177
Rule 93 ... 179
Rule 94 ... 179
Rule 96 ... 180
Appendix: CASES QUOTED IN THE COMMENTARY ... 183
Index: CASES ... 201
Index ... 209

Introduction

The Human Rights Committee has, in its many years of its existence, developed an extensive jurisprudence made up of Concluding Observations prepared in response to State Reports, General Comments on the interpretation of the International Covenant on Civil and Political Rights (ICCPR) and Views expressed in individual cases submitted under the (First) Optional Protocol. The Views concern individuals in concrete situations. State Parties to the Covenant that become a party to the (First) Optional Protocol recognize the competence of the Committee to receive and consider communications from individuals. The Human Rights Committee deals with the communications and delivers the most specific interpretation of the Covenant whereby it applies the ICCPR to the individual cases, which are brought to it under Article 1 of the (First) Optional Protocol. General Comments and Concluding Observations supplement this jurisprudence. Article 40 (4) of the Covenant authorizes the Committee to transmit general comments, as it may be deemed appropriate to the States Parties. On the basis of this authorization, the Committee has issued more than thirty comments. In a number of the Comments, the Human Rights Committee has expressed its opinion on the meaning of specific Covenant rights. The third element of the jurisprudence of the Human Rights Committee is to be found in the Concluding Observations. They are the result of the compulsory monitoring system under the ICCPR. State Parties have to, according to Article 40 (1) of the Covenant, submit reports on the measures they have adopted in order to give effect to the rights recognized in the Covenant. The Human Rights Committee studies these reports and publishes concluding observations, after a public dialog between the Committee and the State Party, in which indications to the interpretation of ICCPR rights can be found.

This book unites all elements of the jurisprudence of the Human Rights Committee. The views, which concern individuals in concrete situations, form the core of the book. The ICCPR as a human rights treaty confers rights on individuals. The latter are the bearers of the rights and the ones who, with their complaints to the Human Rights Committee, give the Committee the possibility of clarifying the meaning of these rights. As a consequence of this work by the Human Rights Committee, the ICCPR truly becomes part of the "International Bill of Human Rights".

This short commentary is based on the practice of the Human Rights Committee. Articles where such a practice exists are followed by an interpretation that is based on this practice. With this arrangement and the strict orientation on the practice of the Human Rights Committee, those on whom the ICCPR confers rights can see the obligations that States have taken which have ratified the ICCPR. Their information is the most important weapon in the struggle for human rights.

Two fundamental works have to be mentioned in this context. Manfred Nowak's *CCPR Commentary* (1993) and *The International Covenant on Civil and Political Rights* (2000) by Sarah Joseph, Jenny Schultz and Melissa Castan. The extensive information in these books supplements - at least, I hope - this new commentary.

Innsbruck, March 2005 Johann Bair

International Covenant on Civil and Political Rights

G. A. res. 2200 A (XXI), 21 U. N. GAOR Supp. (No. 16) at 52, U. N. Doc. A/6316 (1966), 999 U. N. T. S. 171, entered into force March 23, 1976.

PREAMBLE

The States Parties to the present Covenant,
Considering that, in accordance with the principles proclaimed in the Charter of the United Nations, recognition of the inherent dignity and of the equal and inalienable rights of all members of the human family is the foundation of freedom, justice and peace in the world,
Recognizing that these rights derive from the inherent dignity of the human person,
Recognizing that, in accordance with the Universal Declaration of Human Rights, the ideal of free human beings enjoying civil and political freedom and freedom from fear and want can only be achieved if conditions are created whereby everyone may enjoy his civil and political rights, as well as his economic, social and cultural rights,
Considering the obligation of States under the Charter of the United Nations to promote universal respect for, and observance of, human rights and freedoms,
Realizing that the individual, having duties to other individuals and to the community to which he belongs, is under a responsibility to strive for the promotion and observance of the rights recognized in the present Covenant,
Agree upon the following articles:

According to Article 31 (2) of the Vienna Convention on the Law of Treaties, 1155 U. N. T. S. 331, entered into force on January 27, 1980, the context for the purpose of the interpretation of a treaty comprises, in addition to the text and the annexes, its preamble.

PART I

ARTICLE 1

1. All peoples have the right of self-determination. By virtue of that right they freely determine their political status and freely pursue their economic, social and cultural development.
2. All peoples may, for their own ends, freely dispose of their natural wealth and

resources without prejudice to any obligations arising out of international economic co-operation, based upon the principle of mutual benefit, and international law. In no case may a people be deprived of its own means of subsistence.
3. The States Parties to the present Covenant, including those having responsibility for the administration of Non-Self-Governing and Trust Territories, shall promote the realization of the right of self-determination, and shall respect that right, in conformity with the provisions of the Charter of the United Nations.

In accordance with the purposes and principles of the Charter of the United Nations, Article 1 enshrines an inalienable right of all peoples. General Comment No.: 12. The extinguishing of inherent aboriginal rights is incompatible with it. Concluding Comments on Canada (1999) UN doc. CCPR/C/79/Add. 105.

Article 1 (1)

All peoples have the right of self-determination. By virtue of that right they freely determine their political status and freely pursue their economic, social and cultural development.

The right of *self-determination* is of particular importance because its realization is an essential condition for the effective guarantee and observance of individual human rights and for the promotion and strengthening of those rights. E. P. et al. v. Colombia (318/88). It applies to all peoples and not merely to colonized peoples. Concluding Comments on Azerbaijan (1994) UN doc. CCPR/C/79/Add. 38. The question of whether a community is a *people* is not an issue for the Committee to address under the Optional Protocol to the Covenant. The Optional Protocol provides a recourse procedure for individuals claiming that their rights have been violated. Article 1 deals with rights conferred upon peoples as such. Lubicon Lake Band v. Canada (167/84). Kitok v. Sweden (197/85). An *individual* cannot claim to be the victim of a violation of the right of self-determination enshrined in Article 1. Wilson v. Australia (1239/04). Marshall v. Canada (205/86). Also, a group of individuals cannot claim to be the victim of such a violation. What a group of individuals can claim is that they are commonly affected by a violation of a right guaranteed in part III of the Covenant. Mahuika et al. v. New Zealand (547/93). Diergaardt et al. v. Namibia (760/96).
However, although the Committee does not have the competence under the Optional Protocol to consider a communication alleging a violation of the right

to self-determination protected in Article 1, A. B. et al. v. Italy (413/90), R. L. et al. v. Canada (358/89), it interprets Article 1 where this is relevant in determining whether rights protected by the Covenant have been violated. Gillot et al. v. France (932/00). Without expressing a view on the definition of the concept of peoples as referred to in this Article, the Committee thus considered it not unreasonable to limit participation in local referendums to persons concerned by the future of the territory they are living in, who have proven sufficiently strong ties to that territory. Gillot et al. v. France (932/00).

Article 1 (2)

All peoples may, for their own ends, freely dispose of their natural wealth and resources without prejudice to any obligations arising out of international economic cooperation, based upon the principle of mutual benefits, and international law. In no case may a people be deprived of its own means of subsistence.

This provision affirms a particular aspect of the economic content of the right of self-determination. It entails corresponding duties for all States and the international community. General Comment No.: 12. Article 1 (2) cannot be, on its own, the subject of a complaint by an individual. Hom v. The Philippines (1169/03).

Article 1 (3)

The States Parties to the present Covenant, including those having responsibility for the administration of Non-Self-Governing and Trust Territories, shall promote the realization of the right of self-determination, and shall respect that right, in conformity with the provisions of the Charter of the United Nations.

Article 1 (3) imposes, according to the Committee, specific obligations on State Parties, not only in relation to their own peoples but vis-à-vis all peoples, who have not been able to exercise or have been deprived of the possibility of exercising their right to self-determination. The obligations exist irrespective of whether a people entitled to self-determination depend on a State Party to the Covenant or not. All State Parties to the Covenant have to take positive action to facilitate a realization of, and respect for, the right of peoples to self-determination. Such positive action must, however, be consistent with the States' obligations under the Charter of the United Nations and under international law in particular. General Comment No.: 12.

PART II

ARTICLE 2

1. Each State Party to the present Covenant undertakes to respect and to ensure to all individuals within its territory and subject to its jurisdiction the rights recognized in the present Covenant, without distinction of any kind, such as race, colour, sex, language, religion, political or other opinion, national or social origin, property, birth or other status.
2. Where not already provided for by existing legislative or other measures, each State Party to the present Covenant undertakes to take the necessary steps, in accordance with its constitutional processes and with the provisions of the present Covenant, to adopt such legislative or other measures as may be necessary to give effect to the rights recognized in the present Covenant.
3. Each State Party to the present Covenant undertakes:
(a) To ensure that any person whose rights or freedoms as herein recognized are violated shall have an effective remedy, notwithstanding that the violation has been committed by persons acting in an official capacity;
(b) To ensure that any person claiming such a remedy shall have his right thereto determined by competent judicial, administrative or legislative authorities, or by any other competent authority provided for by the legal system of the State, and to develop the possibilities of judicial remedy;
(c) To ensure that the competent authorities shall enforce such remedies when granted.

Article 2 leaves it to the State Parties to choose their method of implementation in their territories within the framework set out in that Article. The obligation under the Covenant is not only confined to the respect of human rights. States have rather to ensure that all individuals under their jurisdiction enjoy these rights. General Comment No.: 3.
The provisions of Article 2, which lay down general obligations for State Parties, cannot in isolation give rise to a claim in a communication under the Optional Protocol. Rogerson v. Australia (802/98). R. L. M. v. France (363/89). G. B. v. France (348/89). S. G. v. France (347/88). S. E. v. Argentina (275/88). Individuals under the Optional Protocol cannot invoke allegations of a violation of this Article, without reference to other specific Articles of the Covenant. A. M. v. Finland (398/90). C. E. A. v. Finland (316/88).

Article 2 (1)

Each State Party to the present Covenant undertakes to respect and to ensure to all individuals within its territory and subject to its jurisdiction the rights recognized in the present Covenant, without distinction of any kind, such as race, colour, sex, language, religion, political or other opinion, national or social origin, property, birth or other status.

In general, the rights set forth in the Covenant apply to everyone, without distinction of any kind. The State Parties have to carry out all their legal commitments, whether under domestic law or under agreements with other states, in a manner consistent with this principle. T. v. Australia (706/96). The enjoyment of rights and freedoms on an equal footing, however, does not mean identical treatment in every instance. The Committee refers to examples that can be found in the Covenant: Article 6 (5), which prohibits the death sentence from being imposed on persons below 18 years of age. The same paragraph also prohibits that sentence from being carried out on pregnant women; Article 10 (3), which requires the segregation of juvenile offenders from adults, and Article 25, which guarantees certain political rights, differentiating on grounds of citizenship. General Comment No.: 18. Then there is Article 13, which applies only to aliens. General Comment No.: 15.

Article 2 (1) ensures to all individuals within a State Party's *territory* the rights recognized in the Covenant. Kindler v Canada (470/91). Ng v. Canada (469/91). Acosta v. Uruguay (110/81). Estrella v. Uruguay (74/80). It does not imply that the State Parties cannot be held accountable for violations of rights under the Covenant, which its agents commit upon the territory of another State, whether with the acquiescence of the Government of that State or in opposition to it. Casariego v. Uruguay (56/79). Burgos v. Uruguay (52/79). The Committee also does not interpret this provision as limiting the obligations of a State Party to citizens within its own territory. Nunez v. Uruguay (108/81). Martins v. Uruguay (57/79). In the case of citizens resident abroad, the Covenant imposes obligations on both the State of residence and the State of nationality. Montero v. Uruguay (106/81). The State of nationality has to issue passports to citizens resident abroad. The Committee sees a passport as a means of enabling an individual to leave any country, including his own. It derives from the very nature of that right, in the case of citizens resident abroad, that the Covenant imposes obligations not only on the State of residence but also on the State under whose *jurisdiction* the issuing of passports lies. Lichtensztejn v. Uruguay (77/80).

Article 2 (1) obliges the State Parties to ensure that all individuals within its territory and subject to its jurisdiction are free from *discrimination*. Consequently, the courts of the State Parties are under an obligation to protect individuals against discrimination, whether this occurs within the public sphere

or among private parties in the quasi-public sector of, for example, employment. Nahlik v. Austria (608/95).
The term *sex* in Article 2 (1) also includes sexual orientation. Toonen v. Australia (488/92).

Article 2 (2)

Where not already provided for by existing legislative or other measures, each State Party to the present Covenant undertakes to take the necessary steps, in accordance with its constitutional processes and with the provisions of the present Covenant, to adopt such legislative or other measures as may be necessary to give effect to the rights recognized in the present Covenant.

The method of application of the Covenant varies among different legal systems. The State Parties have to adopt the necessary legislative or other measures to give effect to the rights recognized in the Covenant. State Parties that have accepted the legal obligation to make the provisions of the Covenant effective also have the obligation to adopt appropriate measures to give legal effect to the *Views* of the Committee as to the interpretation and application of the Covenant in particular cases arising under the Optional Protocol. This includes the Committee's Views under Rule 86 of the Rules of Procedure on the desirability of *interim measures* of protection, to avoid irreparable damage to the victim of the alleged violation. Roberts v. Barbados (504/92). Bradshaw v. Barbados (489/92). The determination of the question whether and when an Article of the Covenant has acquired direct effect in the domestic law of a State Party is a matter of domestic law and does not come within the competence of the Committee. A. P. L. - v. d. M. v. The Netherlands (478/91). Araujo-Jongen v. The Netherlands (418/90).

Article 2 (3)

Each State Party to the present Covenant undertakes:
(a) To ensure that any person whose rights or freedoms as herein recognized are violated shall have an effective remedy, notwithstanding that the violation has been committed by persons acting in an official capacity;
(b) To ensure that any person claiming such a remedy shall have his right thereto determined by competent judicial, administrative or legislative authorities, or by any other competent authority provided for by the legal system of the State, and to develop the possibilities of judicial remedy;
(c) To ensure that the competent authorities shall enforce such remedies when granted.

Article 2 (3), requires that State Parties make reparation to individuals whose Covenant rights have been violated. Without reparation, the obligation to provide an effective remedy, which is central to the efficacy of the Article, is not discharged. General Comment No.: 31.
Article 2 (3) is not mentioned in the list of non-derogable provisions in Article 4 (2), but it constitutes, according to the Committee, a treaty obligation inherent in the Covenant as a whole. Even if a State Party, during a state of emergency, and to the extent that such measures are strictly required by the exigencies of the situation, introduces adjustments to the practical functioning of its procedures governing judicial or other remedies, it must comply with the fundamental obligation, under Article 2 (3), of providing an effective remedy. General Comment No.: 29.

Article 2 (3) a

Each State Party to the present Covenant undertakes:
To ensure that any person whose rights or freedoms as herein recognized are violated shall have an effective remedy, notwithstanding that the violation has been committed by persons acting in an official capacity;

A literal reading of this provision seems to require that an actual breach of one of the guarantees of the Covenant be formally established as a necessary prerequisite to obtaining remedies. Such a reading is, according to the Committee, in contradiction to Article 2 (3) b, which obliges State Parties to ensure the determination of the right to remedy by a competent judicial, administrative or legislative authority, a guarantee that would be void if it were not available in the event of a violation which had not yet been established. Kazantzis v. Cyprus (972/01). Article 2 (3) a constitutes a general undertaking by States. Individuals cannot invoke it in isolation. M. G. B. et al. v. Trinidad and Tobago (268/87). Therefore, the right to a remedy arises only after a violation of a right that can be considered by the Committee is invoked. S. E. v Argentina (275/88).
A State Party to the Covenant has to provide remedies for any violation of the provisions of the Covenant. Article 2 (3) a ensures that any person whose rights or freedoms are violated has an *effective* remedy. Weiss v. Austria (1086/02). Vargas-Machuca v. Peru (906/00). Chambala v. Zambia (856/99). Kelly v. Jamaica (537/93). Remedies have to be available and effective in relation to claims of violations of Covenant rights. Kennedy v. Trinidad and Tobago (845/99). Magana ex-Philibert v. Zaire (90/81). Effective remedies are disciplinary, administrative or criminal proceedings against a perpetrator. Croes v. The Netherlands (164/84). Purely disciplinary and administrative remedies do

not constitute adequate and effective remedies within the scope of this provision in the event of particularly serious violations of human rights, notably in the event of an alleged violation of the right to life. Bautista de Arellana v. Colombia (563/93). Vicente et al. v. Colombia (612/95). But it has to be noted that this Article does not provide for a right to see another person criminally prosecuted. S. E. v. Argentina (275/88). H. C. M. A. v. The Netherlands (213/86). Article 2 (3) a is violated if there is no competent court to which a person can appeal during his arbitrary detention. Massiotti et al. v. (25/78). The deportation of a person before he can exercise his right to appeal against the rejection of his application for a stay of deportation is in contradiction to Article 2 (3) a. Judge v. Canada (829/98).

Article 2 (3) b

Each State Party to the present Covenant undertakes:
To ensure that any person claiming such a remedy shall have his right thereto determined by competent judicial, administrative or legislative authorities, or by any other competent authority provided for by the legal system of the State, and to develop the possibilities of judicial remedy;

Article 2 (3) b obliges State Parties to ensure the determination of the right to remedy by a competent judicial, administrative or legislative authority. It provides protection to alleged victims if their claims are sufficiently well-founded to be arguable under the Covenant. A State Party is not required, on the basis of Article 2 (3) b, to make procedures available no matter how unmeritorious claims may be. Kazantzis v. Cyprus (972/01).

Article 2 (3) c

Each State Party to the present Covenant undertakes:
To ensure that the competent authorities shall enforce such remedies when granted.

Decisions by the authorities of a State in a person's favour have to be enforced by them. Gedumbe v. Democratic Republic of the Congo (641/95).

ARTICLE 3

The States Parties to the present Covenant undertake to ensure the equal right of men and women to the enjoyment of all civil and political rights set forth in the present Covenant.

Article 3 cannot in isolation give rise to a claim in a communication under the Optional Protocol. It primarily deals with the prevention of discrimination. General Comment No.: 4. Article 3 implies that all human beings should enjoy the rights provided for in the Covenant on an equal basis and in their totality. The full effect of this provision is impaired whenever any person is denied the full and equal enjoyment of any right. General Comment No.: 28. Whenever restrictions are placed on a right guaranteed by the Covenant, this has to be done without discrimination on the ground of sex. Whether the restriction in itself would be in breach of that right regarded in isolation is, according to the Committee, not decisive in this respect. It is the enjoyment of the rights, which must be secured without discrimination. Therefore, legislation, which only subjects foreign spouses of a State Party's women to restrictions, but not foreign spouses of a State Party's men, is discriminatory with respect to the women. Aumeeruddy-Cziffra et al. v. Mauritius (35/78). In addition, the fact that a woman is not entitled to sue, because, according to the law, when a woman is married, only the husband is entitled to represent matrimonial property before a Court, constitutes a discrimination on the ground of sex. Avellanal v. Peru (202/86).

Equality before the law and equal protection of the law without any discrimination constitutes a basic and general principle relating to the protection of human rights. The Committee recognizes that this principle sometimes requires a State Party to take *affirmative action* in order to diminish or eliminate conditions, which cause or help to perpetuate discrimination prohibited by the Covenant. Such action may involve granting certain preferential treatment in specific matters for a period of time to the part of the population concerned as compared with the rest of the population. As long as such action is needed to correct discrimination in fact, it is a case of legitimate differentiation under the Covenant. Differentiation of treatment does not constitute discrimination, if the criteria for such differentiation are reasonable and objective and if the aim is to achieve a purpose which is legitimate under the Covenant. General Comment No.: 18.

ARTICLE 4

1. In time of public emergency which threatens the life of the nation and the existence of which is officially proclaimed, the States Parties to the present Covenant may take measures derogating from their obligations under the present Covenant to the extent strictly required by the exigencies of the situation, provided that such measures are not inconsistent with their other obligations under international law and do not involve discrimination solely on the ground of race, colour, sex, language, religion or social origin.

2. No derogation from articles 6, 7, 8 (paragraphs 1 and 2), 11, 15, 16 and 18 may be made under this provision.
3. Any State Party to the present Covenant availing itself of the right of derogation shall immediately inform the other States Parties to the present Covenant, through the intermediary of the Secretary-General of the United Nations, of the provisions from which it has derogated and of the reasons by which it was actuated. A further communication shall be made, through the same intermediary, on the date on which it terminates such derogation.

On the one hand, Article 4 allows for a State Party to derogate unilaterally, and on a temporal basis, from a part of its obligations under the Covenant. On the other hand, Article 4 subjects both this very measure of derogation, as well as its material consequences, to a specific regime of safeguards. The restoration of a state of normalcy where full respect for the Covenant can once again be secured is, for the Committee, the predominant objective of a State Party derogating from the Covenant. Measures derogating from the provisions of the Covenant must therefore be of an exceptional and temporary nature. General Comment No.: 29.

Article 4 (1)

In time of public emergency which threatens the life of the nation and the existence of which is officially proclaimed, the States Parties to the present Covenant may take measures derogating from their obligations under the present Covenant to the extent strictly required by the exigencies of the situation, provided that such measures are not inconsistent with their other obligations under international law and do not involve discrimination solely on the ground of race, colour, sex, language, religion or social origin.

Before a State can move to invoke Article 4, two fundamental conditions must be met: the situation must amount to a *public emergency* which *threatens the life of the nation*, and the State Party must have *officially proclaimed* a state of emergency. General Comment No.: 5. The latter requirement is, according to the Committee, essential for the maintenance of the principles of legality and rule of law at times when they are most needed. Although the substantive right to take derogatory measures does not depend on a formal notification being made pursuant to Article 4 (3) of the Covenant, a State Party concerned is duty bound, when it invokes Article 4 (1) of the Covenant in proceedings under the Optional Protocol, to give a sufficiently detailed account of the relevant facts to show that a situation of the kind described in Article 4 (1) of the Covenant exists or has existed in the country concerned. Montejo v. Colombia (64/79). Borda v.

Colombia (46/79). Zapala v. Uruguay (44/79). Lanza et al. v. Uruguay (8/77). Ramirez v. Uruguay (4/77). A Presidential Decree that merely refers to specific circumstances without, however, specifying the nature and extent of derogations from the rights provided for in domestic legislation and in the Covenant, and without demonstrating that these derogations are strictly required, and how long they are to last, violates this provision. Busyo et al. v. Democratic Republic of the Congo (933/00). Courts must have the power to examine the legality of the declaration of emergency and of the different measures taken during the state of emergency. Concluding Comments on Sri Lanka (1995) UN doc. CCPR/C/79/Add. 56. Legal provisions governing the introduction and administration of a state of emergency have to be clear. Concluding Comments on Nepal (1994) UN doc. CCPR/C/79/Add. 42.
When proclaiming a state of emergency with consequences that entail derogation from any provision of the Covenant, States must, according to the Committee, act within their constitutional and other provisions of law that govern such proclamation and the exercise of emergency powers. Not every disturbance or catastrophe qualifies as a public emergency that threatens the life of the nation. Measures are limited to the extent strictly required by the *exigencies of the situation*. This condition requires that State Parties provide careful justification not only for their decision to proclaim a state of emergency, but also for any specific measures based on such a proclamation. By merely invoking the existence of a state of siege, a State Party cannot evade the obligations which it has undertaken by ratifying the Covenant. Silva et al. v. Uruguay (34/78).
Article 4 of the Covenant cannot be read as justification for derogation from the Covenant if such derogation entails a breach of the State's other *international obligations*, whether based on treaty or general international law. General Comment No.: 4. A measure of derogation may also not involve *discrimination*. General Comment No.: 18.

Article 4 (2)

No derogation from articles 6, 7, 8 (paragraphs 1 and 2), 11, 15, 16 and 18 may be made under this provision.

The fact that some of the provisions of the Covenant are listed in Article 4 (2) as not being subject to derogation does not, according to the Committee, mean that other Articles in the Covenant may be subjected to derogations at will, when a threat to the life of the nation exists. The legal obligation to narrow down all derogations to those strictly required by the *exigencies of the situation* establishes, for State Parties, a duty to conduct a careful analysis under each

Article of the Covenant based on an objective assessment of the actual situation. Article 4 (2) explicitly prescribes that *no derogation* from the following Articles may be made: Article 6 (right to life), Article 7 (prohibition of torture or cruel, inhuman or degrading punishment, or of medical or scientific experimentation without consent), Article 8 (1) and (2) (prohibition of slavery, slave trade and servitude), Article 11 (prohibition of imprisonment because of inability to fulfil a contractual obligation), Article 15 (the principle of legality in the field of criminal law; the requirement of both criminal liability and punishment being limited to clear and precise provisions in the law that were in place and applicable at the time the act or omission took place, except in cases where a later law imposes a lighter penalty), Article 16 (the recognition of everyone as a person before the law), and Article 18 (freedom of thought, conscience and religion). The rights enshrined in these provisions are non-derogable by the very fact that they are listed in Article 4 (2). General Comment No.: 29.
It has to be mentioned that the Committee, also in provisions that are not listed in this Article, sees *elements that cannot be made subject to lawful derogation* under Article 4. Therefore, if an action conducted under the authority of a State constitutes a basis for individual criminal responsibility for a *crime against humanity* by the persons involved in that action, Article 4 cannot be used as justification that a state of emergency exempted the State in question from its responsibility in relation to the same conduct. Hence, the codification of crimes against humanity, for jurisdictional purposes, in the Rome Statute of the International Criminal Court, U. N. Doc. 2187 U. N. T. S. 90, entered into force July 1, 2002, is of relevance in the interpretation of Article 4 of the Covenant. And, although the respect for the *inherent dignity of the human person*, prescribed in Article 10 of the Covenant, is not separately mentioned in the list of non-derogable rights, here the Committee is of the opinion that the Covenant expresses a norm of general international law not subject to derogation. Also, the prohibitions against *taking of hostages*, *abductions* or *unacknowledged detention* are not subject to derogation. The Committee justifies the absolute nature of these prohibitions, even in times of emergency, by their status as norms of general international law. The rights of persons belonging to *minorities* include, according to the Committee, elements that must be respected in all circumstances. This is reflected in the *prohibition against genocide* in international law, in the inclusion of a non-discrimination clause in Article 4 itself, as well as in the non-derogable nature of Article 18. As confirmed by the Rome Statute of the International Criminal Court, *deportation* or *forcible transfer of population* without grounds permitted under international law, in the form of forced displacement by expulsion or other coercive means from the area in which the persons concerned are lawfully present, constitutes a crime against

humanity. Therefore, the legitimate right to derogate from Article 12 of the Covenant during a state of emergency can never, according to the Committee, justify such measures. Moreover, no declaration of a state of emergency made pursuant to Article 4 (1) may be invoked as justification for a State Party to engage itself in, contrary to Article 20, *propaganda for war*, or in *advocacy of national, racial or religious hatred* that would constitute incitement to discrimination, hostility or violence. Article 2 (3) of the Covenant requires a State Party to the Covenant to provide *remedies* for any violation of the provisions of the Covenant. This clause is not mentioned in the list of non-derogable provisions, but it constitutes, according to the Committee, a treaty obligation inherent in the Covenant as a whole. Even if a State Party, during a state of emergency, and to the extent that such measures are strictly required by the exigencies of the situation, introduces adjustments to the practical functioning of its procedures governing judicial or other remedies, the State Party must comply with the fundamental obligation, under Article 2 (3) of the Covenant, to provide a remedy that is effective. The Committee is also of the opinion that it is inherent in the protection of rights explicitly recognized as non-derogable, that they must be secured by procedural guarantees, including, often, judicial guarantees. Therefore, the provisions of the Covenant relating to *procedural safeguards* may, according to the Committee, never be made subject to measures that would circumvent the protection of non-derogable rights. As Article 6 of the Covenant is non-derogable in its entirety any trial leading to the imposition of the death penalty during a state of emergency must conform to the provisions of the Covenant, including all the requirements of Articles 14 and 15. Procedural safeguards are based on the principles of legality and the rule of law. These principles are, according to the Committee, inherent in the Covenant as a whole. They require that fundamental requirements of fair trial must be respected during a state of emergency. Therefore, only a court of law may try and convict a person for a criminal offence. The *presumption of innocence* must be respected. And the right to take proceedings before a court to enable the court to decide without delay on the lawfulness of a detention must also not be diminished by a State Party's decision to derogate from the Covenant. General Comment No.: 29.

The qualification of a right as a non-derogable does not, according to the Committee, mean that no *limitations* or *restrictions* would ever be justified. The Committee sees the permissibility of restrictions or limitations independent of the issue of derogability. It refers in this context to Article 18, a provision that includes a specific clause on restrictions in its paragraph 3. States that interfere with the freedom to manifest one's religion or belief must justify their actions to the Committee by referring to the requirements specified in Article 18 (3).

Article 4

The Covenant neither prohibits reservations nor mentions any type of permitted reservations. The same is true of the (First) Optional Protocol. Therefore, the Committee is of the opinion that the State Parties have the possibility of entering reservations of varying significance to their acceptance of the obligations of the Covenant. But the absence of a prohibition on reservations does not, according to the Committee, mean that any reservation is permitted. The matter of reservations under the Covenant and the (First) Optional Protocol is governed by international law. Article 19 (3) of the Vienna Convention on the Law of Treaties, 1155 U. N. T. S. 331, entered into force on January 27, 1980, provides relevant guidance to the Committee. It stipulates that where a reservation is not prohibited by a treaty or falls within the specified permitted categories, a State may make a reservation provided it is not incompatible with the *object and purpose of the treaty*. Even though, unlike some other human rights treaties, the Covenant does not incorporate a specific reference to the object and purpose test, that test governs, according to the Committee, the matter of interpretation and acceptability of reservations. In a treaty, which articulates many civil and political rights, each of the Articles, and their interplay, secures the objectives of the Covenant. It is, according to the Committee, the object and purpose of the Covenant to create *legally binding standards for human rights* by defining certain civil and political rights and placing them in a framework of obligations which are legally binding for those States which ratify the Covenant. Therefore, reservations that offend peremptory norms are not compatible with the object and purpose of the Covenant. Although treaties that are mere exchanges of obligations between States allow them to reserve inter se application of rules of general international law, it is otherwise, according to the Committee, in human rights treaties, which are, for the *benefit of persons*, within their jurisdiction. In such treaties, and especially the Covenant, the rights enshrined belong to the people living in the territory of the State Parties. General Comment No.: 26. Accordingly, provisions in the Covenant that represent customary international law and peremptory norms may not be the subjects of reservations. A State may not reserve the right to engage in slavery, to torture, to subject persons to cruel, inhuman or degrading treatment or punishment, to arbitrarily deprive persons of their lives, to arbitrarily arrest and detain persons, to deny freedom of thought, conscience and religion, to presume a person guilty unless he proves his innocence, to execute pregnant women or children, to permit the advocacy of national, racial or religious hatred, to deny to persons of marriageable age the right to marry, or to deny to minorities the right to enjoy their own culture, profess their own religion, or use their own language. And while reservations to particular clauses of Article 14 may be, according to the Committee, acceptable, a general reservation to the right to a fair trial is it not. The Committee also does not accept a reservation that singles out a certain group of individuals for lesser procedural protection than that which is enjoyed by the rest of the population. Kennedy v. Trinidad and Tobago (845/99).

The Covenant consists for the Committee not merely of the guaranteed rights, but also out of important *supportive guarantees*. These guarantees provide the necessary framework for securing the rights in the Covenant and are thus essential to its object and purpose. Reservations designed to remove these guarantees are not acceptable for the Committee. Therefore, a State cannot make a reservation to Article 2 (3) of the Covenant, indicating that it intends to provide no remedies for human rights violations. Guarantees such as these are an integral part of the structure of the Covenant and underpin its efficacy.

The Covenant envisages, for the better attainment of its stated objectives, a *monitoring role* for the Committee. Reservations that purport to evade that essential element in the design of the Covenant, which is also directed to securing the enjoyment of the rights, are therefore also incompatible with its object and purpose.

The Committee's role under the Covenant, whether under Article 40 or under the Optional Protocols, necessarily entails the interpretation of the provisions of the Covenant and the development of a jurisprudence. Accordingly, a reservation that rejects the Committee's competence to interpret the requirements of any provisions of the Covenant is also contrary to the object and purpose of that treaty. Only the Committee determines whether a specific reservation is compatible with the object and purpose of the Covenant.

It is also for the Committee, as the treaty body to the International Covenant on Civil and Political Rights and its Optional Protocols, to interpret and determine the validity of reservations made to these treaties. The Committee distinguishes reservations from *declarations* or from *statements of policy*. Kennedy v. Trinidad and Tobago (845/99). The intention of the State is, in this context, more important than the form of the instrument. If a statement, irrespective of its name or title, purports to exclude or modify the legal effect of the treaty in its application to the State, it constitutes a reservation. C. L. D. v. France (439/90). R. L. M. v. France (363/89). G. B. v. France (348/89). S. G. v. France (347/88). H. K. v. France (222/87). T. K. v. France (220/87). Conversely, if a so-called reservation merely offers a State's understanding of a provision, but does not exclude or modify that provision in its application to that State, it is not a reservation. The normal consequence of an unacceptable reservation is not that the Covenant will not at all be in effect for the reserving party. The Committee sees such a reservation as severable, in the sense that the Covenant will be operative for the reserving party without benefit of the reservation. General Comment No.: 24.

Article 4

The International Covenant on Civil and Political Rights does not contain any provision regarding its *termination* and does not provide for *denunciation* or *withdrawal*. Consequently, the Committee considers the possibility of termination, denunciation or withdrawal in the light of applicable rules of customary international law, which are reflected in the Vienna Convention on the Law of Treaties. On this basis, the Covenant is not subject to denunciation or withdrawal unless it is established that the parties intended to admit the possibility of denunciation or withdrawal, or a right to do so is implied from the nature of the treaty. Because of the fact that the First Optional Protocol, which was contemporaneously negotiated with the Covenant and adopted, permits State Parties to denounce it while the Covenant does not contain any provision regarding its termination, the Committee concluded that the drafters did deliberately omit any reference to denunciation. In view of this and the circumstance that the Covenant does not have a temporary character typical of other treaties, and the rights enshrined in the Covenant belong to the people living in the territory of the State Party, international law does not, according to the Committee, permit a State, which has ratified or acceded or succeeded to the Covenant, to denounce it or withdraw from it. General Comment No.: 26.

Article 4 (3)

Any State Party to the present Covenant availing itself of the right of derogation shall immediately inform the other States Parties to the present Covenant, through the intermediary of the Secretary-General of the United Nations, of the provisions from which it has derogated and of the reasons by which it was actuated. A further communication shall be made, through the same intermediary, on the date on which it terminates such derogation.

In times of public emergency, the State Party has to inform the international community, Busyo et al. v. Democratic Republic of the Congo (933/00), through the United Nations Secretary-General, of the provisions it has derogated from, of the nature and extent of the derogations it has made, and of the reasons thereof. General Comment No.: 5, 29.

ARTICLE 5

1. Nothing in the present Covenant may be interpreted as implying for any State, group or person any right to engage in any activity or perform any act aimed at the destruction of any of the rights and freedoms recognized herein or at their limitation to a greater extent than is provided for in the present Covenant.

2. There shall be no restriction upon or derogation from any of the fundamental human rights recognized or existing in any State Party to the present Covenant pursuant to law, conventions, regulations or custom on the pretext that the present Covenant does not recognize such rights or that it recognizes them to a lesser extent.

Article 5 is a general undertaking by States and cannot be invoked by individuals under the Optional Protocol, without reference to other specific Articles of the Covenant. A. M. v. Finland (398/90). M. G. B. v. Trinidad and Tobago (268/87).

Article 5 (1)

Nothing in the present Covenant may be interpreted as implying for any State, group or person any right to engage in any activity or perform any act aimed at the destruction of any of the rights and freedoms recognized herein or at their limitation to a greater extent than is provided for in the present Covenant.

The Committee interprets Article 5 (1) in line with Article 2 (1), which places the obligation upon a State Party to *respect* and to *ensure* rights recognized in the Covenant "to all individuals within its territory and subject to its jurisdiction". A State Party may not perpetrate violations of the Covenant that it cannot perpetrate on its own territory on the territory of another State. Casariego v. Uruguay (56/79). Burgos v. Uruguay (52/79).

Article 5 (2)

There shall be no restriction upon or derogation from any of the fundamental human rights recognized or existing in any State Party to the present Covenant pursuant to law, conventions, regulations or custom on the pretext that the present Covenant does not recognize such rights or that it recognizes them to a lesser extent.

On the pretext that the Covenant does not recognize certain rights, or that it recognizes them to a lesser extent, none of the fundamental human rights recognized or existing in any State Party may be restricted. General Comment No.: 27.

PART III

ARTICLE 6

1. Every human being has the inherent right to life. This right shall be protected by law. No one shall be arbitrarily deprived of his life.
2. In countries which have not abolished the death penalty, sentence of death may be imposed only for the most serious crimes in accordance with the law in force at the time of the commission of the crime and not contrary to the provisions of the present Covenant and to the Convention on the Prevention and Punishment of the Crime of Genocide. This penalty can only be carried out pursuant to a final judgement rendered by a competent court.
3. When deprivation of life constitutes the crime of genocide, it is understood that nothing in this article shall authorize any State Party to the present Covenant to derogate in any way from any obligation assumed under the provisions of the Convention on the Prevention and Punishment of the Crime of Genocide.
4. Anyone sentenced to death shall have the right to seek pardon or commutation of the sentence. Amnesty, pardon or commutation of the sentence of death may be granted in all cases.
5. Sentence of death shall not be imposed for crimes committed by persons below eighteen years of age and shall not be carried out on pregnant women.
6. Nothing in this article shall be invoked to delay or to prevent the abolition of capital punishment by any State Party to the present Covenant.

Article 6 enunciates a right from which no derogation is permitted even in times of public emergency that threaten the life of the nation. General Comment No.: 6, 29. The right enshrined in this Article is, according to the Committee, the supreme right of the human being. Therefore, the deprivation of life by the authorities of a State Party is always a matter of the utmost gravity. The standard way of ensuring the protection of the right to life is to criminalize threats to it. Concluding Comments particularly criticized: lenient laws regarding infanticide committed to protect the honour of a woman, Concluding Comments on Paraguay (1995) UN doc. CCPR/C/79/Add. 48, tolerance of the practice of female genital mutilation, Concluding Comments on Gambia (2004) UN doc. CCPR/CO/75/GMB, the easy availability of firearms to the public, Concluding Comments on The United States of America (1995) UN doc. CCPR/C/79/Add. 106, the existence of paramilitary groups, Concluding Comments on Guatemala (1995) UN doc. CCPR/C/79/Add. 63. The State Parties also have to take into account the necessary economic and social measures to address problems such as homelessness, Concluding Comments on Canada (1999) UN doc. CCPR/C/79/Add. 105, family planning, Concluding Comments on Equatorial Guinea (2004) UN doc. CCPR/CO/79/GNQ, or clandestine abortions, Concluding Comments on Peru (1996) UN doc. CCPR/C/79/Add. 72, that threaten the right to life.

Article 6 (1)

Every human being has the inherent right to life. This right shall be protected by law. No one shall be arbitrarily deprived of his life.

The expression *inherent right to life* cannot, according to the Committee, properly be understood in a restrictive manner. Hence, the protection of this right requires that States adopt positive measures such as the prevention of wars, reduce infant mortality, Concluding Comments on Brazil (1996) UN doc. CCPR/C/79/Add. 66, and increase life expectancy by eliminating malnutrition and epidemics. Concluding Comments on Nepal (1994) UN doc. CCPR/C/79/Add. 42. General Comment No.: 6, 14. Article 6 (1) implies an obligation on the part of the State Parties to protect the right to life of every person within their territory and under their jurisdiction. Nuclear waste in dumpsites near a town raises serious issues, with regard to the obligation of a State Party to protect human life. E. H. P. et al. v. Canada (67/80). Designing, testing, manufacture, possession and deployment of nuclear weapons are among the greatest threats to the right to life that confront mankind today. General Comment No.: 14. But these threats do not place persons in the position to claim to be victims whose right to life is violated or under imminent prospect of violation. E. W. et al. v. The Netherlands (429/90). The Committee decided the question whether the conduct of underground nuclear tests by a State Party results in a violation of the right to life on the available information. It came to the conclusion that if it is not possible to ascertain the validity or correctness of the contention that nuclear tests will further deteriorate the geological structure of atolls on which the tests are carried out, further fissurate the limestone caps of these atolls, and thereby increase the likelihood of an accident of catastrophic proportions, because even in concerned scientific circles this contention is highly controversial, a person cannot claim to be a victim whose right to life is violated or is under a real threat of violation. Bordes et al. v. France (645/95). The mere requirement to do military service is no violation of the right to life. A. R. U. v. The Netherlands (509/92). T. W. M. B. v. The Netherlands (403/90). J. P. K. v. The Netherlands (401/90).

The requirements that the right shall be *protected by law* and that no one shall be *arbitrarily deprived* of his life mean that the law must strictly control and

limit the circumstances in which a person may be deprived of his life by the authorities of a State Party. Baboeram-Adhin et al. v. Suriname (146/83, 148/83-154/83). Concluding Comments on The United States of America (1995) UN doc. CCPR/C/79/Add. 50. Concluding Comments on Cyprus (1995) UN doc. CCPR/C/79/Add. 39. The protection against arbitrary deprivation of life, which is explicitly required by the third sentence of Article 6 (1), is of paramount importance. Every action of law enforcement authorities has to be *proportionate* to the requirements of law enforcement. The authorization to use lethal force without lawful reasons violates Article 6 (1). Chongwe v. Zambia (821/98). Law enforcement has to be justified by *necessity*. Own defence or that of others, or to effect the arrest or prevent the escape of persons can justify the violation of the right to life. Law enforcement action without warning to the victims and without giving them any opportunity to surrender or to offer any explanation of their presence or intentions that leads to the loss of lives violates the right to life. Inasmuch as such an action is made justifiable as a matter of state law by the legislation of a State Party, the law of this State Party does not adequately protect the right to life. Guerrero v. Colombia (45/79). Before resorting to the use of deadly force, all measures to arrest a person suspected of being in the process of committing *acts of terror* must be exhausted. "Targeted killings" (killings of those identified by the State Party as suspected terrorists) may not be used as a deterrent or punishment. Concluding Comments on Israel (2003) UN doc. CCPR/CO/78/ISR. A State Party has failed in taking effective measures to protect the right to life if a person is killed after the need for force no longer exists or his death is the unfortunate result of confusion on the side of the law enforcement authorities. Burrell v. Jamaica (546/93).
In circumstances that may involve a violation of the right to life, State Parties have to establish facilities and procedures to *investigate thoroughly*, by an appropriate *impartial body*, cases. Laureano v. Peru (540/93). Mojica v. Dominican Republic (449/91). Miango Muiyo v. Zaire (194/85). Rafael v. Colombia (181/84). Rubio v. Colombia (161/83). Purely disciplinary and administrative remedies do not constitute adequate and effective remedies in the event of an alleged violation of the right to life. Vicente et al. v. Colombia (612/95). Arellana v. Colombia (563/93). The right to life is ensured by the investigation of killings, by bringing to justice any persons found to be responsible for the death of other persons, by paying compensation to the surviving families. Baboeram et al. v. Suriname (146, 148-154/83). A State Party that does not take the necessary measures against the persons responsible for murder does not guarantee the right to life. Coronel et al. v. Colombia (778/97). Threats and harassment by agents of a State Party, which lead to an attempt on the life of a person, violate, in the absence of any investigation by the

State Party who is responsible, Article 6 (1). Vaca v. Colombia (859/99). The responsibility of State agents for the disappearance and subsequent death of a person makes a State Party directly responsible for the disappearance and subsequent murder. Vicente et al. v. Colombia (612/95).

A person who is in *custody* has to be protected by the authorities by appropriate measures. Barbato v. Uruguay (84/81). A State Party takes on the responsibility to care for their life by arresting and detaining individuals. Barbato et al. v. Uruguay (84/81). It has to organize its detention facilities in such a way that it knows about the state of health of the detainees. Lack of financial means cannot reduce this responsibility. Lantsov v. Russian Federation (763/97).

The *mandatory imposition of the death penalty* constitutes arbitrary deprivation of life in circumstances where the death penalty is imposed without regard to a defendant's personal circumstances or the circumstances of the particular offence. Carpo et al. v. The Philippines (1077/02).

A State Party also acts arbitrarily if it deports a person to a State in which he is under sentence of death, before he can exercise all his rights to challenge that *deportation.* Judge v. Canada (829/98). In this context, Article 6 (1) must be read together with Article 6 (2), which does not prohibit the imposition of the death penalty for the most serious crimes. A State Party that intends to deport a person to a State that retains capital punishment, violates the provision if the person is exposed to a real risk of a violation of Article 6 (2). Therefore, the State Parties must be mindful of the possibilities for the protection of life when exercising their discretion in the application of extradition treaties. The Committee expects that a State, which has abandoned capital punishment, gives serious consideration to its own chosen policy in making its decision. A State that does this is not necessarily required to refuse to extradite or to seek assurances that capital punishment will not be imposed. Only if a decision to extradite without assurances is taken arbitrarily or summarily are the obligations under Article 6 violated. Cox v. Canada (539/93). Kindler v. Canada (470/91). Ng v. Canada (469/91).

Article 6 (2)

In countries which have not abolished the death penalty, sentence of death may be imposed only for the most serious crimes in accordance with the law in force at the time of the commission of the crime and not contrary to the provisions of the present Covenant and to the Convention on the Prevention and Punishment of the Crime of Genocide. This penalty can only be carried out pursuant to a final judgement rendered by a competent court.

It follows from Article 6 (2) that State Parties are not obliged to abolish the death penalty totally. But it has to be quite an *exceptional measure*. Article 6 (2) requires that capital punishment be imposed only for the most serious crimes, in circumstances not contrary to the Covenant and other instruments, and that it be carried out pursuant to a final judgment rendered by a competent court. A. R. J. v. Australia (692/96). Cox v. Canada (539/93). Kindler v. Canada (470/91). Ng v. Canada (469/91). A mandatory imposition of a death sentence under circumstances that do not fall into the category *most serious crimes* violates Article 6 (2). Lubuto v. Zambia (390/90). The State Parties are obliged to limit the use of the death penalty and to abolish it for other than the most serious crimes. The expression "most serious crimes" must be read restrictively. General Comment No.: 6. The use of firearms that does not produce the death or wounding of any person does not belong to this category of crimes. Lubuto v. Zambia (390/90). Political or economic offences cannot be characterized as "most serious crimes." Concluding Comments on Libyan Arab Jamahiriya (1998) UN doc. CCPR/C/79/Add. 101. Also not included are acts of apostasy, committing a third homosexual act, illicit sex, embezzlement by officials, and theft by force, Concluding Comments on Sudan (1997) UN doc. CCPR/C/79/Add. 85, evasion of military service several times or non-violent infringements, Concluding Comments on Iraq (1997) UN doc. CCPR/C/79/Add. 84, trafficking in toxic or dangerous wastes, Concluding Comments on Cameroon (1994) UN doc. CCPR/C/79/Add. 33, corruption and adultery, Concluding Comments on Islamic Republic of Iran (1993) UN doc. CCPR/C/79/Add. 25, or robbery, Concluding Comments on Republic of Korea (1992) UN doc. CCPR/C/79/Add. 6. A premeditated murder constitutes a very serious crime. Kindler v. Canada (470/91).

The provision that a sentence of death may be imposed only *in accordance with the law* and *not contrary to the provisions of the Covenant* implies that the procedural guarantees therein prescribed must be observed, including the right to a fair hearing by an independent tribunal and the presumption of innocence. Levy v. Jamaica (719/96). The imposition of a sentence of death upon conclusion of a trial in which the provisions of the Covenant have not been respected constitutes a violation of the right to life. Kurbanov v. Tajikistan (1096/02). Both the substantive and the procedural law in the application of which a death penalty is imposed may not be contrary to the provisions of the Covenant. Consequently, the failure of a State Party to respect requirements of the ICCPR leads to the conclusion that a death sentences pronounced against a person contrary to the provisions of the Covenant violates Article 6 (2). Brown v. Jamaica (775/97), Daley v. Jamaica (750/97), McLeod v. Jamaica (734/97), Marshall v. Jamaica (730/96), Taylor Patrick v. Jamaica (707/96), Taylor

Desmond v. Jamaica (705/96), Shaw v. Jamaica (704/96), McLawrence v. Jamaica (702/96), Yasseen et al. v. Guyana (676/96), Morrison McCordie v. Jamaica (663/95), Johnson v. Jamaica (588/94), Price v Jamaica (572/94), Kelly v. Jamaica (537/93), Richards v. Jamaica (535/93), Steadman v. Jamaica (528/93), Phillip v. Trinidad and Tobago (594/92), Peart et al. v. Jamaica (464/91, 482/91), Graham et al. v. Jamaica (461/91), Wright Osborne et al. v. Jamaica (459/91), Champagnie et al. v. Jamaica (445/91), Currie v. Jamaica (377/89), Collins. v. Jamaica (356/89), Grant v. Jamaica (353/88), Wright Clifton v. Jamaica (349/89), Simmonds v. Jamaica (338/88), Hamilton v. Jamaica (333/88), Berry v. Jamaica (330/88), Francis v. Jamaica (320/88), Campbell v. Jamaica (307/88), Little v. Jamaica (283/88), Smith v. Jamaica (282/88), Kelly v. Jamaica (253/87), Reid v. Jamaica (250/87), Campbell v. Jamaica (248/87), Pinto v. Trinidad and Tobago (232/87), Henry v. Jamaica (230/87), Mbenge v. Zaire (16/77) - **Article 14**. Legal assistance has to be available at all stages of criminal proceedings in capital cases. Hendricks v. Guyana (838/98). The State Parties have to provide for a right of appeal. Mansaraj et al. v. Sierra Leone (839/98 - 841/98). The carrying out of an execution when the execution of the sentence is still under challenge constitutes a violation of Article 6 (2). Ashby v. Trinidad and Tobago (580/94).

Article 6 (3)

When deprivation of life constitutes the crime of genocide, it is understood that nothing in this article shall authorize any State Party to the present Covenant to derogate in any way from any obligation assumed under the provisions of the Convention on the Prevention and Punishment of the Crime of Genocide.

Article 6 (4)

Anyone sentenced to death shall have the right to seek pardon or commutation of the sentence. Amnesty, pardon or commutation of the sentence of death may be granted in all cases.

In addition to the procedural guarantees, anyone who is *sentenced to death* has the particular right to seek *pardon* or *commutation* of the sentence. General Comment No.: 6. The wording of the provision does not prescribe a particular procedure for the modalities of the exercise of the prerogative of mercy. Accordingly, State Parties retain discretion for spelling out the modalities of the exercise of the rights. These discretionary measures by the executive can be subject to a wide range of considerations. Thompson v. Saint Vincent and the Grenadines (806/98). But it is not allowed for the State Parties to determine the modalities in a way that effectively negates the rights enshrined in this Article. Kennedy v. Trinidad and Tobago (845/99).

Article 6 (5)

Sentence of death shall not be imposed for crimes committed by persons below eighteen years of age and shall not be carried out on pregnant women.

It is incumbent on the State Parties to make enquiries if any doubt is raised as to whether an accused in a capital case is a minor or not. Perkins v. Jamaica (733/97). State Parties also have to protect those who are mentally retarded from the death penalty. Concluding Comments on The United States of America (1995) UN doc. CCPR/C/79/Add. 50.

Article 6 (6)

Nothing in this article shall be invoked to delay or to prevent the abolition of capital punishment by any State Party to the present Covenant.

This provision refers generally to the abolition of the death penalty. All measures of abolition are considered as progress in regard to the enjoyment of the right to life. General Comment No.: 6.

ARTICLE 7

No one shall be subjected to torture or to cruel, inhuman or degrading treatment or punishment. In particular, no one shall be subjected without his free consent to medical or scientific experimentation.

Even in situations of public emergency such as those referred to in Article 4, no derogation from the provisions of Article 7 is allowed and its provisions must remain in force. General Comment No.: 7. The aim of the provisions is to protect both the dignity and the physical and mental integrity of an individual. It is the duty of the State Parties to afford everyone protection through legislative and other measures as may be necessary against the acts prohibited by this Article, whether inflicted by people acting in their official capacity, outside their official capacity, or in a private capacity. Concluding Comments on Yemen (2002) UN doc. CCPR/CO/75/YEM - domestic violence. The competent authorities must investigate allegations of a violation of Article 7. The Committee considers such allegations as extremely serious. They require prompt investigations. Blanco v. Nicaragua (328/88). Motta v. Uruguay (11/77). Amnesties are generally incompatible with the duty of the State Parties to investigate allegations of a violation. General Comment No.: 20. Investigations have to be conducted in a manner that ensures their independence and credibility. Concluding Comments on Lithuania (2004) UN doc. CCPR/CO/80/LTU. Concluding Comments on Hong Kong, United Kingdom of Great Britain and Northern Ireland (1996) UN doc. CCPR/C/79/Add. 69. Where members of a State's security forces are accused, witnesses have to be afforded protection against reprisals, intimidation, threats and harassment. Concluding Comments on Brazil (1996) UN doc. CCPR/C/79/Add. 66. An order from a superior officer or public authority cannot excuse a violation of Article 7. Economic or budgetary considerations can make compliance with the obligations of Article 7 difficult, but also do not constitute or invoke a justification or extenuating circumstance that excuses a violation of Article 7. Mukong v. Cameroon (458/91). Adequate sanctions against persons who are found to have violated this Article have to be imposed. Concluding Comments on Italy (1998) UN doc. CCPR/C/79/Add. 94. Persons alleged to have committed serious violations have to be suspended from official duties during the investigation of allegations and, if found guilty, dismissed from public service in addition to any other punishment. Concluding Comments on Serbia and Montenegro (2004) UN doc. CCPR/CO/81/SEMO.

The assessment of what constitutes *torture or cruel inhuman or degrading treatment* falling within the meaning of the Article depends on all the circumstances of the case, such as the duration and manner of the treatment, its physical or mental effects as well as the sex, age and state of health of the victim. Article 7 is violated if persons, including small children, are in the course of the search of a house, terrified and verbally abused. García v. Colombia (687/96). *Prolonged judicial proceedings* do not, per se, constitute cruel, inhuman and degrading treatment, even if they are a source of mental strain and tension for detained persons. Griffiths v. Jamaica (274/88). Reid v. Jamaica (250/87). This also applies to appeal and review proceedings in cases involving capital punishment. The Committee makes, in such cases, an assessment of the particular circumstances of each case. Pratt et al. v. Jamaica (210/86, 225/87). Martin v. Jamaica (317/88). Kindler v. Canada (470/91).

An element of delay between the lawful imposition of a sentence of death and the exhaustion of available remedies is, according to the Committee, in judicial systems that provide for a review of criminal convictions and sentences inherent in the review of a sentence. The Committee does not want to make such an element of delay a factor that turns detention on death row into a violation of the Covenant. By doing so, the Committee avoids to convey to the State Parties retaining the death penalty the message that they should carry out a capital sentence as expeditiously as possible after it is imposed. For the Committee, life on death row, harsh as it may be, is preferable to death. Johnson v. Jamaica (588/94). Hence, the Committee does not consider as cruel, inhuman or degrading treatment, prolonged periods of detention under a severe custodial regime on death row, in the absence of some further compelling circumstances, Daley v. Jamaica (750/97), Taylor Desmond v. Jamaica (705/96), Simpson v. Jamaica (695/96), Wanza v. Trinidad and Tobago (683/96), Teesdale v. Trinidad and Tobago (677/96), Smart v. Trinidad and Tobago (672/95), McIntosh v. Jamaica (640/95), Walker v. Jamaica (639/95), Amore v. Jamaica (634/95), Campbell v. Jamaica (618/95), Thomas v. Jamaica (614/95), Leehong v. Jamaica (613/95), Morrison v. Jamaica (611/95), Henry v. Jamaica (610/95), Adams v. Jamaica (607/94), Hylton v. Jamaica (600/94), Spence v. Jamaica (599/94), Grant v. Jamaica (597/94), Chaplin v. Jamaica (596/94), Bennett v. Jamaica (590/94), Reynolds v. Jamaica (587/94), Jones v. Jamaica (585/94), Bickaroo v. Trinidad and Tobago (555/93), Richards v. Jamaica (535/93), Thomas v. Jamaica (532/93), Lewis v. Jamaica (527/93), Graham et al. v. Jamaica (461/91), if the convicted person is merely availing himself or herself of appellate remedies. Simms v. Jamaica (541/93). The circumstance that a person has to spend **seven years** on death row does not, per se, violate the Covenant, in the absence of further compelling circumstances. Gonzales v. Trinidad and Tobago (673/95). Stephens v. Jamaica (373/89). A delay of **ten years** between judgements is disturbingly long. Barrett et al. v. Jamaica (270, 271/88). Over **11 years** on death row is a matter of serious concern. Forbes v. Jamaica (649/95). Johnson v. Jamaica (588/94). LaVende v. Trinidad and Tobago (554/93)- **18 years**.

It is incompatible with Article 7 that a State Party does not explain the reasons for a person's stay in the death cell. Pennant v. Jamaica (647/95) – **two weeks**. Where the State Parties duly follow the applicable procedures, a delay between the issuing of a warrant for an execution and its stay, during which time a person is detained in a special cell, does not constitute a violation of Article 7. Martin v. Jamaica (317/88) - **17 days**. But a delay of close to **20 hours** from the time a stay of execution is granted, to the time a person is notified and removed from his death cell, constitutes cruel and inhuman treatment within the meaning of Article 7. Pratt et al. v. Jamaica (210/86, 225/87). The fact that a person is taken to the gallows after a warrant for his execution has been issued and is removed from there before the scheduled execution, does not constitute cruel, inhuman or degrading treatment, if the person is removed from the gallows immediately after the stay of execution has been granted. Thompson v. Saint Vincent and the Grenadines (806/98) - **fifteen minutes** before execution.

Whereas the imposition of the *death penalty* under certain limited circumstances is allowed, any method of execution provided for by law must be designed in such a way as to avoid conflict with Article 7. Executions must not take place in public. Concluding Comments on the Islamic Republic Iran (1993) UN doc. CCPR/C/79/Add. 25. They have to inflict on a person the least possible physical and mental suffering. Execution by gas asphyxiation does not meet this test. Therefore, it constitutes cruel and inhuman treatment. Ng v. Camada (469/91). Lethal injection is not in violation of Article 7. Kindler v. Canada (470/91). Cox v. Canada (539/93).

Mental suffering and anguish as a consequence of being sentenced to death can be exacerbated by the treatment in, as well as the conditions of, the detention. Aggravating factors that lead to long-term psychological damage constitute a violation of Article 7. Wilson v. The Philippines (868/99). The Committee also saw such a violation when a warrant for execution was issued and read to a person of unsound mind. R. S. v. Trinidad and Tobago (684/96). Also, continued detention of a person when the State Party was aware of the person's mental condition and failed to take the steps necessary to ameliorate the mental deterioration violated Article 7. C. v. Australia (900/99).

The *disappearance* of persons is, in absence of any cooperation with the Committee on the part of the State Party, inseparably linked to treatment that amounts to a violation of Article 7. Mojica v. Dominican Republic (449/91). Muiyo v. Zaire (194/85). *Enforced disappearance* of persons means arrest, detention or abduction of persons by, or with the authorization, support or acquiescence of, a State or a political organization, followed by a refusal to acknowledge that deprivation of freedom or to disclose information concerning the fate or whereabouts of those persons, with the intention of removing them from the protection of the law for a prolonged period of time. Any act of such disappearance constitutes a violation of the right not to be subjected to torture or to cruel, inhuman or degrading treatment or punishment. Sarma et al. v. Sri Lanka (950/00). Arellana v. Colombia (563/93). Anguish and stress caused to a mother by the disappearance of her daughter and by the continuing uncertainty concerning her fate and whereabouts amount to psychological torture, if the State Party does not take immediate and effective steps to establish what has happened to the daughter. Quinteros v. Uruguay (107/81). The failure of authorities' to notify a mother of the scheduled date for the execution of her son, and the subsequent persistent failure to notify her of the location of her son's grave amounts to *inhuman treatment.* Staselovich et al. v. Belarus (887/99). Schedko et al. v. Belarus (886/99).

Arm twisting and **putting** a pistol **in the mouth**, Casafranca v. Peru (981/01), **suffocation** in water, Ramirez v. Uruguay (4/77), **electric shocks**, Kanana v. Zaire (366/89), Rodriguez v. Uruguay (322/88), Acosta v. Uruguay (162/83), Gilboa v. Uruguay (147/83), **blows**, Kennedy v. Trinidad and Tobago (845/99),

Howell v. Jamaica (798/98), Robinson v. Jamaica (731/96), Chung v. Jamaica (591/94), Johnson Clive v. Jamaica (592/94), Pennant v. Jamaica (647/95), Johnson Colin v. Jamaica (653/95), Morrison McCordie v. Jamaica (663/95), Gallimore v. Jamaica (680/96), McTaggart v. Jamaica (749/97), Henry v. Trinidad and Tobago (752/97), Henry v. Jamaica (610/95), Johnson v. Jamaica (592/94), Reynolds v. Jamaica (587/94), Bailey v. Jamaica (334/88), Thomas v. Jamaica (321/88), Collins v. Jamaica (240/87), **slaps, kicks**, Kurbanov v. Tajikistan (1096/02), **squeezing fingers** with pieces of wood placed between them, Muteba v. Zaire (124/82), **breaking** of the jaw, Burgos v. Uruguay (52/79), **rubbing** salt water into the nasal passages of a person, and letting him spend the night handcuffed to a table and a chair, without being given as much as a glass of water, García v. Ecuador (319/88), **blindfolding and dunking** a person in a canal, Vicente et al. v. Colombia (612/95), constitute, since they fail to respect a persons inherent and individual *human dignity*, torture or cruel and inhuman treatment within the grounds of the Article. The use of handcuffing, hooding, shaking or sleep deprivation, either alone or in combination, as *interrogation techniques* constitute a violation of Article 7 in any circumstances. Concluding Comments on Israel (1998) UN doc. CCPR/C/79/Add. 93. *Female genital mutilation* is contrary to human dignity and violates the right to protection against cruel, inhuman and degrading treatment. Concluding Comments on Lesotho (1999) UN doc. CCPR/C/79/Add. 106.

The use of harsh punitive measures, including frequent resort to solitary confinement, the lack of fair and open procedures for deciding on disciplinary measures against prisoners accused of breaking the rules, the inadequate protection for prisoners who complain of reprisals by prison warders, the lack of a credible system for investigating complaints by prisoners, and the frequent use of protective measures, such as leather handcuffs raised serious questions of compliance with Article 7. Concluding Comments on Japan (1998) UN doc. CCPR/C/79/Add. 102.

Certain minimum standards regarding the *conditions of detention* must be observed regardless of a State Party's level of development. These include minimum floor space and cubic content of air for each prisoner, adequate sanitary facilities, clothing, which shall in no manner be degrading or humiliating, provision of a separate bed, and provision of food of nutritional value adequate for health and strength. These are the minimum requirements that always have to be observed, even if economic or budgetary considerations may make compliance with these obligations difficult. Mukong v. Cameroon (458/91). Detention in conditions detrimental to the health of a person constitutes a breach of Article 7. Massera v. Uruguay (5/77). Twelve or seventeen link shackles to which detainees are bound during transport to and from prison to minimize the flight risk after an assessment, as well as stripping and subjecting prisoners to cavity searches after each visit to ensure the safety and security of a prison, do not violate Article 7. Cabal et al. v. Australia (1020/01). But this Article is violated if a person is shackled and blindfolded for **five days**, Jijon et al. v. Ecuador (277/88), or more, Carballal v. Uruguay (33/78) - **5 months**. Weinberger v. Uruguay (28/78) - **10 months**. Also the soaking of a prison cell or the bedding of a prisoner with water, mock executions, Muteba v. Zaire (124/82), Young v. Jamaica (615/95), and inadequate food, Smith and Stewart v. Jamaica (668/95), violate Article 7. Food and drink are inadequate if a person is deprived of them for **four days**. Birhashwirwa et al. v. Zaire (241, 242/87). *The following are incompatible with Article 7:* Threats to a prisoner by officials, Boodoo v. Trinidad and Tobago (721/96), Hylton v. Jamaica (407/90), Rubio et al. v. Colombia (161/83), Estrella v. Uruguay (74/80), ridicule and strain in the death cell awaiting execution, Clement Francis v. Jamaica (606/94), emptying a urine bucket over a prisoner's head, throwing his food and water on the floor and his mattress out of the cell, Victor Francis v. Jamaica (320/88), denial of adequate medical care, Whyte v. Jamaica (732/97), Linton v. Jamaica (255/87), Barrett et al. v. Jamaica (270, 271/88), inadequate medical treatment for a mental condition while detained on death row, Williams v. Jamaica (609/95), displaying a prisoner to the press in a cage, Campos v. Peru (577/94), chaining a prisoner to a bed spring on the floor with minimal clothing and severe rationing of food for a period of 3 1/2 months and keeping him incommunicado in a basement cell measuring 2 m by 1 1/2 meters for a period of one month, Wight v. Madagascar (115/82), keeping a person in a cell measuring 20 by 5 meters, where approximately 125 accused persons are being held, and where, owing to a lack of space, some detainees have to sit on excrement, Portorreal v. Dominican Republic (188/84), holding a prisoner for the period of 10 years alone in a cell measuring 6 feet by 14 feet and letting him out only for three and half hours a day without providing him with recreational facilities or books, Edwards v. Jamaica (529/93), locking up a prisoner for 23 hours a day in a cell with no mattress or other bedding, adequate sanitation, ventilation or electric lighting, Sextus v. Trinidad and Tobago (818/98). Brown v. Jamaica (775/97).

A person who is unable to see her family, relatives or legal representative is kept *incommunicado*. Shaw v. Jamaica (704/96). The prevention of contact with the outside world for **8 months** or more constitutes inhuman treatment within the grounds of Article 7. Laureano v. Peru (540/93). Tshishimbi v. Zaire (542/93). Polay Campos v. Peru (577/94). Marais v. Madagascar (49/79). El-Megreisi v. Libyan Arab Jamahiriya (440/90).

For a *punishment* to be degrading, the humiliation or debasement involved must exceed a particular level and must, in any event, entail other elements beyond the mere fact of deprivation of liberty. Vuolanne v. Finland (265/87). Corporal punishment constitutes cruel, inhuman or degrading treatment or punishment contrary to Article 7. Sooklal v. Trinidad and Tobago (928/00). Higginson v. Jamaica (792/98). Osbourne v. Jamaica (759/97). Matthews v. Trinidad and Tobago (569/93). Concluding Comments on Lesotho (1999) UN doc. CCPR/C/79/Add. 106. Concluding Comments on Iraq (1997) UN doc. CCPR/C/79/Add. 84 - branding. Concluding Comments on Libyan Arab Jamahiriya (1998) UN doc. CCPR/C/79/Add. 101 - amputation and flogging.
Article 7 prohibits a State Party from exposing a person to the necessary and foreseeable consequence of treatment contrary to this provision as a result of his *deportation.* A. R. J. v. Australia (692/96). In this context, the right to be free from torture requires not only that the State Parties refrain from torture. They also have to take steps of due diligence to avoid a threat to an individual of torture from third parties. Ahani v. Canada (1051/02). The Committee deemed no cruel, inhuman or degrading treatment in the deportation of an individual in his 30s from the only country in which he grew up and, as a result, permanent separation from his family and close relatives. Canepa v. Canada (558/93). Stewart v. Canada (538/93).
Article 7 expressly prohibits *medical or scientific experimentation* without the free consent of the person concerned. Non-therapeutic research may not be conducted on minors or mentally ill patients on the basis of surrogate consent. Concluding Comments on the United States of America (1995) UN doc. CCPR/C/79/Add. 50.
A person cannot claim to be a victim of a violation of Articles 7 by mere reference to the requirement to do *military service.* A. R. U. v. The Netherlands (509/92). C. B. D. v. The Netherlands (394/90).
The *burden of proof* for the violation of Article 7 does not rest alone with the victim, but also with the State Party. The Committee grants that the victim and the State Party do not always have equal access to the evidence. In most cases even, only the State Party alone has access to the relevant information. Telitsin v. Russian Federation (888/99). It is in such a case incumbent upon the State Party to refute the allegations in detail. Bleier v. Uruguay (30/78). Mukong v. Cameroon (458/91). Vicente et al. v. Colombia (612/95). Chung v. Jamaica (591/94). A refutation of allegations in general terms is not sufficient. Vasilskis v. Uruguay (80/80). Valcada v. Uruguay (9/77).

ARTICLE 8

1. No one shall be held in slavery; slavery and the slave-trade in all their forms shall be prohibited.
2. No one shall be held in servitude.
3. (a) No one shall be required to perform forced or compulsory labour;
(b) Paragraph 3 (a) shall not be held to preclude, in countries where imprisonment with hard labour may be imposed as a punishment for a crime, the performance of hard labour in pursuance of a sentence to such punishment by a competent court;
(c) For the purpose of this paragraph the term "forced or compulsory labour" shall not include:
(i) Any work or service, not referred to in subparagraph (b), normally required of a person who is under detention in consequence of a lawful order of a court, or of a person during conditional release from such detention;
(ii) Any service of a military character and, in countries where conscientious objection is recognized, any national service required by law of conscientious objectors;
(iii) Any service exacted in cases of emergency or calamity threatening the life or well-being of the community;
(iv) Any work or service which forms part of normal civil obligations.

Article 4 (2) of the Covenant explicitly prescribes that no derogation from Article 8 (1) and (2) may be made. General Comment No.: 29. For the purposes of the Slavery Convention, 60 L.N.T.S. 253, that entered into force March 9, 1927, *slavery* is defined as a the status or condition of a person over whom any or all of the powers attaching to the right of ownership are exercised. *Slave trade* includes all acts involved in the capture, acquisition or disposal of a person with intent to reduce him to slavery; all acts involved in the acquisition of a slave with a view to selling or exchanging him; all acts of disposal by sale or exchange of a slave acquired with a view to being sold or exchanged, and, in general, every act of trade or transport in slaves. According to the Supplementary Convention on the Abolition of Slavery, the Slave Trade, and Institutions and Practices Similar to Slavery, 226 U.N.T.S. 3, entered into force April 30, 1957, *serfdom* belongs to institutions and practices that are similar to slavery. The Supplementary Convention defines serfdom as the condition or status of a tenant who is by law, custom or agreement bound to live and labour on land belonging to another person and to render some determinate service to such other person, whether for reward or not, and is not free to change his status. Other institutions and practices mentioned in the Supplementary

Convention as similar to slavery are: (i) Debt bondage, that is, the status or condition arising from a pledge by a debtor of his personal services or of those of a person under his control as security for a debt, if the value of those services as reasonably assessed is not applied towards the liquidation of the debt or the length and nature of those services are not respectively limited and defined. (ii) Any institution or practice whereby: (a) A woman, without the right to refuse, is promised or given in marriage on payment of a consideration in money or in kind to her parents, guardian, family or any other person or group. (b) The husband of a woman, his family, or his clan, has the right to transfer her to another person for value received or otherwise. (c) A woman, on the death of her husband, is liable to be inherited by another person. (iii) Any institution or practice whereby a child or young person under the age of 18 years, is delivered by either or both of his natural parents or his guardian to another person, whether for reward or not, with a view to the exploitation of the child or young person or of his labour. State Parties have the duty to take effective measures to eradicate bonded labour, Concluding Comments on India (1997) UN doc. CCPR/C/79/Add. 81, and forced prostitution. Trafficking of women and others for the purposes of prostitution is an act tantamount to slavery. Concluding Comments on Italy (1998) CCPR/C/79/Add. 94. State Parties have to severely punish under law persons who directly profit from forced labour . Concluding Comments on Brazil (1996) UN doc. CCPR/C/79/Add. 66.
The Convention concerning Forced or Compulsory Labour (ILO No. 29), 39 U.N.T.S. 55, entered into force May 1, 1932, defines the term *forced or compulsory labour* as all work or service which is exacted from any person under the menace of any penalty and for which the said person has not offered himself voluntarily. It does not include: (a) Any work or service normally required of a person who is under detention in consequence of a lawful order of a court, or of a person during conditional release from such detention. (b) The institution of compulsory military service. T. W. M. B. v. The Netherlands (403/90). J. P. K. v. The Netherlands (401/90). C. B. D. v. The Netherlands (394/90). (c) National service required by law of conscientious objectors. Jarvinen v. Finland (295/88). (d) Any service exacted in cases of emergency or calamity threatening the life or well-being of the community. (e) Any work or service which forms part of normal civil obligations. The prohibition of forced or compulsory labour does not prevent the State Parties from imposing the performance of hard labour in pursuance of a sentence to such punishment by a competent court as a punishment for a crime.

ARTICLE 9

1. Everyone has the right to liberty and security of person. No one shall be subjected to arbitrary arrest or detention. No one shall be deprived of his liberty except on such grounds and in accordance with such procedure as are established by law.
2. Anyone who is arrested shall be informed, at the time of arrest, of the reasons for his arrest and shall be promptly informed of any charges against him.
3. Anyone arrested or detained on a criminal charge shall be brought promptly before a judge or other officer authorized by law to exercise judicial power and shall be entitled to trial within a reasonable time or to release. It shall not be the general rule that persons awaiting trial shall be detained in custody, but release may be subject to guarantees to appear for trial, at any other stage of the judicial proceedings, and, should occasion arise, for execution of the judgement.
4. Anyone who is deprived of his liberty by arrest or detention shall be entitled to take proceedings before a court, in order that court may decide without delay on the lawfulness of his detention and order his release if the detention is not lawful.
5. Anyone who has been the victim of unlawful arrest or detention shall have an enforceable right to compensation.

An illegal and prohibited activity by a State Party, such as *enforced disappearance* as it is contained in Article 7 (2) i of the Rome Statute of the International Criminal Court, U. N. Doc. 2187 U. N. T. S. 90, entered into force July 1, 2002, that leads to the arrest, detention or abduction of persons by, or with the authorization, support or acquiescence of, a State or a political organization, followed by a refusal to acknowledge that deprivation of freedom or to give information on the fate or whereabouts of those persons, with the intention of removing them from the protection of the law for a prolonged period of time, constitutes, in the absence of specific and effective measures to prevent the disappearance of individuals and establish facilities and procedures to investigate thoroughly by an appropriate impartial body, cases of missing and disappeared persons in circumstances, which may involve Government officials, Rafael et al. v. Colombia (181/84), Bleier v. Uruguay (30/78), a violation of Article 9 in its entirety. Sarma et al. v. Sri Lanka (950/00). *Administrative detention* may not be objectionable in circumstances where the person concerned constitutes a clear and serious threat to society that cannot be contained in any other manner. But the guarantees enshrined in Article 9 fully apply also in such instances. Schweizer v. Uruguay (66/80). The punishment of indeterminate detention in respect of possible future offences is inconsistent with Article 9. Concluding Comments on New Zealand (1995) CCPR/C/79/Add. 47. The mere detention for questioning of an individual on return to his country of nationality in relation to his conviction by another State does not of itself amount to a necessary and foreseeable breach of Article 9. T. v. Australia (706/96).

Article 9 (1)

Everyone has the right to liberty and security of person. No one shall be subjected to arbitrary arrest or detention. No one shall be deprived of his liberty except on such grounds and in accordance with such procedure as are established by law.

Although in the Covenant the only reference to the right to security of the person is to be found in Article 9 (1), there is, according to the Committee, no evidence that narrows the concept of the right to security only to situations of formal deprivation of liberty. Paragraph 1 is applicable to all deprivations of liberty, whether in criminal cases or in other cases such as, for example, mental illness, vagrancy, drug addiction, educational purposes, immigration control, etc. General Comment No.: 8. State Parties are under an obligation to take reasonable and appropriate measures to protect the *liberty and security* of persons. Legislation and administrative measures have to be put in place to correct deficiencies. *Threats* against a person, Truong v. Canada (743/97), Tshishimbi v. Zaire (542/93), Mojica v. Dominican Republic (449/91), or *attacks* on a person create an objective need for a State Party to provide a person with protective measures to guarantee the security. Vaca v. Colombia (859/99). Dias et al. v. Angola (711/96). Bahamonde v. Equatorial Guinea (468/91). Páez v. Colombia (195/85). Bwalya v. Zambia (314/88). In cases of *domestic violence*, State Parties have to provide hostels and refuges for family members suffering from domestic violence. Concluding Comments on Poland (1999) UN doc. CCPR/C/79/Add. 110. Allegations made by a representative of a State Party, acting under immunity, on the state-owned media that put the life of a person at risk, violate the right to security. Jayawardena v. Sri Lanka (916/00). Also, a State Party that refuses to carry out independent investigations after a person is shot at and wounded by State authorities violates Article 9 (1). Chongwe v. Zambia (821/98). Leehong v. Jamaica (613/95). Administrative detention of vagrants is a matter of concern. Concluding Comments on Ukraine (1995) UN doc. CCPR/C/79/Add. 52.

The Committee does not equate the term *arbitrary* with *against the law*. It interprets it more broadly to include elements of inappropriateness, injustice and lack of predictability. Therefore, the remand in custody pursuant to lawful arrest must not only be *lawful* but *reasonable* under all the circumstances. Furthermore, remand in custody must be *necessary* under all the circumstances, for example, to prevent flight, interference with evidence or the recurrence of crime. The element of proportionality becomes relevant in this context. A. v. Australia (560/93). Mukong v. Cameroon (458/91). *Flight* from an open facility makes detention reasonable for a limited time until the administrative procedures relating to the case are completed. Jalloh v. The Netherlands (794/98). In addition, the privilege that protects a *lawyer-client relationship* intends to protect the client and not the lawyer. A client who waives the privilege frees the lawyer from his duty of confidentiality and obliges him to assist the State in mounting a case. The detention of a lawyer in such a case for not cooperating with a State Party is only arbitrary if the lawyer himself is a suspect. Van Alphen v. The Netherlands (305/88). In any case, a State Party has to show why it is necessary to detain a person. Spakmo v. Norway (631/95). In particular, it has to be demonstrated that, in the light of the particular circumstances, there were no less invasive means of achieving the same ends by, for example, the imposition of reporting obligations, sureties or other conditions. Baban et al. v. Australia (1014/01). The detention of a person for **more than a year** in order to force him to reveal the whereabouts of another person is, in the absence of any criminal charge, arbitrary and in contradiction to Article 9 (1). Mbenge et al. v. Zaire (16/77)

A *substitution of the death penalty* with life imprisonment, with a prospect of parole in the future, is not a re-sentencing tainted with arbitrariness. Reece v. Jamaica (796/98).

Every decision to keep a person in detention must be based on grounds and procedures established by law, General Comment No.: 8, and has to be open to review periodically so that the grounds justifying the detention can be assessed. A. v. New Zealand (754/97). Assessment after threatening and aggressive behaviour of a person followed by a committal order based on an opinion of three psychiatrists and continuing periodical review of the situation by a panel of psychiatrists precludes the qualification of the deprivation of the liberty as unlawful or arbitrary. A v. New Zealand (754/1997). Provisions of law under which a convicted person remains legally subject to deprivation of freedom until the expiry of the sentence, notwithstanding the remission he may have earned, do not affect the guarantees against arbitrary arrest or detention set out in Article 9. A. R. S. v. Canada (91/81). Requiring *repentance* from detainees as a condition of their release from custody raises serious questions about the compatibility with Article 9 (1). Concluding Comments in Islamic Republic of Iran (1993) UN doc. CCPR/C/79/Add. 25.

There is, according to the Committee, no basis for the claim that it is, per se, arbitrary to detain individuals requesting *asylum*. The Covenant does not recognize the right of aliens to enter or reside in the territory of a State Party. Therefore, it is a matter for the State Parties to decide whom they will admit to their territories. General Comment No.: 15. Aliens who arrive by boat, without dependents, with their identity in doubt and claiming to be from a State suffering serious internal disorder can, in the light of these factors and the fact that they can apply for release, be detained without violation of Article 9 (1). Bakhtiyari et al. v. Australia (1069/02) - **seven months**. But mandatory detention of an alien until he is removed or granted a permit to stay violates the Covenant. C. v. Australia (900/99).
The act of *abduction* into a State Party's territory by agents of the State Party constitutes an arbitrary arrest and detention. García v. Ecuador (319/88). Casariego v. Uruguay (56/79). Burgos v. Uruguay (52/79). Casariego v. Uruguay (56/79). Borda v. Colombia (46/79). The same has to be said of an arrest for holding political views. Mukong v. Cameroon (458/91). Minanga v. Zaire (366/89). Blanco v. Nicaragua (328/88). Portorreal v. Dominican Republic (188/84). Jaona v. Madagascar (132/82). Quinteros et al. v. Uruguay (107/81).
Arrest on suspicion of having committed an offence can justify detention. Borisenko v. Hungary (852/99). Campbell v. Jamaica (248/87). But detention as a "*temporary preventive measure*" for up to **10 days** on the initiative of a prosecutor is incompatible with Article 9. Concluding Comments on Ukraine (2001) UN doc. CCPR/CO/73/UKR. Preventive detention for up to **15 days** in cases of terrorism, drug trafficking and espionage raises serious issues with regard to Article 9. Concluding Comments on Peru (1996) CCPR/C/79/Add. 67. Article 9 (1) is violated if preventive detention lasts for **22 days**, whereas the law provides for a period of 15 days. Casafranca v. Peru (981/01).
In any event, detention must not continue beyond the period for which the State can provide appropriate justification. A. v. Australia (560/93). It is arbitrary to keep a prisoner in custody after a sentence of imprisonment has been fully served, a judicial order of release issued, or an amnesty decreed. Chambala v. Zambia (856/99). Jijón v. Ecuador (277/88). Mpandanjila et al. v. Zaire (138/83). Bouton v. Uruguay (37/78). Carballal v. Uruguay (33/78). Massiotti et al. v. Uruguay (25/78). Lanza et al. v. Uruguay (8/77). Bazzano v. Uruguay (5/77). Ramirez v. Uruguay (4/77).
A State Party that deprives the liberty of a person *contrary to the laws of the state* violates Article 9 (1). Bolaños v. Ecuador (238/87). The principle of legality is also violated if an individual is arrested or detained on grounds that are not clearly established in domestic legislation. McLawrence v. Jamaica v. Jamaica (702/96). An arrest following an international agreement on

cooperation in criminal matters between State Parties violates the Covenant if there is no request for arrest by a party of the agreement. Domukovsky et al. v. Georgia (623/95, 624/95, 626/95, 627/95). If there is no legal basis for an arrest, there is also none for the continuing detention. Sarma et al. v. Sri Lanka (950/00). Detention in the absence of any arrest warrants is illegal. Coronel et al. v. Colombia (778/97). Arredondo v. Peru (688/96). Vicente et al. v. Colombia (612/95). Arellana v. Colombia (563/93). Laureano v. Peru (540/93). Bahamonde v. Equatorial Guinea (468/91). Minanga v. Zaire (366/89). Conteris v. Uruguay (139/83). Magana ex-Philibert v. Zaire (90/81). A warrant that is issued more than **three days** after the arrest, in contravention of national legislation, which stipulates that a warrant must be issued within 72 hours of arrest, violates Article 9 (1). Gridin v. Russian Federation (770/97).

Article 9 (2)

Anyone who is arrested shall be informed, at the time of arrest, of the reasons for his arrest and shall be promptly informed of any charges against him.

Article 9 (2) covers the situation of persons being remanded in custody pending the result of police investigations. Kelly v. Jamaica (253/87). The first part of the Article requires that anyone "who is arrested shall be informed" sufficiently of the reasons for his arrest to enable him to take immediate steps to secure his release if he believes that the reasons given are invalid or unfounded. Campbell v. Jamaica (248/87). Caldas v. Uruguay (43/79). The authorities have to inform a person about the substance of a complaint against him. This can necessitate the suspension of police formalities until an official interpreter arrives, so that a person can be duly informed in the presence of a legal counsel about the reasons of the arrest. Hill et al. v. Spain (526/93) - **15 hours.** It is not sufficient simply to inform a person that he is arrested without any further information. Caldas v. Uruguay (43/79). If during **50 hours** of detention, a person is not informed on the reasons for his arrest, Article 9 (2) is violated even if the person is released after this time. Portorreal v. Dominican Republic (188/84). A delay of **seven days**, Kurbanov v. Tajikistan (1096/02), or more to inform a person about the reasons of the arrest violates Article 9 (2). McLawrence v. Jamaica (702/96) - **3 weeks**. Kalenga v. Zambia (326/88) - **1 month**. Kelly v. Jamaica (253/87). Birhashwirwa et al. v. Zaire (241/87, 242/87) - **more than one month**. Jaona v. Madagascar (132/82), Magana ex-Philibert v. Zaire (90/81) - **several months**. Domukovsky et al. v. Georgia (623/95, 624/95, 626/95, 627/95), Miha v. Equatorial Guinea (414/90) - **more than 1 year**.

The second part of Article 9 (2) is only applicable to persons against whom *criminal charges* are brought. General Comment No.: 8. They have to be

promptly informed about the criminal charges against them. A period of **three days** from the time of arrest until a person is formally informed about the charges against him does not amount to a violation of the right to be promptly informed of the charges against him. Pennant v. Jamaica (647/95). A delay of **9 days**, Morrison McCordie v. Jamaica (663/95), violates Article 9 (2). Taylor v. Jamaica (707/96) - **26 days**. Morrison Everton v. Jamaica (635/95) - **3 to 4 weeks**. Zapala v. Uruguay (44/79), Carballal v. Uruguay (33/78), Bazzano et al. v. Uruguay (5/77) - **several months**. Conteris v. Uruguay (139/83) - **2 years**. Budgetary constraints may cause impediments to the proper administration of justice. But they cannot justify the violation of the Covenant. Fillastre et al. v. Bolivia (336/88).
A State Party is not absolved from its obligation under Article 9 (2) to inform someone of the reasons of his arrest and of the charges against him because of the arresting officer's opinion that the arrested person is aware of them. Grant v. Jamaica (597/94). A person who surrenders himself to the police is fully aware of the reasons for which he is detained. Bennett v. Jamaica (590/94). Stephens v. Jamaica (373/89). If it is absolutely clear to a person, or he is aware of the reasons for his arrest in general terms, for example, his arrest and subsequent detention are for involvement in a certain crime, formal information about the charges and the reasons for the arrest need not be given by the authorities. Pennant v. Jamaica (647/95). Freemantle v. Jamaica (625/95). In addition, although no interpreter is present during an arrest, the circumstances of the arrest can make it wholly unreasonable to argue that a person is unaware of the reasons for his arrest. Griffin v. Spain (439/92).

Article 9 (3)

Anyone arrested or detained on a criminal charge shall be brought promptly before a judge or other officer authorized by law to exercise judicial power and shall be entitled to trial within a reasonable time or to release. It shall not be the general rule that persons awaiting trial shall be detained in custody, but release may be subject to guarantees to appear for trial, at any other stage of the judicial proceedings, and, should occasion arise, for execution of the judgement.

Article 9 (3) requires that any person arrested or detained be brought promptly before a judge or other officer authorized by law to exercise judicial power. The Committee determines the meaning of the term *promptly* in paragraph 3 of Article 9 on a case-by-case basis. Kennedy v. Trinidad and Tobago (845/99). General Comment No.: 8. It is a matter of concern for the Committee if the maximum period of detention of **48 hours** before being brought to a judge or magistrate be extended to 96 hours by a senior police officer. Concluding Comments on Zimbabwe (1998) CCPR/C/79/Add. 89. In general, delays shall not exceed **a few days**. McLawrence v. Jamaica (702/96). Stephens v. Jamaica (373/89). **Seventy-three hours** of detention without being brought before a judge do not raise any issue under Article 9 (3). Houwen v. The Netherlands (583/94). However, in the absence of an explanation for the delay **three**, Borisenko v. Hungary (852/99), or more days violate Article 9 (3). Freemantle v. Jamaica (625/95) - **4 days**. Jijón v. Ecuador (277/88) - **5 days**. Kurbanov v. Tajikistan (1096/02), McLawrence v. Jamaica (702/96), Grant v. Jamaica (597/94) - **7 days** Morrison McCordic v. Jamaica (663/95) - **9 days**. Forbes v. Jamaica (649/95) - **14 days**. Marshall v. Jamaica (730/96) - **21 days**. Casafranca v. Peru (981/01) - **22 days**. Perkins v. Jamaica (733/97), Whyte v. Jamaica (732/97), Taylor Patrick v. Jamaica (707/96) - **26 days**. Bennett v. Jamaica (590/94), Motta v. Uruguay (11/77) - **28 days**. Pennant v. Jamaica (647/95), Campbell v. Jamaica (248/87) - more than **4 weeks**. Kelly v. Jamaica (253/87) - **5 weeks**. Daley v. Jamaica (750/97) - **6 weeks**. Penarrieta et al. v. Bolivia (176/84), Carballal v. Uruguay (33/78) - more than **6 weeks**. Birhashwirwa et al. v. Zaire (241/87, 242/87) - close to **8 weeks**. Jones v. Jamaica (585/94), Berry v. Jamaica (330/88) - **10 weeks**. Leehong v. Jamaica (613/95), Pena et al. v. Venezuela (156/83), Kalenga v. Zambia (326/88), Muteba et al. v. Zaire (124/82), Magana ex-Philibert v. Zaire (90/81), Barbato et al. v. Uruguay (84/81), Bouton v. Uruguay (37/78), Touron v. Uruguay (32/78), Weinberger v. Uruguay (28/78) - **several months**. Bwalya v. Zambia (314/88), Schweizer v. Uruguay (66/80), Altesor v. Uruguay (10/77) - more than **1 year**. Wolf v. Panama (289/88) - **several years**. A delay of **one week** in a capital case is not compatible with Article 9 (3). McLawrence v. Jamaica (702/96).

It is inherent to the proper exercise of judicial power that an authority, which is independent, objective and impartial in relation to the issues dealt with, exercises it. The Committee did not regard a public prosecutor as having the institutional objectivity and impartiality necessary to be considered an officer authorized to exercise judicial power within the grounds of Article 9 (3). Zheludkova v. Ukraine (726/96). Kulomin v. Hungary (521/92). Bahamonde v. Equatorial Guinea (468/91).

Under Article 9 (3), anyone arrested or detained on a criminal charge shall be entitled to trial within a reasonable time. The Committee assesses what *reasonable time* constitutes on case-by-case basis. Koné v. Senegal (386/89). The lack of adequate budgetary appropriations for the administration of criminal justice does not justify unreasonable delays in the adjudication of criminal cases. Nor does the fact that investigations into a criminal case are, in essence, carried out by way of written proceedings justify such delays. Fillastre et al. v.

Bolivia (336/88). A delay of **5 months**, Zapala v. Uruguay (44/79), or more between the arrest and the trial, which remain unexplained by a State Party and during which a person is in detention, is unreasonable. It constitutes a violation of Article 9 (3). Izquierdo v. Uruguay (73/81) - **7 months**. Sequeira v. Uruguay (6/77), Weinberger v. Uruguay (28/78) - **10 months**. Perkins v. Jamaica (733/97), Lewis v. Jamaica (708/96), McLawrence v. Jamaica (702/96), Teesdale v. Trinidad and Tobago (677/96), Walker v. Jamaica (639/95), Muteba et al. v. Zaire (124/82), Borda et al. v. Colombia (46/79), Netto et al. v. Uruguay (8/77), Bazzano et al. v. Uruguay (5/77) - more than **1 year**. Evans v. Trinidad and Tobago (908/00), Boodoo v. Trinidad and Tobago (721/96), Taylor Patrick v. Jamaica (707/96), Taylor Desmond v. Jamaica (705/96), Shaw v. Jamaica (704/96), Finn v. Jamaica (617/95), Hamilton v. Jamaica (616/95), Henry et al. v. Jamaica (571/94), Steadman v. Jamaica (528/93), Smart v. Trinidad and Tobago (672/95), Brown et al. v. Jamaica (665/95), Neptune v. Trinidad and Tobago (523/92), Conteris v. Uruguay (139/83), Burgos v. Uruguay (52/79) - more than **2 years**. Hendricks v. Guyana (838/98), Whyte v. Jamaica (732/97) - more than **3 years**. Sahadeo v. Guyana (728/96), Shalto v. Trinidad and Tobago (447/91) more than **4 years**. Elahie v. Trinidad and Tobago (533/93), Pena et al. v. Venezuela (156/83), Antonaccio v. Uruguay (63/79) - more than **7 years**.

Article 9 (3) allows *pre-trial detention* as an exception. Cagas et al. v. The Philippines (788/97). Bolanos v. Ecuador (238/87). Pre-trial detention may be necessary, for example, to ensure the presence of the accused at the trial, avert interference with witnesses and other evidence, or the commission of other offences. W. B. E. v. The Netherlands (432/90). In this regard, there do not have to be any offences for which pre-trial detention is obligatory. Concluding Comments on Argentina (2000) CCPR/CO/70/ARG. The maximum duration of pre-trial detention may not be determined according to the applicable penalty. Concluding Comments on Spain (1996) CCPR/C/79/Add. 61. Generally *bail* has to be granted, except in situations where the likelihood exists that the accused would abscond or destroy evidence, influence witnesses or flee from the jurisdiction of the State Party. The mere fact that the accused is a foreigner does not, in itself, imply that he may be held in detention pending trial. Hill et al. v. Spain (526/93). **Three years** in detention prior to release on bail entailed a violation of Article 9 (3). Sooklal v. Trinidad and Tobago (928/00).

In cases involving serious charges such as homicide or murder, and where the accused is denied bail by the court, the accused must be tried in as expeditious a manner as possible. The period of nearly **14 months** of pre-trial detention does not constitute, in capital murder cases, a violation of Article 9 (3). McTaggart v. Jamaica (743/97). Thomas v. Jamaica (614/95). A delay of **a year and a half** is a matter of concern, but does not amount to a violation of Articles 9 (3) if the preliminary enquiry takes place during that period. Morrison Everton v. Jamaica (635/95). Substantial reasons must be presented in order to justify a **22-month or more** delay until trial. Sextus v. Trinidad and Tobago (818/98). Very exceptional reasons must be presented in order to justify delays of **more than three years**. Francis et al. v. Trinidad and Tobago (899/99).

Article 9 (4)

Anyone who is deprived of his liberty by arrest or detention shall be entitled to take proceedings before a court, in order that that court may decide without delay on the lawfulness of his detention and order his release if the detention is not lawful.

The Committee considers disciplinary punishment that leads to a degree of social isolation normally associated with arrest and detention as a *deprivation of liberty* by detention in the sense of Article 9 (4). Solitary confinement for a period of 10 days in a cell measuring 2 x 3 meters, permission to leave the cell solely for purposes of eating, going to the toilet and taking air for half an hour every day, prohibition to talk to other detainees or to make any noise in the cell, control of the correspondence and personal notes is a disciplinary punishment that exceeds the normal restrictions that military life entails. Vuolanne v. Finland (265/87).

Whenever a decision depriving a person of his liberty is taken by an administrative body or authority, Article 9 (4) obliges the State Party concerned to make the right of recourse to a court of law available to the person detained. A court, and it does not matter whether the court is civilian or military, has the *legality of the detention* to determine that a higher degree of objectivity and independence is ensured. Torres v. Finland (291/88). A court review of the lawfulness of detention may not be limited to the examination of the mere compliance of the detention with domestic law but must include the possibility to order release if the detention is incompatible with the requirements of the Covenant. Baban et al. v. Australia (1014/01). What is decisive is that such reviews are real, and not merely formal, in their effects. Bakhtiyari et al. v. Australia (1069/02). A State Party that allows that authorities do not comply with a court's release order violates Article 9 (4). Massiotti et al. v. Uruguay (25/78). Article 9 (4) is also violated if a person is unable to take proceedings before a court to determine the lawfulness of an arrest for **three days**. Hammel v. Madagascar (155/83). But it is up to a detained person to preserve the opportunity that Article 9 (4) gives to him. He has to take proceedings before a court by applying for a review. Stephens v. Jamaica (373/89).

Preventive detention (indefinite detention until release) for reasons of public security must be controlled by Article 9 (4). General Comment No.: 8. **Two and a half years** of detention, for preventive purposes, before the non-parole period arising under the sentence of preventive detention expires, violates the right under Article 9 (4) to approach a court for the determination of the lawfulness of the detention. Rameka et al. v. New Zealand (1090/02*)*. Also, "prompt security measures" that make recourse to habeas corpus unavailable violate the Covenant. Conteris v. Uruguay (139/83). Barbato v. Uruguay (084/81). Borda et al. v. Colombia (46/79). Zapala v. Uruguay (44/79). Caldas v. Uruguay (43/79). Bouton v. Uruguay (37/78). Carballal v. Uruguay (33/78). Touron v. Uruguay (32/78). Weinberger v. Uruguay (28/78). Motta v. Uruguay (11/77). Altesor v. Uruguay (10/77). Valcada v. Uruguay (9/77). Netto et al. v. Uruguay (8/77). Sequeira v. Uruguay (6/77). Bazzano et al. v. Uruguay (5/77). Ramirez v. Uruguay (4/77).

Article 9 (5)

Anyone who has been the victim of unlawful arrest or detention shall have an enforceable right to compensation.

This provision governs the granting of compensation for detention that is unlawful either under the terms of domestic law or within the meaning of the Covenant. A v. Australia (560/93). Anyone who has been the victim of unlawful arrest or detention has an enforceable right to compensation. Paraga v. Croatia (727/96). Blanco v. Nicaragua (328/88). Bolanos v. Ecuador (238/87). Article 9 (5) is violated if under a State Party's jurisdiction, a person cannot seek compensation for detention. Chambala v. Zambia (856/99). However, the fact that a detained person is subsequently acquitted does not, in and of itself, render the pre-trial detention unlawful. Uebergang v. Australia (963/01). W. B. E. v. The Netherlands (432/90).

ARTICLE 10

1. All persons deprived of their liberty shall be treated with humanity and with respect for the inherent dignity of the human person.

2. (a) Accused persons shall, save in exceptional circumstances, be segregated from convicted persons and shall be subject to separate treatment appropriate to their status as unconvicted persons;

(b) Accused juvenile persons shall be separated from adults and brought as speedily as possible for adjudication.

3. The penitentiary system shall comprise treatment of prisoners the essential aim of which shall be their reformation and social rehabilitation. Juvenile offenders shall be segregated from adults and be accorded treatment appropriate to their age and legal status.

The United Nations Standard Minimum Rules for the Treatment of Prisoners, adopted Aug. 30, 1955 by the First United Nations Congress on the Prevention of Crime and the Treatment of Offenders, U.N. Doc. A/CONF/611, annex I, E.S.C. res. 663C, 24 U.N. ESCOR Supp. (No. 1) at 11, U.N. Doc. E/3048 (1957), amended E.S.C. res. 2076, 62 U.N. ESCOR Supp. (No. 1) at 35, U.N. Doc. E/5988 (1977), constitute, for the Committee, valuable guidelines for the interpretation of this Article. Potter v. New Zealand (632/95). The Article applies to anyone deprived of liberty under the laws and authority of a State Party who is held in prisons, hospitals, detention camps, correctional institutions or in banishment. Mpandanjila et al. v. Zaire (138/83).

Article 10 (1)

All persons deprived of their liberty shall be treated with humanity and with respect for the inherent dignity of the human person.

Article 10 (1), of the Covenant provides that all persons deprived of their liberty shall be treated with *humanity* and with *respect for the inherent dignity* of the human person. Ultimate responsibility for the observance of this principle rests, according to the Committee, with the State Parties. They have to care that all institutions where persons are lawfully held against their will, not only in prisons but also in hospitals - particularly psychiatric hospitals - detention camps, correctional institutions or elsewhere, are treated with humanity. General Comment No.: 9. Conditions in places of detention have to be regulated by law. Places of detention have regularly to be visited by magistrates or other independent bodies. Concluding Comments on Sri Lanka (1995) UN doc. CCPR/C/79/Add. 56. Women prisoners have to be guarded only by female warders. Concluding Comments on Cambodia (1999) CCPR/C/79/Add. 108. The use of cage-beds as a measure of restraint in social care homes or psychiatric institutions is incompatible with Article 10 (1). Concluding Comments on Slovakia (2003) CCPR/CO/78/SVK.

Article 10 (1) is generally applicable to persons deprived of their liberty, whereas paragraph 2 deals with accused, as distinct from convicted, persons only. Article 10 (1) supplements Article 7 with regard to the treatment of all persons deprived of their liberty and imposes on State Parties a positive obligation toward persons who are particularly vulnerable. General Comment

No.: 21. Cruel and inhuman treatment within the meaning of Article 7 also entails a violation of Article 10, which requires that detained persons be treated with respect for their human dignity. Reynolds v. Jamaica (587/1994). Ortega v. Ecuador (481/1991). El-Megreisi v. Libyan Arab Jamahiriya (440/1990). M'Boissona v. Central African Republic (428/1990). Kanana v. Zaire (366/1989). Soogrim v. Trinidad and Tobago (362/1989). Bailey v. Jamaica (334/1988). Blanco v. Nicaragua (328/1988). Thomas v. Jamaica (321/1988). Francis v. Jamaica (320/1988). Linton v. Jamaica (255/87).
The humane treatment and the respect for the dignity of all persons deprived of their liberty is, for the Committee, a basic standard of universal application which does not depend entirely on material resources. The modalities and conditions of detention may vary with the available resources. General Comment No.: 9. But adequate **medical care** during detention has to be provided. Howell v. Jamaica (798/98). Whyte v. Jamaica (732/97). Taylor Desmond v. Jamaica (705/96). Simpson v. Jamaica (695/96). Teesdale v. Trinidad and Tobago (677/96). - eye glasses. Smith v. Jamaica (668/95) - loss of sight in one eye. Henry v. Jamaica (610/95). Lewis v. Jamaica (527/93) - skin condition. Magana ex-Philibert v. Zaire (90/81). Basic **sanitary facilities** to detained persons also have to be provided. Inadequate **food**, Phillip v. Jamaica (594/92), Hill et al. v. Spain (526/93), or occasional deprivation of food, Kalenga v. Zambia (326/88), Wolf v. Panama (289/88), to detained individuals, and the total absence of **recreational facilities** do not meet the requirements of this Article. Kelly v. Jamaica (253/87). Deidrick v. Jamaica (619/95). Five minutes per day for personal hygiene and five minutes for exercise in the open air, Párkányi v. Hungary (410/90), sharing a cell with mentally ill inmates, Reece v. Jamaica (796/98), having a pipe carrying waste water with foul odour close to the cell or the rations room where food is prepared, Bennett v. Jamaica (590/94), Matthews v. Trinidad and Tobago (569/93), keeping prisoners in overcrowded cells, Kennedy v. Trinidad and Tobago (845/99), Neptune v. Trinidad and Tobago (523/92) - 5 to 10 detainees in a cell measuring 6 by 9 feet, Sextus v. Trinidad and Tobago (818/98), Lantsov v, Russian Federation (763/97), Henry v. Jamaica (752/97), Blaine v. Jamaica (696/96), Shaw v. Jamaica (704/96), McTaggart v. Jamaica (749/97), or requiring them to share mattresses, Yasseen v. Republic of Guyana (676/96), are not compatible with Article 10 (1). Circumstances such as a prison infested with rats, lice, cockroaches, Campbell v. Jamaica (618/95), very hot in summer and very cold in winter, Lluberas v. Uruguay (123/82), no windows, Wanza v. Trinidad and Tobago (683/96), or only steel bars open to the cold and the wind, human faeces all over the floor, sea water for showers, urine soaked blankets and mattresses or only a piece of sponge and old newspapers to sleep on, Elahie v. Trinidad and

Tobago (533/93), violate Article 10 (1). Griffin v. Spain (493/92). Confinement in a cell for 23 hours each day, Morgan et al. v. Jamaica (720/96), Levy v. Jamaica (719/96), McLeod v. Jamaica (734/97), Polay Campos v. Peru (577/94), Forbes v. Jamaica (649/95), except for an average of 15 minutes twice everyday to empty the slops bucket, Pennant v. Jamaica (647/95), no provision of mattress or bedding for the concrete bunk, no integral sanitation, Johnson v. Jamaica (653/95), inadequate ventilation and no natural lighting are contrary to Article 10 and violate the right to be treated with humanity and with respect for the inherent dignity of the human person. Taylor v. Jamaica (707/96).

Authorities that disclose to a prisoner that the prerogative of mercy will not be exercised and his early release denied because of his human rights complaints reveal a lack of humanity. Such behaviour amounts to a treatment that fails to respect the person's dignity. Pinto v. Trinidad and Tobago (512/92).

The beating of a detained person constitutes a violation of Article 10 (1). McTaggart v. Jamaica (749/97). Marshall v. Jamaica (730/96). Gallimore v. Jamaica (680/96). Pennant v. Jamaica (647/95). Walker and Richards v. Jamaica (639/95). Chaplin v. Jamaica (596/94). Chung v. Jamaica (591/94). Jones v. Jamaica (585/94). Berry v. Jamaica (330/88) - in the face. Solorzano v. Venezuela (156/83).

A person who is unable to see her family, relatives or legal representative is kept *incommunicado*. The State Parties have to allow prisoners under necessary supervision to communicate with their family and reputable friends at regular intervals, by correspondence as well as by receiving visits. Estrella v. Uruguay (74/80). State Parties who hold detainees incommunicado for **weeks** or **months**, Caldas v. Uruguay (43/79) - **6 weeks**, Penarietta v. Bolivia (176/84), Conteris v. Uruguay (139/83) - **over 3 months**, Cubas Simones v. Uruguay (70/81), Casariego v. Uruguay (56/79) - **4 months**, Romero v. Uruguay (85/81), Machado v. Uruguay (83/81) - **more than 5 months**, Lluberas v. Uruguay (123/82) - **6 months**, Pietraroia v. Uruguay (44/79), Altesor v. Uruguay (10/77), Valentini de Bazzano v. Uruguay (5/77) - **several months**, or even as little as a period of **15 days**, Arzuaga Gilboa v. Uruguay (147/83), violate Article 10 (1).

A failure to make available a cell that is big enough to hold two persons is insufficient explanation for requiring two prisoners to alternately stand and sit, even if only for an hour, within such an enclosure. Cabal v. Australia (1020/01).

The Article is also violated, if a person is detained in a moist and dark room, where the electric light is on day and night, Thompson v. Saint Vincent and Grenadines (806/98), R. S. v. Trinidad and Tobago (684/96), Teesdale v. Trinidad and Tobago (677/96), in solitary confinement in enforced darkness, Freemantle v. Jamaica (625/95), Finn v. Jamaica (617/95),without anything to keep a person occupied, Robinson v. Jamaica (731/96), for years in a cell

measuring 6 by 9 feet, with no sanitation except for a slop pail, no natural light, being allowed out of the cell only **once a day** for a **short time**, Boodoo v. Trinidad and Tobago (721/96), Taylor Desmond v. Jamaica (705/96), Edwards v. Jamaica (529/93) - about **one hour**, Lewis v. Jamaica (708/96) - **five minutes**, or **once**, Kennedy v. Trinidad and Tobago (845/99), **or twice a week,** during which the person is restrained in handcuffs, Evans v. Trinidad and Tobago (908/00), and with wholly inadequate food that does not take into account the particular dietary requirements. Evans v. Trinidad and Tobago (908/00).
Detention in solitary confinement for a period as long as **13 years** is a measure of such gravity, and of such fundamental impact on the individual, that it requires the most serious and detailed justification. Confinement for such a lengthy period, on the sole basis of the presumed political opinion, fails to meet the burden of justification. Kang v. Republic of Korea (878/99).
The violent and abusive behaviour both of prison guards, Perkins v. Jamaica (733/97), Elahie v. Trinidad and Tobago (533/93), and of other inmates, particularly when the prison authorities acquiesce in it, Daley v. Jamaica (750/97), violate the right of a prisoner to be treated with humanity. Wilson v. The Philippines (868/99). This right is also violated if the authorities burn personal belongings of a prisoner without justification, Howell v. Jamaica (798/98), and consistently deny access without explanation to medical records. Zheludkova v. Ukraine (726/96). Malnutrition, lack of sunshine and exercise, as well as nervous problems created by tension and ill-treatment that lead to the breakdown of the physical and mental health of a person in detention are incompatible with Article 10 (1). Schweizer v. Uruguay (66/80). A prisoner who is paralyzed in both legs and is unable to move from his cell, unless other inmates carry him, may not be obliged to pay other inmates in order to remove his slop bucket from the cell. Hamilton v. Jamaica (616/95).

Article 10 (2) a

Accused persons shall, save in exceptional circumstances, be segregated from convicted persons and shall be subject to separate treatment appropriate to their status as unconvicted persons;

The requirement of Article 10 (2) a that accused persons shall, save in exceptional circumstances, be segregated from convicted persons means, according to the Committee, that they have to be kept in separate quarters but not necessarily in separate buildings. The *segregation* is required in order to emphasize the status of accused persons as unconvicted persons who at the same time enjoy the right to be presumed innocent as stated in Article 14 (2). General

Comment No.: 21. Unconvicted persons have to be subjected to separate treatment appropriate to their status as unconvicted persons. Wolf v. Panama (289/88). Berry v. Jamaica (330/88). The arrangement that convicted persons work as food servers and cleaners in the remand area of a prison is not incompatible with the Article, provided that contacts between the two classes of prisoners are kept strictly to a minimum necessary for the performance of those tasks. Pinkney v. Canada (27/77). The provision is violated where a detained person is kept with convicted prisoners in a cell. Lewis v. Jamaica (708/96). Griffin v. Spain (493/92).

Article 10 (2) b

Accused juvenile persons shall be separated from adults and brought as speedily as possible for adjudication.

This Article calls, inter alia, for accused juvenile persons to be separated from adults. A State Party fails to discharge its obligations under this Article in so far as it keeps minors among adult prisoners. Thomas v. Jamaica (800/98) - 15 years old. Article 10 does not indicate any limits of juvenile age. This is, according to the Committee, to be determined by each State Party in the light of relevant social, cultural and other conditions. But the State Parties have to take Article 6 (5) into consideration. It suggests that all persons under the age of 18 should be treated as juveniles, at least in matters relating to criminal justice. General Comment No.: 21. Persons between the age of sixteen and eighteen have to be considered as child or youthful offenders. Concluding Comments on Cyprus (1994) CCPR/C/79/Add. 39.

Article 10 (3)

The penitentiary system shall comprise treatment of prisoners the essential aim of which shall be their reformation and social rehabilitation. Juvenile offenders shall be segregated from adults and be accorded treatment appropriate to their age and legal status.

No penitentiary system may, according to the Committee, be solely retributory. The essential aim of every penitentiary system has to be the reformation and social rehabilitation of the prisoners. Therefore, State Parties have to provide teaching, education and re-education, vocational guidance and training as well as work programs for prisoners inside and outside the penitentiary establishment. General Comment No.: 21. Detention in solitary confinement for a period as long as 13 years fails to meet the requirement that the essential aim of detention is reformation and social rehabilitation. Kang v. Republic of Korea (878/99). Juvenile offenders have to be segregated from adults and be accorded treatment appropriate to their age and legal status. A person who is 15 years old at the point of his sentencing may not to be kept among adult prisoners when still a minor. Thomas v. Jamaica (800/98).

ARTICLE 11

No one shall be imprisoned merely on the ground of inability to fulfil a contractual obligation.

Article 4 (2) of the Covenant explicitly prescribes that no derogation from this provision may be made. It can therefore never become necessary to derogate from this Article during a state of emergency. General Comment No.: 29. State Parties that imprison persons for contractual debts have to abolish this practice. Concluding Comments on Uganda (2004) CCPR/CO/80/UGA.
The choice offered to a prisoner to accept release under the system of mandatory supervision or to continue to serve his sentence, does not result in a contractual obligation with penalties for failure of fulfilment if the person concerned chooses release and signs a mandatory supervision certificate. A. R. S. v. Canada (91/81).

ARTICLE 12

1. Everyone lawfully within the territory of a State shall, within that territory, have the right to liberty of movement and freedom to choose his residence.
2. Everyone shall be free to leave any country, including his own.
3. The above-mentioned rights shall not be subject to any restrictions except those, which are provided by law, are necessary to protect national security, public order (ordre public), public health or morals or the rights and freedoms of others, and are consistent with the other rights recognized in the present Covenant.
4. No one shall be arbitrarily deprived of the right to enter his own country.

Liberty of movement is an indispensable condition for the free development of a person. Article 12 does not guarantee an unrestricted right to travel from one country to another. In particular, it confers no right for a person to enter a country other than his own. Nunez v. Uruguay (108/81). But the permissible limitations, which may be imposed on the rights protected under Article 12, may not, according to the Committee, nullify the principle of liberty of movement. They have to be governed by the requirement of necessity and by the need for

consistency with the other rights recognized in the Covenant. State Parties have to allow foreigners who investigate human rights violations to enter their territory. Concluding Comments on Mexico (1999) UN doc. CCPR/C/79/Add. 109. They must also ensure that the rights guaranteed in this provision are protected not only from public but also private interference. General Comment No.: 27. Therefore, the confiscation of passports of foreign workers by employers is incompatible with Article 12. The State Parties have to take effective measures to protect the rights of these foreign workers by preventing such confiscation and by providing an accessible and effective means for the recovery of the passports. Concluding Comments on Lebanon (1997) UN doc. CCPR/C/79/Add. 78.
The Rome Statute of the International Criminal Court, U. N. Doc. 2187 U. N. T. S. 90, entered into force July 1, 2002, confirms to the Committee that deportation or forcible transfer of population without grounds permitted under international law, in the form of forced displacement, by expulsion or other coercive means from the area in which the persons concerned are lawfully present, constitutes a crime against humanity. The legitimate right to derogate from Article 12 of the Covenant during a state of emergency can never justify such measures. General Comment No.: 29.

Article 12 (1)

Everyone lawfully within the territory of a State shall, within that territory, have the right to liberty of movement and freedom to choose his residence.

The right to liberty of movement relates to the whole *territory* of a State, including all parts of federal States. Persons are entitled to move from one place to another and to establish themselves in a place of their choice. Ackla v. Togo (505/92). The enjoyment of this right may not be made dependent on any particular purpose or reason for the person wanting to move or stay in a place. General Comment No.: 27. In principle, citizens of a State are always *lawfully* within the territory of that State. The question whether an alien is lawfully within the territory of a State is a matter governed by domestic law, which may subject the entry of an alien to the territory of a State to restrictions. The Committee considers an alien, who stays in a State illegally because the expulsion order cannot be enforced due to the situation in his home country, to be lawfully within the territory. Celepli v. Sweden (456/91).
Once a person is lawfully within a territory, any restrictions on his or her rights, as well as any treatment different from that accorded to nationals, have to be justified by the State Party. Internal banishment without justification violates the right to move freely. Birhashwirwa et al. v. Zaire (241, 242/87). Mpaka-Nsusu

v. Zaire (157/83). Mpandanjila et al. v. Zaire (138/83). Measures preventing women from moving freely or from leaving the country by requiring them to have the consent or the escort of a male person constitute a violation of the right to liberty of movement. General Comment No.: 27.

Article 12 (2)

Everyone shall be free to leave any country, including his own.

Freedom to *leave the territory* of a State may not, according to the Committee, be made dependent on any specific purpose or in the period of time the individual chooses to stay outside the country. Thus, travelling abroad as well as departure for permanent emigration are covered, Likewise, the right of an individual to determine the State of destination is part of the legal guarantee. And as the scope of Article 12 (2) is not restricted to persons lawfully within the territory of a State, an alien being legally expelled from a country is likewise entitled to elect the State of destination, subject to the agreement of that State. General Comment No.: 27.
In order to enable an individual to enjoy the rights guaranteed by Article 12 (2), the Committee imposes obligations on both the State of residence and the State of nationality. International travel usually requires appropriate documents, in particular a passport. Therefore, the right to leave a country includes the right to obtain the necessary travel documents. The issuing of passports is normally incumbent on the State of nationality of the individual. The refusal by that State to issue a passport or prolong its validity deprives a person of the right to leave the country of residence and to travel elsewhere. Bahamonde v. Equatorial Guinea (468/91). Miha v. Equatorial Guinea (414/90). Kalenga v. Zambia (326/88). Bwalya v. Zambia (314/88). Nunez v. Uruguay (108/81). Martins v. Uruguay (57/79). The Committee does not regard the issuing of an identity and travel document by the State of residence as a sufficient substitute for the issuing of a valid passport by the State of nationality. Montero v. Uruguay (106/81). Lichtensztejn v. Uruguay (77/80).

Article 12 (3)

The above-mentioned rights shall not be subject to any restrictions except those, which are provided by law, are necessary to protect national security, public order (ordre public), public health or morals or the rights and freedoms of others, and are consistent with the other rights recognized in the present Covenant.

This provision provides for exceptional circumstances in which rights under paragraphs 1 and 2 may be restricted. Only *restrictions* that are recognized in the Covenant are permissible. They do not have to, according to the Committee, impair the essence of the rights. The relation between right and restriction, norm and exception, may not be reversed. Precise criteria have to guide those charged with their execution. Law must establish any limitations on the freedom of movement. Concluding Comments on Sudan (1997) UN doc. CCPR/C/79/Add. 85. It is not sufficient, according to the Committee, that restrictions serve permissible purposes. They must also be necessary to protect them, and be proportionate to the interest to be protected. The least intrusive instrument among those, which might achieve the desired result, has to be selected. These conditions are not met if an individual is prevented from leaving a country merely on the grounds that he or she is the holder of State secrets, Concluding Comments on Belarus (1997) UN doc. CCPR/C/79/Add. 86, or if an individual is prevented from travelling internally without a specific permit. Internal banishment without justification violates the right to move freely. Birhashwirwa et al. v. Zaire (241, 242/87). Mpaka-Nsusu v. Zaire (157/83). Mpandanjila et al. v. Zaire (138/83).

On the other hand, the conditions are met by restrictions on access to military zones on *national security* grounds, or limitations on the freedom to settle in areas inhabited by indigenous or minorities communities. The aim to protect the resources of a reservation and *preserve the identity of* its *people* justifies restrictions on the freedom to choose the residence. Lovelace v Canada (24/77). Pending *judicial proceedings* justify restrictions on an individual's right to leave his country. But where the judicial proceedings are unduly delayed, a constraint upon the right to leave the country is not justified. Rio v. Peru (263/87). Restrictions of the freedom of movement of individuals who have not yet performed their *military service* are in principle considered necessary for the protection of national security and public order. Peltonen v. Finland (492/92).

Once an alien is lawfully within a territory, his freedom of movement within the territory and his right to leave that territory may, according to the Committee, only be restricted in accordance with this provision. Differences in treatment in this regard between aliens and nationals, or between different categories of aliens, need to be justified under Article 12 (3). General Comment No. 15. An alien who is an active supporter of a group that advocates violent action can be restricted in his movement for reasons of national security. Karker v. France (833/98). Also, suspicions of involvement in *terrorist activities* justify, for reasons of national security, restrictions on the freedom of movement. Celepli v. Sweden (456/91).

Bureaucratic barriers affect the enjoyment of the rights of individuals to move freely, to leave a country, including their own, and to take up residence. The Committee sees such barriers in: Provisions requiring individuals to apply for permission to change their residence; the necessity to seek the approval of the local authorities of the place of destination, as well as delays in processing written applications; the lack of access for applicants to the competent authorities and lack of information regarding requirements; the requirement of applying for special forms through which the proper application documents for the issuance of a passport can be obtained; the need for supportive statements from employers or family members; the exact description of the travel route; the issuance of passports only on payment of high fees substantially exceeding the cost of the service rendered by the administration; Concluding Comments on Iraq (1997) UN doc. CCPR/C/79/Add. 84; unreasonable delays in the issuance of travel documents; restrictions on family members travelling together; the requirement of a repatriation deposit or a return ticket; the requirement of an invitation from the State of destination or from people living there; the requirement of an exit visa for foreign workers and refugees. Concluding Comments on Gabon (2000) UN doc. CCPR/CO/70/GAB.
Restrictions permissible under Article 12 (3) need to be consistent with the fundamental principles of equality and non-discrimination. General Comment No.: 27. Thus, the Committee sees a clear violation of the Covenant if the rights enshrined in Article 12 (1) and (2) are restricted by making distinctions of any kind, such as on the basis of race, colour, sex, language, religion, political or other opinion, national or social origin, property, birth or other status. Measures preventing women from moving freely or from leaving the country by requiring them to have the consent or the escort of a male person constitute a violation of the right to liberty of movement. Concluding Comments on Lebanon (1997) UN doc. CCPR/C/79/Add. 78.

Article 12 (4)

No one shall be arbitrarily deprived of the right to enter his own country.

Article 12 (4) guarantees, according to the Committee, that even interference provided for by law has to be in accordance with the provisions, aims and objectives of the Covenant and must be, in any event, reasonable in the particular circumstances. Punishment by exile is not compatible with the Covenant. Concluding Comments on Dominican Republic (1993) UN doc. CCPR/C/79/Add. 18. If a person cannot return from involuntary exile in safety to the own country, a State Party has not ensured the right to remain in, return to and reside in that country. Vaca v. Colombia (859/99).

The wording of this Article does not distinguish between nationals and aliens. The Committee identifies the persons entitled to exercise the guaranteed right, as stated in Article 12 (4), by interpreting the meaning of the phrase *his own country*. The scope of the words "his own country" is broader than the concept "country of his nationality". Stewart v. Canada (538/93). It is, according to the Committee, neither constituted by, nor limited to, nationality in a formal sense, that is, nationality acquired at birth or by conferral. The phrase "his own country" embraces, an individual who, because of his special ties to or claims in relation to a given country, cannot be considered a mere alien. A country to whom a person has no connection by reason of birth, descent or residence but whose nationality he has involuntarily acquired and lost in a time he is unaware of any claim to the citizenship is not the person's own country. Toala et al. v. New Zealand (675/95). Also, a person who enters a State under the State's immigration laws and who is subject to the conditions of those laws cannot regard that State as his own country when he has not acquired its nationality and continues to retain the nationality of his country of origin. An exception might only arise in limited circumstances, such as where unreasonable impediments are placed on the acquisition of nationality. Canepa v. Canada (558/93).

A State Party may not, by stripping a person of his or her nationality or by expelling an individual to a third country, arbitrarily prevent this person from returning to his or her own country. General Comment No.: 27. The Committee does not consider a person an alien if he, as a national of a country, has been stripped of his nationality in violation of international law. Also, individuals whose country of nationality has been incorporated into, or transferred to, another national entity, and to whom the nationality is denied, are not considered aliens.

The right of a person to enter his or her own country recognizes the special relationship of a person to that country. It implies, according to the Committee: The right to remain in one's own country; the entitlement of a person to come to a country for the first time, if he was born outside and has the State's nationality; the prohibition of enforced population transfers or mass expulsions to other countries. In no case may a person be arbitrarily deprived of the right to enter his or her own country. This applies to all State action, legislative, administrative and judicial. A State Party that prevents an alien from returning to his own country, by restraining him or deporting him to a third country, violates Article 12 (4). General Comment No.: 15.

ARTICLE 13

An alien lawfully in the territory of a State Party to the present Covenant may be expelled therefrom only in pursuance of a decision reached in accordance with law and shall, except where compelling reasons of national security otherwise require, be allowed to submit the reasons against his expulsion and to have his case reviewed by, and be represented for the purpose before, the competent authority or a person or persons especially designated by the competent authority.

The purpose of this Article is to prevent arbitrary expulsions by entitling each alien to a decision in his own case. It directly regulates only the procedure and not the substantive grounds for expulsion. Nevertheless, the Committee considered an expulsion of a person as both untenable and incompatible with the spirit of the Covenant because his activities as a corresponding member of Amnesty International and of the Human Rights Committee and as a barrister had in the view of the State Party discredited the State Party. Hammel v. Madagascar (155/83). Article 13 is applicable to all procedures aimed at the obligatory departure of an alien, whether described in national law as expulsion or otherwise. Giry v. Dominican Republic (193/85). It protects those aliens who are lawfully in the territory of a State Party. V. R. M. B. v. Canada (236/87). This means that the Committee takes national law concerning the requirements for entry and stay into account in determining the scope of Article 13, Maroufidou v. Sweden (58/79), and that illegal entrants and aliens, in particular who have stayed longer than the law or their permits allow are not covered by its provisions. However, if the legality of an alien's entry or stay is in dispute, any decision on this point leading to his expulsion or deportation has to be taken in accordance with this Article. General Comment No.: 15. If a State Party pleads reasons of national security in connection with proceedings to deport a person, the Committee does not test a sovereign State's evaluation of an alien's security rating. J. R. C. v. Costa Rica (296/88). V. R. M. B. v. Canada (236/87). The fact that, for urgent reasons of public security, a person is not allowed to submit reasons against his expulsion before the expulsion order is issued, does not violate Article 13, if the opportunity is later given to him with the help of a counsel to have his case reviewed by a competent authority. Karker v. France (833/98). States are fully entitled to vigorously protect their territory against the menace of criminal activities by entering into extradition treaties with other States. The practice under such treaties must comply with Article 13. Giry v. Dominican Republic (193/85). The State Parties also have to follow the formal extradition procedures under the treaties and may not deprive a person of procedural safeguards which they have agreed to in such treaties. García v. Ecuador (319/88).

ARTICLE 14

1. All persons shall be equal before the courts and tribunals. In the determination of any criminal charge against him, or of his rights and obligations in a suit at law, everyone shall be entitled to a fair and public hearing by a competent, independent and impartial tribunal established by law. The press and the public may be excluded from all or part of a trial for reasons of morals, public order (ordre public) or national security in a democratic society, or when the interest of the private lives of the parties so requires, or to the extent strictly necessary in the opinion of the court in special circumstances where publicity would prejudice the interests of justice; but any judgement rendered in a criminal case or in a suit at law shall be made public except where the interest of juvenile persons otherwise requires or the proceedings concern matrimonial disputes or the guardianship of children.
2. Everyone charged with a criminal offence shall have the right to be presumed innocent until proved guilty according to law.
3. In the determination of any criminal charge against him, everyone shall be entitled to the following minimum guarantees, in full equality:
(a) To be informed promptly and in detail in a language which he understands of the nature and cause of the charge against him;
(b) To have adequate time and facilities for the preparation of his defence and to communicate with counsel of his own choosing;
(c) To be tried without undue delay;
(d) To be tried in his presence, and to defend himself in person or through legal assistance of his own choosing; to be informed, if he does not have legal assistance, of this right; and to have legal assistance assigned to him, in any case where the interests of justice so require, and without payment by him in any such case if he does not have sufficient means to pay for it;
(e) To examine, or have examined, the witnesses against him and to obtain the attendance and examination of witnesses on his behalf under the same conditions as witnesses against him;
(f) To have the free assistance of an interpreter if he cannot understand or speak the language used in court;
(g) Not to be compelled to testify against himself or to confess guilt.
4. In the case of juvenile persons, the procedure shall be such as will take account of their age and the desirability of promoting their rehabilitation.
5. Everyone convicted of a crime shall have the right to his conviction and sentence being reviewed by a higher tribunal according to law.
6. When a person has by a final decision been convicted of a criminal offence and when subsequently his conviction has been reversed or he has been

pardoned on the ground that a new or newly discovered fact shows conclusively that there has been a miscarriage of justice, the person who has suffered punishment as a result of such conviction shall be compensated according to law, unless it is proved that the non-disclosure of the unknown fact in time is wholly or partly attributable to him.
7. No one shall be liable to be tried or punished again for an offence for which he has already been finally convicted or acquitted in accordance with the law and penal procedure of each country.

This Article aims at ensuring the proper administration of justice and applies to all courts and tribunals whether ordinary or specialized. The rights set forth in this Article constitute the *minimum standards*, Mukunto v. Zambia (768/97), that establish the *concept of fair trial*. This includes different elements. Among these are, the respect for the principles of equality of arms, of adversary proceedings, of expeditious proceedings, Fei v. Colombia (514/92), Casanovas v. France (441/90), Hermoza v. Peru (203/86), and preclusion of ex officio reformatio in peius (ex officio correction worsening an earlier verdict). Morael v. France (207/86). Specific instructions by a judge to a jury are beyond the scope of application of Article 14, unless it can be ascertained that the instructions to the jury were clearly arbitrary or amounted to a denial of justice, or that the judge manifestly violated his obligation of impartiality. Henry v. Jamaica (230/87). Reynolds v. Jamaica (229/87). Sawyers et al. v. Jamaica (226, 256/87). Information that is available to a judge and that can be very serious in its implications for the decision of a jury has to be brought to the jury's attention by the judge. An omission of such information constitutes a denial of justice. Wright v Jamaica (349/89).
The Committee is not a "fourth instance" competent to re-evaluate findings of fact or to review the application of domestic legislation. The appellate courts of the State Parties have to evaluate the facts and the evidence in a particular case. Meurs v. The Netherlands (215/86). Article 14 guarantees procedural equality. It does not guarantee equality of results or absence of error on the part of a competent tribunal. B. D. B. et al. v. The Netherlands (273/88). The *commutation of a sentence* also does not attract the guarantees of Article 14. Kennedy v. Trinidad and Tobago. (845/98). A right of appeal in *civil matters* cannot be derived from it. I. P. v. Finland (450/91).

Article 14 (1)

All persons shall be equal before the courts and tribunals. In the determination of any criminal charge against him, or of his rights and obligations in a suit at law, everyone shall be entitled to a fair and public hearing by a competent, independent and impartial tribunal established by law. The press and the public may be excluded from all or part of a trial for reasons of morals, public order (ordre public) or national security in a democratic society, or when the interest of the private lives of the parties so requires, or to the extent strictly necessary in the opinion of the court in special circumstances where publicity would prejudice the interests of justice; but any judgement rendered in a criminal case or in a suit at law shall be made public except where the interest of juvenile persons otherwise requires or the proceedings concern matrimonial disputes or the guardianship of children.

The principle of equality before the courts and tribunals is expressly referred to in this Article. General Comment No.: 18. Equality encompasses the idea that no person stands outside the law. A concept, which restricts the right of individuals to pursue civil remedies against the President in the courts for anything done in his private capacity, is therefore incompatible with this provision. Concluding Comments on Zambia (1996) UN doc. CCPR/C/79Add. 62.

The notion of equality before the courts and tribunals also encompasses the very *access to the courts*. Hence, the application of a law that only husbands entitles to represent matrimonial property in court denies women equality before courts. Avellanal v. Peru (202/86). Where a backlog of cases pending before the courts exists, the State Parties have to improve the effectiveness of the judicial process. Concluding Comments on Brazil (1996) UN doc. CCPR/C/79/Add. 66. A situation, in which an individual's attempts to seize the competent jurisdictions of his grievances are systematically frustrated, runs counter to the guarantees of Article 14 (1). Bahamonde v. Equatorial Guinea (468/91). High legal costs are a particular concern where satisfactory legal aid is missing. Concluding Comments on Norway (1999) CCPR/C/79/Add. 112. Administrative, prosecutorial or judicial authorities of a State Party may not lay such a cost burden on an individual that his access to court is prevented de facto. Lindon v. Australia (646/95). A State Party violates Article 14 (1), if no legal aid is available to a person before a court. Kennedy v. Trinidad and Tobago (845/99) - Constitutional Court. Aliev v. Ukraine (781/97) - Supreme Court. Legal assistance must be provided free of charge where a convicted person seeking review of irregularities in a trial has insufficient means to meet the costs. Henry v. Trinidad and Tobago (752/97), Taylor Desmond v. Jamaica (705/96), Kelly v. Jamaica (537/93), Currie v. Jamaica (377/89) - criminal trial.

Article 14 (1) speaks of *criminal proceedings* and *suits at law*. The concept of suit at law is based on the nature of the right in question. Y. L. v. Canada (112/81). It encompasses the regulation of the activities of professional bodies

and the scrutiny of such regulations by the courts. It applies not only to criminal matters but also to litigation concerning rights and obligations of a civil nature. Morael v. France (207/86). The term also possibly encompasses immigration hearings and deportation proceedings. V. M . R. B. v. Canada (236/87). A procedure concerning the dismissal from employment constitutes the determination of rights and obligations in a suit at law. Casanovas v. France (441/90). The determination of any rights or obligations in a suit at law entitles a person to a fair and public hearing. J. L. v. Australia (491/92).
Neither jury trial nor preliminary examination is in itself required by this Article in order to render a trial *fair*. Wilson v. Australia (1239/04). The absence of either or both of these elements does not necessarily make a trial unfair. Trial before courts other than the ordinary courts is not necessarily, per se, a violation of the entitlement to a fair hearing. Kavanagh v. Ireland (819/98). But State Parties have to revise their laws to the effect of excluding military courts′ jurisdiction over civilians. Concluding Comments on Slovakia (2003) CCPR/CO/78/SVK. Where civilians are subjected to military penal procedures, they have to substantiate that they are in effect deprived of basic judicial guarantees aimed at ensuring fair trial. Borda et al. v. Colombia (46/79).
A *trial in absentia* is compatible with Article 14 when the accused is summoned in a timely manner and informed of the proceedings against him. Maleki v. Italy (699/96). Mbenge v. Zaire (16/79). The requirements of a fair trial are not respected where a person is denied the opportunity to personally attend proceedings. Wolf v. Panama (289/88). Where the right to a fair trial in a suit at law requires that an individual is able to participate in person in court proceedings, a State Party is under obligation to allow that the individual is present at the hearing, even if the person is a non-resident alien. Said v. Norway (767/97). A person who is only informed about the date of a hearing before an appellate instance after the hearing has taken place is unable to communicate with his representative with regard to the appeal. Such appeal proceedings do not meet the requirements of a fair trial. Thomas Alrick v. Jamaica (272/88). Article 14 (1) is violated if a person is not provided with any reasons for the length of the non parole-period, and is not given the opportunity either to make any contribution to the procedure, or to appeal against the sentence imposed on him by a judge, who, when fixing the non-parole period, exercises the discretionary power conferred on him. Gallimore v. Jamaica (680/96).
The right to a fair trial before an independent and impartial tribunal does not encompass an absolute right to have a certain *witness* testify in court on trial. Therefore, it does not necessarily amount to a violation of due process, if all possible steps are taken to secure the presence of a witness in court. McLawrence v. Jamaica (702/96). In a case involving the death penalty, a judge

has to adjourn a trial and to issue a subpoena to secure the attendance of a witness in court. Furthermore, the police have to make transportation available if the witness has no means to attend the trial. Grant v. Jamaica (353/88). An in-court identification of the accused is not incompatible with the guarantee of a fair trial. Piandiong et al. v. The Philippines (869/99). Detention of witnesses in view of obtaining their testimony is an exceptional measure. It must be regulated by strict criteria in law, and in practice, to guarantee a fair trial. Campbell v. Jamaica (307/88).

It is the duty of a Court that is not constrained by any prescribed time limit to ensure that each party can challenge the documentary evidence which the other files or wishes to file and, if need be, to adjourn proceedings. Jansen-Gielen v. The Netherlands (846/99). The refusal of a trial judge to order an adjournment to allow a person to have legal representation, when several adjournments have already been ordered when the prosecution's witnesses were unavailable or unready, violates the *equality of arms* between the parties. Robinson v. Jamaica (223/87). The principle of equality of arms is also not respected where an indictment is not served. Wolf v. Panama (289/88). An extradition in breach of a stay issued by a Court and the inability to appeal an adverse decision of a Court, while the Prosecutor is able to appeal, amount to a violation of the right to equality before the courts. Weiss v. Austria (1086/02). But the entry into force of new procedural rules and the fact that these are applicable from the time of their entry into force does not, in themselves, constitute a violation of the principle of equality of all persons before the courts. Orejuela v. Colombia (848/99).

Another element of the principle of fair trial is that justice is rendered without *undue delay*. A State Party has to explain why a case is pending for several years. Fei v. Colombia (514/92), Hermoza v. Peru (203/86), Rio v. Peru (263/87) - **7 years**. The complexity of a case can justify prolonged proceedings. Casanovas v. France (441/90) - more than **2 years** (dismissal from civil service). Morael v. France (207/86) - **3 years** (bankruptcy).

An important safeguard in the interest of the individual and of society at large is the *publicity of hearings*. Only under exceptional circumstances must a hearing not be open to the public in general, including members of the press. State Parties have to justify a trial without a public hearing. Estrella v. Uruguay (74/80). In cases where the public is excluded from the trial, the *judgement* must, with certain strictly defined exceptions, be made public. General Comment No.: 13. Any judgement rendered in a criminal case or in a suit at law has to be delivered in public, Touron v. Uruguay (32/78), and made public. Weinberger v. Uruguay (28/78). Only where the interest of juvenile persons otherwise requires, or in proceedings concerning matrimonial disputes or the guardianship of children, R. M. v. Finland (301/88), may a judgement not be made public. The publicity of hearings is a duty upon the State Parties that is not dependent on any request by an interested party. Both domestic legislation and judicial practice must provide for the possibility of the public attending, if members of the public so wish. Meurs v. the Netherlands (215/86). Usually a hearing may not be limited only to a particular category of persons. But the failure by a trial court to control the hostile atmosphere and pressure created by the public in the courtroom, which makes it impossible for the defence counsel to properly cross-examine the witnesses and present his defence, violates the right to a fair trial. Gridin v. Russian Federation (770/97). Labour disputes that are argued in an oral hearing before a court, also fall within the requirement, in Article 14 (1), that suits at law be held in public. Meurs v. The Netherlands (215/86). The absence of oral hearings in appellate proceedings raises no issue under Article 14. R. M. v. Finland (301/88).

The right to be tried by an independent and impartial tribunal is an absolute right that suffers no exception. Political implications of a case cannot justify a court's inaction or delays in judicial proceedings. Rio v. Peru (263/87). The State Parties have to establish a clear demarcation between the competence of the executive and judicial bodies. Concluding Comments on Romania (1999) UN doc. CCPR/C/95/Add. 7. A situation where the functions and competences of the judiciary and the executive are not clearly distinguishable or where the latter is able to control or direct the former is incompatible with the notion of an *independent and impartial tribunal.* Bahamonde v. Equatorial Guinea (468/91). The power of a president to appoint and remove judges subject only to ratification by the National Assembly without any safeguard or inquiry by an independent judicial tribunal is incompatible with Article 14 (1). Concluding Comments on Zambia UN docs. (1996) UN doc. CCPR/C/79/Add. 62. Also, the fact that judges enjoy immovability only after 10 years of work is incompatible with the independence of the judiciary. Concluding Comments on Algeria (1998) UN doc. CCPR/C/79/Add. 95. The election of judges by popular vote for a fixed maximum term of six years does not ensure their independence and impartiality. Concluding Comments on Armenia (1998) UN doc. CCPR/C/79/Add. 100. The dismissal of a judge by the executive several years before the expiry of the term for which he had been appointed, constituted, in the absence of an effective judicial protection, an attack on the independence of the judiciary. Pastukhov v. Belarus (814/98).

The fact that a person is first acquitted and then ordered for retrial by a "faceless" Chamber of a Court raises issues under Article 14 (1). Casafranca v. Peru (981/01). A court consisting of faceless judges deprives a person of the right to be tried by an impartial tribunal since he cannot refuse the judges. In

this system, neither the independence nor the impartiality of the judges is guaranteed. Arredondo, v. Peru (688/96). Vivanco v. Peru (678/96). Campos v. Peru (577/94).
Justice has to be administered by qualified and trained persons. Concluding Comments on The United States of America (1995) UN doc. CCPR/C/79/Add. 50. They have to be informed about human rights instruments. Concluding Comments on Mali (2003) UN doc. CCPR/CO/77/MLI. Impartiality of the court implies that judges must not harbour preconceptions about the matter put before them, and that they must not act in ways that promote the interests of one of the parties. A President of a Court who publicly, before a case is heard, supports a decision under review (dismissal of a judge) damages the equitable hearing of the case. Busyo et al. v. Democratic Republic of the Congo (933/00). Where law lays down the grounds for disqualification of a judge, it is incumbent upon a court to consider ex officio these grounds and to replace members of the court falling under the disqualification criteria. The Committee does not consider a trial flawed by the participation of a judge who, under domestic statutes, should have been disqualified, to be fair or impartial. Appellate instances can correct the irregularities of proceedings before lower court instances. However, in this case, only oral proceedings that enable appellate instances to determine whether the procedural flaw had indeed affected the verdict of a lower Court correct the procedural irregularities. Karttunen v. Finland (387/89).

Article 14 (2)

Everyone charged with a criminal offence shall have the right to be presumed innocent until proved guilty according to law.

The *presumption of innocence* is violated if a person is tried in circumstances in which, irrespective of the legislative provisions, he cannot effectively enjoy the safeguards of fair trial. Lanza et al. v. Uruguay (8/77). Bazzano et al. v. Uruguay (5/77). It is therefore the duty of all public authorities to refrain from prejudging the outcome of a trial. Gridin v. Russian Federation (770/97). Denial of bail does not a priori affect the right of a person to be presumed innocent. Cagas et al. v. The Philippines (788/97).
Article 14 (2) lays the burden of proof of the charge on the prosecution. The accused has the benefit of doubt. No guilt can be presumed until the charge has been proved beyond *reasonable doubt*. General Comment No.: 13.
Article 14 (2) is applicable only to persons charged with a *criminal offence*. Morael v. France (207/86). The punishment of the owner of a vehicle for not identifying the driver of the vehicle reported for committing a traffic offence falls outside the scope of application of this provision. López v. Spain (777/97) -

non-cooperation with the authorities. Article 14 (2) also does not apply to proceedings for compensation after an acquittal. W. B. E. v. The Netherlands (432/90).
Pre-trial detention can affect the right to be presumed innocent. Cagas et al. v. The Philippines (788/97) - more than **nine years**. On the other hand, *detention for preventive purposes*, that is, protection of the public once a punitive term of imprisonment has been served, does not offend the presumption of innocence. Rameka et al. v. New Zealand (1090/02). The decision to try a person before a Special Criminal Court does not, of itself, violate Article 14 (2). Kavanagh v. Ireland (819/98). But a system of "faceless" judges fails to safeguard the presumption of innocence. Campos v. Peru (577/94).

Article 14 (3)

In the determination of any criminal charge against him, everyone shall be entitled to the following minimum guarantees, in full equality:

This Article prescribes minimum guarantees in *criminal proceedings*. General Comment No.: 13. In the determination of any criminal charge against him, everyone is entitled, in full equality, to these minimum guarantees. General Comment No.: 18. Custody proceedings are outside the scope of this Article. A. J. v. G. v. The Netherlands (1142/02).

Article 14 (3) a

In the determination of any criminal charge against him, everyone shall be entitled to the following minimum guarantees, in full equality:
To be informed promptly and in detail in a language which he understands of the nature and cause of the charge against him;

Among the minimum guarantees in criminal proceedings prescribed by this Article, the first concerns the right of everyone *to be informed* of the charge against him in a language that he understands. The provision applies to all cases of criminal charges, including those of persons not in detention. The right to be informed of the charge promptly requires that information be given as soon as a competent authority first makes the charge. The right arises when in the course of an investigation a court or an authority of the prosecution decides to take procedural steps against a person suspected of a crime or publicly names him as such. Williams v. Jamaica (561/93). The specific requirements of this Article are met by stating the charge either orally or in writing, provided that the information indicates both the law and the alleged facts on which the charge is

based. General Comment No.: 13. The duty to inform the accused under Article 14 (3) a is, according to the Committee, more precise than that for arrested persons under Article 9 (2). As long as Article 9 (3) is complied with, the details of the nature and cause of the charge need not necessarily be provided to an accused person immediately upon arrest. McLawrence v. Jamaica (702/96). But a delay in presenting the charges to a detained person can affect the possibilities of a detained person to defend himself, in a manner that constitutes a violation of Article 14 (3) a. Kurbanov v. Tajikistan (1096/02).
The requirement of prompt information, however, only applies once the individual has been formally charged with a criminal offence. It does not apply to those remanded in custody pending the result of police investigations. The latter situation is covered by Article 9 (2). Kelly v. Jamaica (253/87).

Article 14 (3) b

In the determination of any criminal charge against him, everyone shall be entitled to the following minimum guarantees, in full equality:
To have adequate time and facilities for the preparation of his defence and to communicate with counsel of his own choosing;

What *adequate time* is depends on the circumstances of each case. Grant v. Jamaica (353/88). Berry v. Jamaica (330/88). Sawyers et al. v. Jamaica (226, 256/87). If a counsel or an accused feels inadequately prepared, it is incumbent upon him or her to request an adjournment. Henry v. Jamaica (610/95). Wright v. Jamaica (349/89). Thomas Alrick v. Jamaica (272/88). A delay in the transmittal of a person's letter to his counsel does not raise an issue in respect of this Article if this delay does not adversely affect the right to prepare adequately the defence. Tomlin v. Jamaica (589/94) - **two and a half months**.
The term *facilities* includes access to documents and other evidence, which the accused requires to prepare his case. The failure of a State Party to produce police documents, which may have contained evidence in favour of an accused, denies the accused access to documents, which he requires to prepare his case. Yasseen et al. v. Republic of Guyana (676/96). The right of access to documents does not entail that an accused, who does not understand the language used in a court, has the right to be furnished with translations of all relevant documents in a criminal investigation, provided that the relevant documents are made available to his counsel. Hill v. Spain (526/93). Harward v. Norway (451/91). The term *facilities* also includes the opportunity to engage and communicate with a counsel. When the accused does not want to defend himself in person or requests a person or an association of his choice, he must be able to have recourse to a *counsel*. Article 14 (3) b is violated if a person is forced to accept

an ex officio counsel, although a counsel of his choice is ready to take up the defence. Acosta v. Uruguay (110/81). Scarrone v. Uruguay (103/81). Also, the interrogation of a person who has requested access to a counsel and is denied the access, Kelly v. Jamaica (537/93), constitutes a violation of the Article. A counsel must have the possibility of communicating with the accused in conditions giving full respect for the confidentiality of their communications. Therefore, the fact that a person is unable to consult with his lawyer in private constitutes a violation of Article 14 (3) b. Gridin v. Russian Federation (770/97). Also, other restrictions, influences, pressures or undue interferences violate this provision. General Comment No.: 13.

A person has to be informed with sufficient advance notice about the date of a hearing. A delay jeopardizes his opportunities to prepare himself and to consult with his lawyer. Simmonds v. Jamaica (338/88). **42 days** of detention without access to a legal counsel violates Article 14 (3) b. Caldas v. Uruguay (43/79). Penarrieta et al. v. Bolivia (176/84) - **44 days**. Touron v. Uruguay (32/78) - **7 months**. Wight v. Madagascar (115/82), Weinberger v. Uruguay (28/78) - **10 months**. It is of fundamental importance, particularly in cases involving capital punishment, that a lawyer effectively assists the accused. Kurbanov, v. Tajikistan (1096/02). Aliev v Ukraine (781/97). Robinson v. Jamaica (223/87). Brown v. Jamaica (775/97). Legal assistance must be made available to an accused faced with a capital crime not only to the trial and relevant appeals, but also to any preliminary hearing relating to the case. Marshall v. Jamaica (730/96). Wright et al. v. Jamaica (459/91).

A State Party cannot generally be held responsible for the conduct of a lawyer in court, Reece v. Jamaica (796/98), his lack of preparation or errors, Hankle v. Jamaica (710/96), unless it is or should have been manifest to the judge that the lawyer's behaviour is incompatible with the interests of justice. Daley v. Jamaica (750/97). The requirements of representation require that a person is informed that his counsel does not intend to put arguments to the Court. In such a case the person must have the opportunity to seek alternative representation in order that his concerns are ventilated at appeal level. McLeod v. Jamaica (734/97). Burrell v. Jamaica (546/93).

Article 14 (3) c

In the determination of any criminal charge against him, everyone shall be entitled to the following minimum guarantees, in full equality:
To be tried without undue delay;

Article 14 (3) c and Article 14 (5) are to be read together, in the sense that the right to review of conviction and sentence must be made available without *undue delay* at all instances. Reid v. Jamaica (355/89). Francis v. Jamaica (320/88). The guarantee of Article 14 (3) c relates not only to the time by which a trial should commence, but also the time by which it should end and judgement be rendered. Article 14 (3) c overlaps with Article 9 (3) which guarantees a trial, within reasonable time, or release to anyone arrested or detained on a criminal charge. Article 9 (3) relates to the length of time between arrest and trial. Article 14 (3) c relates to the determination of a criminal charge without regard to arrest or detention. All stages of the determination must, according to the Committee, take place without undue delay. Exceptional circumstances can justify a delay. Where investigations of allegations are of a very complex nature, this complexity may necessitate prolonged proceedings. Wolf v. Panama (289/88) - (fraud) **four and a half years**. A delay of **a year and a half** in bringing an accused to trial is a matter of concern for the Committee. But this concern does not amount to a violation of Article 14 (3) c in a murder case. Morrison Everton v. Jamaica 635/1995. However, if there is no indication that any further investigation is required after the hearing of the sole witness, a delay of **more than one year** until the trial starts violates Article 14 (3) c. Hill et al. v. Spain (526/93). Inadequate staffing or general administrative backlog is not sufficient justification for a delay. Ashby v. Trinidad and Tobago (580/94). Also, a difficult economic situation cannot justify a delay. Lubuto v. Zambia (390/90). The right to be tried without undue delay has to be made effective by the State Parties. Therefore, a procedure must be available in order to ensure that a trial will proceed without undue delay, both in first instance and on appeal. General Comment No.: 13. A delay of **two and a half years** in the production of the transcripts of a trial for the purposes of the appeal, Pinkney v. Canada (27/77), or the failure of a Court of Appeal to issue a written judgement violates the right under Article 14 (3) c. Collins v. Jamaica (356/89). Pratt et al. v. Jamaica (210/86, 225/87) - more than **3 years**. Smith v. Jamaica (282/88) - more than **4 years**. Kelly v. Jamaica (253/87) - almost **5 years**. Francis v. Jamaica (320/88) - more than **9 years**. Currie v. Jamaica (377/89) - **13 years**. Hamilton v. Jamaica (333/88) - no reasoned judgement.

As already mentioned, a State Party must show exceptional reasons to justify delays until trial. A delay of **21 months** or more between arrest and trial and **/23 months** or more between conviction and decision of the appeal violates this provision. Perkins v. Jamaica (733/97) - **21 months**. Sextus v. Trinidad and Tobago (818/98) - **22 months**. Brown v. Jamaica (775/97), Lewis v. Jamaica (708/96) - **23 months**. Thomas Samuel v. Jamaica (614/95) - **/23 months**. Jensen v. Australia (762/97), Brown et al. v. Jamaica (665/95), Morrison McCordie v. Jamaica (663/95), Fuenzalida v. Ecuador (480/91) - **/more than 2 years**. Reece v. Jamaica (796/98), Henry et al. v. Jamaica (571/94) - **/more than**

3 years. Evans v. Trinidad and Tobago (908/00) - **2 years/4years**. Teesdale v. Trinidad and Tobago (677/96), Bennett v. Jamaica (590/94), Johnson v. Jamaica (588/94) - **/more than 4 years**. Neptune v. Trinidad and Tobago (523/92) - **/more than 7 years**. Wanza v. Trinidad and Tobago (683/96) - **/5 years**. Rogerson v. Australia (802/98), Boodoo v. Trinidad and Tobago (721/96), Taylor Patrick v. Jamaica (707/96), Taylor Desmond v. Jamaica (705/96), Shaw v. Jamaica (704/96), McLawrence v. Jamaica (702/96), Smart v. Trinidad and Tobago (672/95), Brown et al. v. Jamaica (665/95), Finn v. Jamaica (617/95), Hamilton v. Jamaica (616/95), Henry et al. v. Jamaica (571/94), Leslie v. Jamaica (564/93), Williams v. Jamaica (561/93), Steadman v. Jamaica (528/93), Neptune v. Trinidad and Tobago (523/92) - more than **2 years**. Francis et al. v. Trinidad and Tobago (899/99), Hendricks v. Guyana (838/98), Whyte v. Jamaica (732/97), Gómez v. Panama (473/91), Seerattan v. Trinidad and Tobago (434/90), Fillastre et al. v. Bolivia (336/88) - more than **3 years**. Filipovich v. Poland (875/99), Cagas et al. v. The Philippines (788/97), Sahadeo v. Guyana (728/96), M´Boissona v. Central African (428/90) - more than **4 years**. Muñoz v. Spain (1006/01) - **5 years**. Sooklal v. Trinidad and Tobago (928/00), Paraga v. Croatia (727/96), Elahie v. Trinidad and Tobago (533/93), Pena et al. v. Venezuela (156/83) - more than **7 years**. A delay of **11 years** in the judicial process at first instance and of more than **13 years** until the rejection of the appeal violates a person's right under Article 14 (3) c. Agudo v. Spain (864/99). Also, new judicial proceedings on charges that **12 years** ago have been investigated and tried with the result of an acquittal violate the Article. Casafranca v. Peru (981/01). Delays in judicial proceedings after the ordering of a re-trial over **22 months** from the ordering of the re-trial to the dismissal of the second appeal are unreasonable within the meaning of Article 14 (3) c. Wright et al. v. Jamaica (459/91). Yasseen et al. v. Guyana (676/96) - **2 years**. Shalto v. Trinidad and Tobago (447/91) - **4 years**. Kennedy v. Trinidad and Tobago (845/99) - **6 years**.

Article 14 (3) d

In the determination of any criminal charge against him, everyone shall be entitled to the following minimum guarantees, in full equality:
To be tried in his presence, and to defend himself in person or through legal assistance of his own choosing; to be informed, if he does not have legal assistance, of this right; and to have legal assistance assigned to him, in any case where the interests of justice so require, and without payment by him in any such case if he does not have sufficient means to pay for it;

All criminal proceedings must provide the person charged with a criminal offence the right to an oral hearing, at which he or she may *appear in person* or be represented by a counsel and may bring evidence and examine the witnesses. Orejuela v. Colombia (848/99). Therefore, in a reclassification procedure in which an offence is reclassified and a non-parole is set, a convicted person must be afforded the opportunity to make submissions prior to the decision of the judge. Bailey v. Jamaica (709/96). Also, the legislation of a State Party has to allow an accused person to *defend himself* in person. Graham et al. v. Jamaica (461/91).

The right to a defence is inalienable in a trial in which the death penalty can be imposed. This right has to be adhered at every instance and without exception. Inalienable is also the right *to be tried in one's presence.* Domukovsky et al. v. Georgia (623, 624, 626, 627/95). Pinto v. Trinidad & Tobago (232/87). Estrella v. Uruguay (74/80). Lopez v. Uruguay (52/79). A convicted person also has the right to be present during the hearing of an appeal. The assignment of legal aid to him and to hear his case in his absence and in the presence of his legal aid attorney violates the right to be tried in his presence. Simmonds v. Jamaica (338/88). When trials *in absentia* are held, exceptionally and for justified reasons, strict observance of the rights of the defence is all the more necessary. General Comment No.: 13. Proceedings in absentia are permissible in the interest of the proper administration of justice, when the accused person, although informed of the proceedings sufficiently in advance, Maleki v. Italy (699/96), declines to exercise his right to be present. A lack of information denies an accused the opportunity to personally attend proceedings. Wolf v. Panama (289/88). Judgement in absentia requires that, notwithstanding the absence of the accused, all due notification has been made to inform him of the date and place of his trial and to request his attendance. Mbenge et al. v. Zaire (16/77).

The part of Article 14 (3) d that guarantees the right of *legal representation* overlaps to a large extent with Article 14 (3) b. Every accused must be able to have the assistance of a counsel of his own choosing to represent him and to prepare and present his defence. Estrella v. Uruguay (74/80). He may not be forced to agree to ex officio legal counsel. Burgos v. Uruguay (52/79). If an accused has made the necessary arrangements to have a lawyer other than the court appointed lawyer of first instance represent him before a Court of Appeal, these arrangements have to be considered by the court. Pinto v. Trinidad and Tobago (232/87). Every charged person is entitled to *free legal assistance* in any case where the *interests of justice* so require and without payment by him in any such case, if he does not have sufficient means to pay for it. But free legal assistance must be seen in the light of the nature of the offences with which a person is charged. If charges are trivial and ordinary and can, in practice, only lead to a small fine, the accused has to substantiate his claim that the interest of justice requires the assignment of legal aid. O. F. v. Norway (158/83). If a person who is charged with a serious offence (rape) does not present any facts to the effect that he has any arguable grounds of appeal to the Legal Aid Board of a State Party, the interests of justice do not require the assignment of legal aid. Z. P. v. Canada (341/88).

It is incumbent upon a State Party to ensure that legal representation provided by the State guarantees *effective representation* in the interests of justice. Borisenko v. Hungary (852/99). This includes consulting with, and informing, the accused, if the counsel intends to withdraw an appeal or to argue before the appeals court that the appeal has no merit. Kelly v. Jamaica (253/87). A trial judge must be apparent that a counsel is not providing effective representation when he notices that the counsel is absent when he starts his summing-up. Brown v. Jamaica (775/97). A Court appointed defence counsel who is not a lawyer does not constitute adequate legal assistance for the preparation of a defence. Vasilskis v. Uruguay (80/80).

It is of fundamental importance in *capital cases* that legal assistance is available at all stages of criminal proceedings. Aliev v. Ukraine (781/97). Marshall v. Jamaica (730/96). Simpson v. Jamaica (695/96). LaVende v. Trinidad and Tobago (554/93), Wright et al. v. Jamaica (459/91). Robinson v. Jamaica (223/87). The requirement that legal assistance must be made available to an accused faced with a capital crime applies not only to the trial and relevant appeals, but also to any preliminary hearing relating to the case. Levy v. Jamaica (719/96). Johnson v. Jamaica (592/94). Wright et al. v. Jamaica (459/91). Robinson v. Jamaica (223/87). A magistrate may not proceed with the deposition of witnesses during a preliminary hearing without allowing the accused an opportunity to ensure the presence of his lawyer. Brown v. Jamaica (775/97). Hendricks v. Guyana (838/98). This holds true even if the unavailability of private counsel is to some degree attributable to the accused, or if the provision of legal assistance entails an adjournment of proceedings. This requirement is also not made unnecessary by efforts which the trial judge otherwise makes to assist the accused in the handling of his defence, in the absence of the counsel. Yasseen et al. v. Guyana (676/96). In cases involving the death penalty, a State Party has to accept a convicted person's arrangement for another attorney to represent him for purposes of the appeal, even if this entails an adjournment of the proceedings. Pinto v. Trinidad and Tobago (232/87). An accused is not entitled to choice of counsel, if he is being provided with a legal aid lawyer, and is otherwise unable to afford legal representation. Teesdale v. Trinidad and Tobago (677/96). Chaplin v. Jamaica (596/94). Grant

v. Jamaica (353/88). But even if an accused is not entitled to choose the counsel provided to him free of charge, the Court has to ensure that the conduct of the trial by the lawyer is not incompatible with the interests of justice. This means that in a capital case, if the counsel for the accused who is not experienced in such cases requests an adjournment because he is unprepared to proceed, the Court must ensure that the accused is given an opportunity to prepare his defence. Phillip v. Trinidad and Tobago (594/92).
It is up to the professional judgement of a counsel to choose the grounds for an appeal, Marshall v. Jamaica (730/96), and to decide whether to seek instructions from the defendant. Teesdale v. Trinidad and Tobago (677/96). A convicted person who is not notified of the name of his court-appointed lawyer until after his appeal is dismissed is effectively prevented from consulting with his lawyer and from giving him instructions in preparation of the appeal. Campbell John v. Jamaica (307/88). In general, a State Party cannot be held accountable for errors made by a defence lawyer. Campbell Barrington v. Jamaica (618/95). Henry v. Jamaica (610/95). It is not the duty of a State Party to question a counsel's professional judgment. Adams v. Jamaica (607/94). This is especially true for *privately retained* lawyers. The failure of them to properly represent a person cannot be attributed to a State Party. H. C. v. Jamaica (383/89). But a court has to ensure that the conduct of a case by a lawyer is not incompatible with the interests of justice. Taylor Desmond v. Jamaica (705/96). When the counsel for an accused concedes, in a capital case, that there is no merit in the appeal, the Court has to ascertain whether the counsel has consulted with the accused and informed him accordingly. If not, the Court must ensure that the accused is so informed and given an opportunity to engage another counsel. Only the opportunity to seek alternative representation secures the accused the possibility to ventilate his concerns in such a case. Sooklal v. Trinidad and Tobago (928/00). McLeod v. Jamaica (734/97). Daley v. Jamaica (750/97). Jones v. Jamaica (585/94). Price v. Jamaica (572/94). Kelly v. Jamaica (537/93). Steadman v. Jamaica (528/93). Collins v. Jamaica (356/89). Reid v. Jamaica (250/87). The withdrawal of an appeal by a counsel without consultation amounts to a violation of Article 14 (3) d. McLeod v. Jamaica (734/97). Smith et al. v. Jamaica (668/95). Morrison McCordie v. Jamaica (663/95). Jones v. Jamaica (585/94). Steadman v. Jamaica (528/93). Graham et al. v. Jamaica (461/91). Collins v. Jamaica (356/89).

Article 14 (3) e

In the determination of any criminal charge against him, everyone shall be entitled to the following minimum guarantees, in full equality:

To examine, or have examined, the witnesses against him and to obtain the attendance and examination of witnesses on his behalf under the same conditions as witnesses against him;

This provision is designed to guarantee the same legal powers to the accused as to the prosecution, in terms of compelling the attendance of witnesses and of examining or cross- examining any witnesses. *Anonymous witnesses* are incompatible with this provision. Concluding Comments on Colombia (1997) UN doc. CCPR/C/79/Add. 76. However, Art. 68 (5) of the Rome Statute of the International Criminal Court, U. N. Doc. 2187 U. N. T. S. 90, entered into force July 1, 2002, has to be mentioned in this context: Where the disclosure of evidence or information may lead to the grave endangerment of the security of a witness or his or her family, the Prosecutor may withhold such evidence or information and, instead, submit a summary thereof. Such measures shall be exercised in a manner that is not prejudicial to, or inconsistent with, the rights of the accused and a fair and impartial trial.

Article 14 (3) e does not provide an unlimited right to obtain the attendance of any witness requested by the accused or his counsel. Gordon v. Jamaica (237/87). But a court's refusal to order expert testimony of crucial importance to a case violates Article 14 (3) e. Fuenzalida v. Ecuador (480/91). Also, the failure to make the police statement of a witness available to the defence seriously obstructs the defence in its cross-examination of a witness. Peart et al. v. Jamaica (464/91, 482/91). In a case involving the death penalty, a judge has to issue a subpoena to secure the attendance of a witness in court. The police has to make transportation available to a witness who has no means to attend the hearing. Grant v. Jamaica (353/88).

In order to guarantee the rights of the defence enshrined in this Article, all criminal proceedings must provide the person charged with the criminal offence with the *right to an oral hearing*, at which he or she may appear in person or be represented by counsel and may bring evidence and examine the witnesses. Orejuela v. Spain (848/99). Article 14 (3) e protects the equality of arms between the prosecution and the defence in the examination of witnesses, but does not prevent the defence from waiving or not exercising its entitlement to cross-examine a prosecution witness during the trial hearing. Compass v. Jamaica (375/89). A counsel exercises his professional judgement by not calling witnesses for the defence. Tomlin v. Jamaica (589/94). A State Party cannot be held accountable for errors made by a defence lawyer, unless it is or should be manifest to the judge that the lawyer's behaviour is incompatible with the interests of justice. Henry v. Jamaica (610/95). Adams v. Jamaica (607/94).

Article 14 (3) f

In the determination of any criminal charge against him, everyone shall be entitled to the following minimum guarantees, in full equality:
To have the free assistance of an interpreter if he cannot understand or speak the language used in court;

The right guaranteed in Article 14 (3) f is of basic importance in cases whereby ignorance of the language used by a court or difficulty in understanding may constitute a major obstacle to the right of defence. General Comment No.: 13. This right applies to aliens as well as to nationals. It is independent of the outcome of the proceedings. Article 14 (3) f does not prohibit the use of one *official court language* by State Parties. Cadoret et al. v. France (323/88, 221/87). Guesdon v. France (219/86). But in a territory where the majority of the population speaks another language, official charge forms and charge sheets, as well as court documents, have not only to be made available in the official court language, but also in the language of the majority of the population of the territory where the court hears a case. Concluding Comments on the United Kingdom of Great Britain and Northern Ireland (Hong Kong) (1995) CCPR/C/79/Add. 57.
There is no right under the Covenant to have court proceedings conducted in the language of one's choice. C. E. A. v. Finland (316/88). But the services of an interpreter have to be made available, if the accused or the witnesses have difficulties in understanding or expressing himself or herself in the court language. Cadoret et al. v. France (221/87, 323/88). The requirement of a fair hearing does not obligate State Parties to make the services of an interpreter available ex officio or upon application to a person whose mother tongue differs from the official court language, if the person is capable of expressing himself adequately in the official language. Z. P. v. Canada (341/88). Barzhig v. France (327/88). With other words: Article 14 (3) f does not imply that the accused be afforded the possibility to express himself in the language which he normally speaks or speaks with a maximum of ease. Guesdon v. France (219/86).

Article 14 (3) g

In the determination of any criminal charge against him, everyone shall be entitled to the following minimum guarantees, in full equality:
Not to be compelled to testify against himself or to confess guilt.

The wording of this Article must be understood in terms of the absence of any direct or indirect physical or psychological pressure from the investigating

authorities on the accused, with a view to obtaining a confession of guilt. Johnson v. Jamaica (588/94). Campbell v. Jamaica (248/87). It is unacceptable to treat an accused person in a manner contrary to Article 7 of the Covenant in order to extract a confession. Berry v. Jamaica (330/88). Kelly v. Jamaica (253/87). The State Parties have to adopt appropriate legislation that places the burden on the State to prove that statements made by accused persons in a criminal case have been given of their own free will, and that statements obtained in violation of Article 7 of the Covenant are excluded from the evidence. Concluding Comments on Romania (1999) UN doc. CCPR/C/79/Add. 111. Provisions that inferences may be drawn from the *silence* of a persons accused of crimes violate various provisions of Article 14. Concluding Comments on United Kingdom of Great Britain and Northern Ireland (1995) UN doc. CCPR/C/79/Add. 55. Also, the principle that juries may draw negative inferences from the silence of an accused person is incompatible with Article 14. Concluding Comments on United Kingdom of Great Britain and Northern Ireland (2001) UN doc. CCPR/CO/73/UK.
The punishment of the owner of a vehicle for not identifying the driver of the vehicle reported for committing a traffic offence falls outside the scope of application of this Article. López v. Spain (777/97).

Article 14 (4)

In the determination of any criminal charge against him, everyone shall be entitled to the following minimum guarantees, in full equality:
In the case of juvenile persons, the procedure shall be such as will take account of their age and the desirability of promoting their rehabilitation.

Juveniles enjoy at least the same guarantees and protection as adults. The term *juvenile person* is not defined in the Covenant. Therefore, it is, according to the Committee, up to the State Parties to determine the minimum age at which a juvenile may be charged with a criminal offence and the maximum age at which a person is still considered to be a juvenile. General Comment No.: 13. However, Article 6 (5) of the Covenant suggests that all persons under the age of 18 should be treated as juveniles, at least in matters relating to criminal justice. General Comment No.: 21. Persons between the age of sixteen and eighteen have to be considered as child or youthful offenders. Concluding Comments on Cyprus (1994) CCPR/C/79/Add. 39.

Article 14 (5)

In the determination of any criminal charge against him, everyone shall be entitled to the following minimum guarantees, in full equality:
Everyone convicted of a crime shall have the right to his conviction and sentence being reviewed by a higher tribunal according to law.

The term *crime* shows that the guarantee of this Article is not confined only to the most serious offences. General Comment No.: 13.
Article 14 (5) does not require a State Party to provide for *several* instances of appeal. However the words *according to law* must be understood to mean that if domestic law provides for several instances of appeal, the convicted person must have effective access to each of them. Douglas et al. v. Jamaica (352/89). Henry v. Jamaica (230/87). What is to be determined according to law are the *modalities* by which the review has to be carried out by a higher tribunal. Montejo v. Colombia (64/79). While the modalities of an appeal may differ among the domestic legal systems of the State Parties, every State Party is under an obligation, under Article 14 (5), to substantially review convictions and sentences. Reid v. Jamaica (355/89).
A State Party violates Article 14 (5), if it does not provide for a right of appeal. Mansaraj et al. v. Sierra Leone (839-841/98) - court martial (capital case). The request for the submission of a supervisory protest does not constitute a right to have one's sentence and conviction reviewed by a higher tribunal. Gelazauskas v. Lithuania (836/98). Article 14 (5) does not require that a Court of Appeal proceeds to a *factual retrial*, but that the Court conducts an evaluation of the evidence presented at the trial and of the conduct of the trial. Perera v. Australia (536/93). A system not allowing for an automatic right to appeal is in conformity with Article 14 (5), as long as the examination of an application for leave to appeal entails a full review, both on the basis of the evidence and of the law, of the conviction and sentence, and as long as the procedure allows for due consideration of the nature of the case. Lumley v. Jamaica (662/95). *Fresh evidence* is not to be evaluated if it was already available during the trial at first instance and, because of a conscious decision of the defence, not used. H. T. B. v. Canada (534/93). Notwithstanding the absence of an *oral hearing*, the totality of the review by a Court of Appeal can satisfy the requirements of Article 14 (5). Bryhn v. Norway (789/97).
Regardless of the name of a remedy, it must meet the requirements for which the Covenant provides. Vázquez v. Spain (701/96). A judicial review that takes place without a hearing and is on matters of law only, falls short of the requirements of Article 14 (5) for a full evaluation of the evidence.

Domukovsky et al. v. Georgia (626-627/95). The inability of a Court, as the sole body of appeal, to review evidence submitted at first instance is tantamount to a violation of Article 14 (5). A Court that expressly states that it is not part of its functions to reconsider the evidence on which the court of first instance has based its conviction denies a convicted person the full review of his conviction and sentence. Fernández v. Spain (1007/01). Semey v. Spain (986/01). Vázquez v. Spain (701/96).

In order to enjoy the right to have his conviction and sentence reviewed by a higher tribunal according to law, a convicted person is entitled to have, within a reasonable time period, access to a duly reasoned, written judgement. Lubuto v. Zambia (390/90). Currie v. Jamaica (377/89). The words according to law imply that the right to a duly reasoned, written judgement must apply to all instances of appeal provided in the domestic law. Bailey v. Jamaica (709/96). Francis v. Jamaica (320/88). Little v. Jamaica (283/88). Henry v. Jamaica (230/87). Pinkney v. Canada (27/77).

A Court of Appeal does not effectively consider an appeal if no lawyer is available to submit any grounds of appeal. Hill et al. v. Spain (526/93). The denial of *legal aid* for an appeal violates Article 14 (5) if it effectively precludes the review of a conviction and sentence. LaVende v. Trinidad and Tobago (554/93). A convicted person also has to be informed by the Court that his legal aid counsel is not going to argue any grounds in support of his appeal. Gallimore v. Jamaica (680/96). Smith et al. v. Jamaica (668/95). But the right to have a conviction reviewed by a higher tribunal is not violated if the counsel for an appellant chooses, in the exercise of his professional judgement, to concentrate on one arguable ground of appeal rather than advance several grounds. Tomlin v. Jamaica (589/94).

Article 14 (5) is violated if a convicted person is obliged to abandon his appeal in exchange for conditional release. Fuenzalida v. Ecuador (480/91).

Article 14 (6)

In the determination of any criminal charge against him, everyone shall be entitled to the following minimum guarantees, in full equality:

When a person has by a final decision been convicted of a criminal offence and when subsequently his conviction has been reversed or he has been pardoned on the ground that a new or newly discovered fact shows conclusively that there has been a miscarriage of justice, the person who has suffered punishment as a result of such conviction shall be compensated according to law, unless it is proved that the non-disclosure of the unknown fact in time is wholly or partly attributable to him.

This Article provides for compensation according to law in certain cases of miscarriage of justice. The conditions for the application of this Article are: (a) A *final* conviction for a criminal offence; (b) Suffering of punishment as a *consequence* of such conviction; and (c) A subsequent reversal or pardon on the grounds of a new or newly discovered fact showing *conclusively* that there has been a miscarriage of justice. W. J. H. v. The Netherlands (408/90). No right to compensation exists if a State Party can prove that the non-disclosure of an unknown fact in time is wholly or partly attributable to the person who is seeking compensation. Muhonen v. Finland (89/81). It has to be noted that, according to Article 9 (5), anyone who has been a victim of unlawful arrest or detention has an enforceable right to compensation.

Article 14 (7)

In the determination of any criminal charge against him, everyone shall be entitled to the following minimum guarantees, in full equality:
No one shall be liable to be tried or punished again for an offence for which he has already been finally convicted or acquitted in accordance with the law and penal procedure of each country.

Article 14 (7) proscribes *retrial* or *punishment* for an offence for which the person has already been finally convicted or acquitted. Jijon et al. v. (277/88). Schweizer v. Uruguay (66/80). It must be distinguished between a *resumption* of a trial justified by exceptional circumstances and a retrial prohibited pursuant to the principle of *ne bis in idem* as contained in this Article. General Comment No.: 13. Article 14 (7) does not guarantee ne bis in idem with respect to the national jurisdictions of two or more states. This provision only prohibits double jeopardy with regard to an offence adjudicated in a given State. A. R. J. v. Australia (692/96). A. P. v. Italy (204/86).

ARTICLE 15

1. No one shall be held guilty of any criminal offence on account of any act or omission, which did not constitute a criminal offence, under national or international law, at the time when it was committed. Nor shall a heavier penalty be imposed than the one that was applicable at the time when the criminal offence was committed. If, subsequent to the commission of the offence, provision is made by law for the imposition of the lighter penalty, the offender shall benefit thereby.
2. Nothing in this article shall prejudice the trial and punishment of any person for any act or omission which, at the time when it was committed, was criminal

according to the general principles of law recognized by the community of nations.

The requirements of both criminal liability and punishment have to be limited to clear and precise provisions in the law that are in place and applicable at the time the act or omission takes place. In cases where a later law imposes a lighter penalty, the offender has to benefit thereof. The Article constitutes, according to the Committee, the principles of legality (*nullum crimen sine lege*/no crime except in accordance with law) and the rule of law (*nulla poena sine lege*/no punishment except in accordance with law) in the field of criminal law. As Article 4 (2) explicitly prescribes, no derogation from Article 15 may be made. Therefore, any trial leading to the imposition of a penalty during a state of emergency must conform to the requirements of this Article. Only a court of law may try and convict a person for a criminal offence. The presumption of innocence must be respected (Article 14 (2)). General Comment No.: 29. Article 15 relates to *criminal offences*, not child custody cases, A. J. v. G. v. The Netherlands (1142/02), or disciplinary measures. Strik v. The Netherlands (1001/01). It prohibits *ex analogia application* of a law to the disadvantage of a person charged with an offence. Kivenmaa v. Finland (412/90).
The creation of vague and insufficiently defined (or "abstract") offences is a matter of concern to the Committee. Concluding Comments on Portugal (1999) CCPR/C/79/Add. 115. Hence, the courts and authorities of the State Parties that have to interprete and apply domestic legislation have to ensure that laws, which are so vague that their application cannot be foreseen, are not interpreted and applied arbitrarily. Kruyt-Amesz et al. v. The Netherlands (664/95).

Article 15 (1)

No one shall be held guilty of any criminal offence on account of any act or omission which did not constitute a criminal offence, under national or international law, at the time when it was committed. Nor shall a heavier penalty be imposed than the one that was applicable at the time when the criminal offence was committed. If, subsequent to the commission of the offence, provision is made by law for the imposition of the lighter penalty, the offender shall benefit thereby.

The Committee interprets the term *criminal offence* in conformity with the term *criminal charge* in Article 14 (3). Rogerson v. Australia (802/98). It bases its interpretation on the principle that the terms and concepts of the Covenant are independent of any particular national system of law and of all dictionary definitions.

Whether the word *penalty* applies to different kinds of penalties, criminal and administrative, depends on its object and purpose. Duzen v. Canada (50/79). Mandatory supervision is not considered as equivalent to a penalty. It is rather seen as a measure of social assistance intended to provide for the rehabilitation of the convicted person, in his own interest. The fact that, even in the event of remission of the sentence being earned, the person concerned remains subject to supervision after his release and does not regain his unconditional freedom, is therefore not characterized as the imposition or re-imposition of a penalty. A. R. S. v. Canada (91/81).
Article 15 (1) is violated if a person is sentenced under a law that is not in force at the time the acts are committed. Casafranca v. Peru (981/01). Where a person is charged for an offence under a Criminal Code and, subsequently, before the person is convicted, the Code is amended and the amendment is applied to the person, the sentence imposed on the person may not be heavier than that applicable at the time of the offence. Westerman v. The Netherlands (682/96). A sentence that does not explain which version of a Criminal Code it applies does not violate Article 15 (1) if the sentence is well within the latitude provided by the earlier law. Filipovich v. Poland (875/99). A criminal law amendment must not result automatically, for those to whom it is applied, in a lighter penalty compared to that under the earlier legislation. This is true where an amendment only entails a modification in the system of dealing with certain cases and leaves the question as to whether the total effect in the individual case will be a lighter penalty to the judge who sentences the offender. The burden of proving that an amended law denies an advantage of the earlier legislation lies with the author of a communication. MacIsaac v. Canada (55/79).

Article 15 (2)

Nothing in this article shall prejudice the trial and punishment of any person for any act or omission which, at the time when it was committed, was criminal according to the general principles of law recognized by the community of nations.

Article 15 (2) allows the trial and punishment of any person who acts criminally according to the general principles of law recognized by the community of nations. It is, according to the Committee, a general principle of law recognized by the community of nations that lethal force to enforce the prohibition to leave one's own country may only be used to meet a proportionate threat. State authorities have therefore to enforce such a prohibition with the appropriate means. Disproportionate use of force is criminal. The international human rights law obliges State Parties to prosecute those suspected of being responsible for the use of disproportionate force. Baumgarten v. Germany (960/00).

ARTICLE 16

Everyone shall have the right to recognition everywhere as a person before the law.

This Article guarantees that one is *legally recognized* as a person. Article 4 (2) explicitly prescribes that no derogation from this Article may be made. General Comment No.: 29. Administrative detention for reasons of State security of persons who do not personally threaten State security but are kept as "bargaining chips" in order to promote negotiations with other parties on releasing detained soldiers or the bodies of deceased soldiers is incompatible with Articles 16. Concluding Comments on Israel (1998) UN doc. CCPR/C/79/Add. 93.
The State Parties have to endeavour to establish the identity of a person and issue identity papers accordingly. The recognition as a person before the law includes the standing in proceedings. Gallicchio et al. v. Argentina (400/90).
A State Party does not violate the right under this Article if it refuses to provide for marriage between homosexual couples. Joslin et al. v. New Zealand (902/99). The acquittal of one accused and the conviction of another as such do not raise issues of recognition as a person. Werenbeck v. Australia (579/94).

ARTICLE 17

1. No one shall be subjected to arbitrary or unlawful interference with his privacy, family, home or correspondence, nor to unlawful attacks on his honour and reputation.
2. Everyone has the right to the protection of the law against such interference or attacks.

The right of privacy is guaranteed against all interferences and attacks whether they emanate from *State authorities* or from *natural* or *legal persons*. General Comment No.: 16. As there are no limitations enumerated in this Article and Article 5 (1) does not allow a State to limit the rights and freedoms of the Covenant to a greater extend than is provided for in the Covenant, the right of privacy may only be limited for the protection of all members of a society against interferences or attacks. As all persons live in a society, the protection of privacy is necessarily relative. The competent public authorities may call for such information relating to an individual's private life, the knowledge of which is essential in the interests of the society. General Comment No.: 16. The notion of *privacy* refers to the sphere of a person's life in which he or she can freely express his or her identity, be it by entering into relationship with others, or alone. A. R. Coeriel et al. v. The Netherlands (453/91).

Article 17 (1)

No one shall be subjected to arbitrary or unlawful interference with his privacy, family, home or correspondence, nor to unlawful attacks on his honour and reputation.

The abduction of a person, the falsification of her birth certificate and her adoption by another person entails numerous acts of arbitrary and unlawful interference with her privacy and family life. Gallicchio et al. v. Argentina (400/90). The expression *arbitrary interference* is, according to the Committee, not confined to procedural arbitrariness. It can even extend to interference provided for under the law. Also, such interference has to be in accordance with the aims and objectives of Article 17 (1). Every interference has to, in any event, be reasonable in the particular circumstances. Serious inconvenience caused by judicial proceedings before different judicial instances is not qualified as arbitrary or unlawful interference with an individual's privacy. Fei v. Colombia (514/92). Also, the fact that a freely made decision, such as cohabitation with a girlfriend without marrying her, has certain legal consequences in the field of social security does not constitute arbitrary or unlawful interference with privacy and family life. Hoofdman v. the Netherlands (602/94).
As already mentioned before, the notion of *privacy* refers to the sphere of a person's life in which he or she can freely express his or her identity. A. R. Coeriel et al. v. The Netherlands (453/91). A person's surname constitutes an important component of one's identity. The protection against arbitrary or unlawful interference with one's privacy includes therefore the protection against arbitrary or unlawful interference with the right to choose and change one's own name. The request to have one's change of name recognized can only be refused on grounds that are reasonable in the specific circumstances of the case. The refusal of the change of a surname on the grounds that the applicant has not shown that the change sought is essential to pursue his religious studies, that the name has religious connotations and that it is uncommon sounding is not reasonable and therefore arbitrary within the meaning of Article 17 (1). A. R. Coeriel et al. v. The Netherlands (453/91). A State Party does not violate Article 17 if it refuses to provide for marriage between homosexual couples. Joslin et al. v. New Zealand (902/99). On the other hand, it is undisputed that adult *consensual sexual activity* in private is covered by the concept of privacy.

State Parties have to protect the freedom of an adult individual's sexual conduct. Concluding Comments on United Republic of Tanzania (1998) UN doc. CCPR/C/79/Add. 97. A prohibition of private homosexual behaviour interferes with a person's privacy. This is true even if the prohibition has not been enforced for a decade. The policy not to initiate criminal proceedings in respect of private homosexual conduct does not amount to a guarantee that no actions will be brought against homosexuals in the future. Hence, the continued existence of provisions, which prohibit private homosexual behaviour, continuously and directly interferes with a person's privacy. The Committee also does not deem a prohibition that is not enforced as essential, necessary and reasonable. Toonen v. Australia (488/92).

The term *family* has to be interpreted to include all those comprising a family as understood in the society of the State Party concerned. *Cultural traditions* have to be taken into account. The relationship to ancestors can be an essential element of identity and play an important role in family life. A State Party that does not consider such traditions and allows the construction of a hotel complex on ancestral burial grounds violates Article 17 (1). Hopu et al. v. France (549/93).

The interference with *family relations* is the inevitable outcome of a deportation. The Committee does not regard it as either unlawful or arbitrary when the deportation order is made under law in furtherance of a legitimate state interest, and due consideration is given in the deportation proceedings to the deportee's family connections. The separation of a person from his family by means of his expulsion is an arbitrary interference with the family and a violation of Article 17 if the separation of the family and its effects on a person are disproportionate to the objectives of removal. The mere fact that one member of a family is entitled to remain in the territory of a State Party does not necessarily mean that requiring other members of the family to leave involves arbitrary interference in family life contrary to Article 17. Winata et al. v. Australia (930/00). No arbitrariness was seen in the case of a person who had an almost continuous record of convictions from age 17 to age 31, who had neither spouse nor children and whose family was not able to provide a help or guidance in overcoming his criminal tendencies and his drug-addiction. Canepa v. Canada (558/93) – immigration at the age of **five**. Also, the removal of a divorced individual who had been residing from age **seven** until his deportation with age thirty in the territory of a State Party, leaving behind his two children and his entire family apart from one brother who lived in the country to which he was deported, was not seen as a violation of Article 17 (1). Stewart v. Canada (538/93). On the other hand, the removal of a mother and her children without awaiting the final determination of the father's and husband's immigration proceedings constituted arbitrary interference in this family. Bakhtiyari et al. v. Australia (1069/02). Also, the decision of a State Party to deport the parents and to compel the family to choose whether the **13-year old** child, who had attained citizenship of the State Party after living there for 10 years, either to remain alone in the country or accompany his parents, constituted arbitrary interference with family life contrary to Article 17. Additional factors that go beyond a simple enforcement of immigration law have to justify the removal of both parents in such a case. Winata et al. v. Australia (930/00).

Article 17 is not applicable if, except for a brief period of 2 years some 17 years ago, a person and her adopted daughter have not lived together as a family. A. S. et al. v. Canada (68/80).

The term *home* has to be understood, according to the Committee, to indicate the place where a person resides or carries out his usual occupation. The common residence of husband and wife is considered as the normal behaviour of a family. A State Party that excludes one of them has to do this without discrimination. A distinction based on sex that interferes with the family life of a couple has to be justified. Aumeeruddy-Cziffra et al. v. Mauritius (35/78) - immigration law.

Article 17 requires that the integrity and confidentiality of *correspondence* is guaranteed *de iure* and *de facto*. Correspondence has to be delivered to the addressee without interception and without being opened or otherwise read. General Comment No.: 16. Prohibitory orders must not be too broad. The broad scope of a prohibitory order, pursuant to the provisions of a Post Office Act, which forbid the transmission of scurrilous material, extended to all mail, whether sent or received, raised for the Committee a question of compatibility with Article 17. J. R. T. et al. v. Canada (104/81). Prison authorities have the right to exercise measures of control and censorship over prisoners' correspondence. Prisoners have to be allowed, under necessary supervision, to communicate with their families and reputable friends at regular intervals by correspondence. Estrella v. Uruguay (74/80). Measures of control or censorship must be subject to legislative provisions that provide the necessary protection against arbitrary application. Pinkney v. Canada (27/77).

Clear legislation setting out the conditions for legitimate interferences with privacy and providing for safeguards against unlawful interferences has to be established. Concluding Comments on the Russian Federation (1995) UN doc. CCPR/C/79/Add. 54 - intrusion into private telephone communication. Concluding Comments on Jamaica (1997) UN doc. CCPR/C/79/Add. 83 - wire-tapping. *Surveillance*, whether electronic or otherwise, interceptions of telephonic, telegraphic and other forms of communication, wire-tapping and recording of conversations are prohibited if there is no independent monitoring

(judicial supervision) of such practices. Concluding Comments on Zimbabwe (1999) UN doc. CCPR/C/79/Add. 110 - postal articles or telegrams. Concluding Comments on Poland (1999) UN doc. CCPR/C/79/Add. 110 - telephone tapping.
A State Party that *searches* a person's home for necessary evidence has to restrict such searches. A search may not amount to harassment. A raid on the home of a family that is carried out illegally without a search warrant violates Article 17 (1). Coronel et al. v. Colombia (778/97). Hooded men who enter a house through the roof at 2 a. m. and who fire a gunshot to compel the occupants to find the keys to the main door violate Article 17 (1), even if they act according to the letter of the law. García v. Colombia (687/96). As far as personal and body search is concerned, such searches have to be carried out in a manner consistent with the *dignity of the person* who is being searched. Persons being subjected to a body search have to be examined by persons of the same sex. General Comment No.: 16. The strip-searching of male and female prisoners in view of the existence of adequate alternative search techniques is incompatible with the concept of privacy. Concluding Comments on United Kingdom of Great Britain and Northern Ireland (1995) UN doc. CCPR/C/79/Add. 55.
The *gathering and holding of personal information* on computers, databanks and other devices, whether by public authorities or private individuals or bodies must be, according to the Committee, regulated by law. Effective measures have to be taken by States to ensure that information concerning a person's private life does not reach the hands of persons who are not authorized by law to receive, process and use it. Every individual has the right to ascertain in an intelligible form whether, and if so, what, personal data is stored in automatic data files, and for what purposes. General Comment No.: 16. If such files contain incorrect personal data or have been collected or processed contrary to the provisions of the law, every individual has the right to request rectification or elimination. Concluding Comments on the Republic of Korea (1999) UN doc. CCPR/C/79/Add. 114.
A State Party that consistently refers to a person in the press as being mentally disturbed and seeks to have a person declared insane, although medical reports contradict such diagnosis, subjects the person to an unlawful attack on his *honour and reputation*. Birhashwirwa et al. v. Zaire (241, 242/87). But the Committee did not attribute articles about a person's alleged involvement in fraudulent procurement policies, as published in local and national newspapers that were supportive of the government in force, to the State Party's authorities. Rio v. Peru (263/87). Every person who complains about an unlawful attack on his honour and reputation has to prove it. Simons v. Panama (460/91) - judicial

proceedings. I. P. v. Finland (450/91) - disclosure of information by tax inspectors. R. L. M. v. Trinidad and Tobago (380/89) - remarks made by a judge in his judicial capacity.

Article 17 (2)

Everyone has the right to the protection of the law against such interference or attacks.

The protection of every member of a society against interference or attacks is, according to the Committee, an obligation for State Parties. They are under a duty to provide the legislative framework prohibiting interference or attacks by *natural* or *legal* persons. Everyone must have the possibility of effectively being able to protect himself against interferences or attacks that occur and to have an *effective remedy*, either civil or criminal, against those responsible. General Comment No.: 16. State Parties have to take measures to investigate with a view to ensuring women rights to privacy allegations that women who seek employment in enterprises are subjected to pregnancy tests and required to respond to intrusive personal questioning. Concluding Comments on Mexico (1999) UN doc. CCPR/C/79/Add. 109.
Article 17 (2) includes effective protection to the right of a parent to regular contact with his or her minor children. While there may be exceptional circumstances in which denying contact is required in the interests of the children and is not unlawful or arbitrary, it is not in the best interest of children, in the absence of such special circumstances, to virtually eliminate one parent's access to them. Fei v. Colombia (514/92). Nor do special circumstances exist if a domestic court of a State Party has ruled that the father may meet his son. When the mother fails to respect this order and the court neither fully enforces nor replaces it with other measures aimed at ensuring the rights recognized in this Article, Article 17 (2) is violated by the State Party. L. P. v. Czech Republic (946/00).

ARTICLE 18

1. Everyone shall have the right to freedom of thought, conscience and religion. This right shall include freedom to have or to adopt a religion or belief of his choice, and freedom, either individually or in community with others and in public or private, to manifest his religion or belief in worship, observance, practice and teaching.
2. No one shall be subject to coercion which would impair his freedom to have or to adopt a religion or belief of his choice.

Article 18

3. Freedom to manifest one's religion or beliefs may be subject only to such limitations as are prescribed by law and are necessary to protect public safety, order, health, or morals or the fundamental rights and freedoms of others.
4. The States Parties to the present Covenant undertake to have respect for the liberty of parents and, when applicable, legal guardians to ensure the religious and moral education of their children in conformity with their own convictions.

The right to freedom of thought, conscience and religion, which includes the freedom to hold beliefs, is far-reaching and profound. No derogation from it may be made (Article 4 (2)). General Comment No.: 29. It encompasses *freedom of thought* on all matters, personal conviction and the commitment to religion or belief, whether manifested individually or in community with others. The provision protects, according to the Committee, theistic, non-theistic and atheistic beliefs, as well as the right not to profess any religion or belief. It distinguishes the freedom of thought, conscience, religion or belief from the freedom to manifest religion or belief. The *freedom to manifest* religion or belief may be exercised either individually or in community with others and in public or private. It encompasses worship, observance, practice and teaching. A State Party may, without violating Article 18, allow competent religious authorities to decide who may teach religion and in what manner it has to be taught. Páez v. Colombia (195/85). The concept of worship extends to, according to the Committee, ritual and ceremonial acts given direct expression to belief, as well as various practices integral to such acts, including the building of places of worship, the use of ritual formulae and objects, the display of symbols, and the observance of holidays and days of rest. The observance and practice of religion or belief include not only ceremonial acts but also such customs as the observance of dietary regulations, the wearing of distinctive clothing or head coverings, participation in rituals associated with certain stages of life, and the use of a particular language customarily spoken by a group. General Comment No.: 22. In addition, the practice and teaching of religion or belief includes, according to the Committee, acts integral to the conduct by religious groups of their basic affairs, such as, inter alia, the freedom to choose their religious leaders, priests and teachers, the freedom to establish seminaries or religious schools and the freedom to prepare and distribute religious texts or publications. However, no manifestation of religions or beliefs may, according to the Committee, amount to *propaganda* for war or advocacy of national, racial or religious hatred that constitutes incitement to discrimination, hostility or violence (Article 20). The *freedom to have or to adopt a religion or belief* necessarily entails for the Committee the freedom to choose a religion or belief, including, inter alia, the right to replace one's current religion or belief with another or to adopt atheistic views, as well as the right to retain one's religion or belief. The fact that a religion is recognized as a *State religion* or that it is established as official or traditional or that its followers comprise the majority of the population is compatible with Article 18 as long as this does not result in any impairment of the freedom under Article 18. General Comment No.: 22.

Article 18 does not imply, especially taking Article 8 (3) c (ii) into account, the right to *conscientious objection*. L. T. K. v. Finland (185/84). On the other side the Committee derives such a right from Article 18, inasmuch as the obligation to use lethal force seriously conflicts with the freedom of conscience and the right to manifest one's religion or belief. General Comment No.: 22. In these cases the legislation of the State Parties has to allow conscientious objection to military service. In addition, it has to be guaranteed that conscientious objectors are able to opt for alternative service. Concluding Comments on Colombia (2004) UN doc. CCPR/CO/80/COL. It is not consistent with the requirements of Article 18 that individuals cannot claim the status of conscientious objectors once they have entered the armed forces. Concluding Comments on Spain (1996) UN doc. CCPR/C/79/Add. 61. The tasks to be performed by conscientious objectors have to be compatible with their convictions. Concluding Comments on the Russian Federation (2003) UN doc. CCPR/CO/79/RUS. The Committee does not evaluate applications for exemption from service in the armed forces under State law. This has to be done by the authorities of the State Parties. Muhonen v. Finland (89/81).

The requirement, despite conscientious objection, of singing the national anthem and saluting the national flag as a condition of attending a State school is an unreasonable requirement and incompatible with Article 18. Concluding Comments on Zambia (1996) UN doc. CCPR/C/79/Add. 62.

A *belief* consisting primarily or exclusively in the worship and distribution of a narcotic drug cannot be brought within the scope of Article 18. M. A. B. et al. v. Canada (570/93).

Article 18 (1)

1. Everyone shall have the right to freedom of thought, conscience and religion. This right shall include freedom to have or to adopt a religion or belief of his choice, and freedom, either individually or in community with others and in public or private, to manifest his religion or belief in worship, observance, practice and teaching.

The right to freedom of conscience does not, as such, imply the right to refuse all obligations imposed by law, nor does it provide immunity from criminal liability in respect of every such refusal. Therefore, the imposition of sanctions

to enforce the performance of military duty after a person fails to satisfy the authorities of a State Party that he has an insurmountable objection of conscience to military service does not violate Article 18 (1). Westerman v. The Netherlands (682/96). Also, the refusal to pay taxes on the grounds of conscientious objection falls outside the scope of protection of this Article. K. V. et al. v. Germany (568/93). J. v. K. et al. v. The Netherlands (483/91). J. P. v. Canada (446/91).
On the other hand an "ideology conversion system" or "oath of law-abidance system" applied by a State Party with the view to alter the political opinion of inmates by offering inducements of preferential treatment within prisons and improved possibilities of parole is incompatible with Article 18 (1). Kang v. Republic of Korea (878/99).

Article 18 (2)

No one shall be subject to coercion which would impair his freedom to have or to adopt a religion or belief of his choice.

No one can be compelled to reveal his thoughts or adherence to a religion or belief. This provision bars, according to the Committee, coercions that impair the right to have or adopt a religion or belief, including the use of threat of physical force or penal sanctions to compel believers or non-believers to adhere to their religious beliefs and congregations, to recant their religion or belief, or to convert. Holders of all beliefs of a non-religious nature enjoy the same protection. General Comment No.: 22. State Parties have to take measures to ensure respect for freedom of religion and belief, and ensure that their laws and policies fully comply with Article 18. Concluding Comments on Morocco (1999) UN doc. CCPR/C/79/Add. 113. Constitutional provisions that require judges to make a declaration with religious references are incompatible with the respect for freedom of religion and belief. Concluding Comments on Ireland (2000) UN doc. CCPR/CO/69/IRL. Adherence to certain religious organizations or beliefs may not constitute one of the main grounds to disqualify individuals from obtaining employment in the public service. Concluding Comments on Germany (2004) UN doc. CCPR/CO/80/DEU. Where registration of religions is required and the registration depends on the number of followers, Article 18 (2) is violated. Concluding Comments on Armenia (1998) CCPR/C/79/Add. 100.

Article 18 (3)

Freedom to manifest one's religion or beliefs may be subject only to such limitations as are prescribed by law and are necessary to protect public safety, order, health, or morals or the fundamental rights and freedoms of others.

This Article does not permit any limitations whatsoever on the freedom of thought and conscience or on the freedom from coercion to have or to adopt a religion or belief. Also the liberty of the parents and guardians to ensure religious and moral education cannot be restricted. These freedoms are protected unconditionally. General Comment No.: 22.
It can never become necessary for a State Party to derogate from Article 18 during a state of emergency. The reference in Article 4 (2) to Article 18 demonstrates to the Committee that the permissibility of restrictions is independent of the issue of derogability. Even in times of the most serious public emergencies, States that interfere with the freedom to manifest one's religion or belief must justify their actions by referring to the requirements specified in Article 18 (3). General Comment No.: 29.
Article 18 (3) permits restrictions on the freedom to manifest religion or belief only if law prescribes limitations and these restrictions are necessary to protect public safety, order, health or morals, or the fundamental rights and freedoms of others. Limitations imposed must be established by *law* and must not be applied in a manner that would vitiate the rights guaranteed in Article 18. Article 18 is not violated if an action by State authorities taken against a person is not aimed at his thoughts or beliefs as such, but rather at the manifestation of those beliefs within a particular context. Ross v. Canada (736/97) - school. The regulation of surnames and the change thereof is a matter of *public order*. Restrictions are therefore permissible under Article 18 (3). Coeriel et al. v. The Netherlands (453/91). The Committee regards legislation requiring that workers be protected from injury and electric shock by the wearing of hard hats as a limitation that is justified. Bhinder v. Canada (208/86) - Sikh.
Restrictions are not allowed, according to the Committee, on grounds not specified in this Article, even if they are allowed as restrictions to other rights protected in the Covenant, such as national security. Limitations may be applied only for those purposes for which they have been prescribed and must be directly related and proportionate to the specific need on which they are predicated. They may not be imposed for discriminatory purposes or applied in a discriminatory manner. The conviction of involvement in reorganizing a dissolved fascist party is based on an act that is of a kind which is removed from

the protection of the Covenant by Article 5. Such an act may be prohibited by law. M. A. v. Italy (117/81).
The concept of *morals* derives, for the Committee, from many social, philosophical and religious traditions. Limitations on the freedom to manifest a religion or belief for the purpose of protecting morals must therefore be based on principles not deriving exclusively from a single tradition. General Comment No.: 22.
Persons already subject to certain legitimate constrains, such as prisoners, continue to enjoy their rights to manifest their religion or belief to the fullest extent compatible with the specific nature of the constraint. Detained Muslims may wear a beard or worship at religious services. Prayer books may not be taken away from them. Boodoo v. Trinidad (721/96).

Article 18 (4)

The States Parties to the present Covenant undertake to have respect for the liberty of parents and, when applicable, legal guardians to ensure the religious and moral education of their children in conformity with their own convictions.

Public education that includes instruction in a particular religion or belief is not, according to the Committee, inconsistent with Article 18 (4) if provision is made for non-discriminatory exemptions or alternatives that accommodate the wishes of parents and guardians. General Comment No.: 22. Therefore, the requirement of provisions of a State Party's legislation that instruction in the study of the history of religion and ethics are given instead of religious instruction to students whose parents or legal guardians object to religious instruction is not, in itself, incompatible with Article 18 (4) if such an alternative course of instruction is given in a neutral and objective way and respects the convictions of parents and guardians who do not believe in any religion. Hartikainen et al. v. Finland (40/78). However, a law that states that individuals professing a certain religion are bound to bring up their children in the same faith is in clear contradiction with Article 18. Concluding Comments on Norway (1999) UN doc. CCPR/C/79/Add. 112.
If a State Party chooses to provide public funding to religious schools, it has to make this funding available without discrimination. This means that providing funding for the schools of one religious group and not for another must be based on reasonable and objective criteria. Waldman v. Canada (694/96). Differential treatment of religious denominations in the allocation of public funds is a matter of concern for the Committee. Concluding Comments on Liechtenstein (2004) UN doc. CCPR/CO/81/LIE.

ARTICLE 19

1. Everyone shall have the right to hold opinions without interference.
2. Everyone shall have the right to freedom of expression; this right shall include freedom to seek, receive and impart information and ideas of all kinds, regardless of frontiers, either orally, in writing or in print, in the form of art, or through any other media of his choice.
3. The exercise of the rights provided for in paragraph 2 of this article carries with it special duties and responsibilities. It may therefore be subject to certain restrictions, but these shall only be such as are provided by law and are necessary:
(a) For respect of the rights or reputations of others;
(b) For the protection of national security or of public order (ordre public), or of public health or morals.

The right to freedom of opinion and expression is of paramount importance in any democratic society. Any restrictions to the exercise of this right must, according to the Committee, meet a strict test of justification. Measures taken against a person have to be necessary for the purposes stated. Disciplinary or other sanctions against a municipal official for writing a critical report to his employer when the latter considers the language as defamatory raise issues under Article 19. Strik v. The Netherlands (1001/01). Article 19 does not provide for the right to conscientious objection L. T. K. v. Finland (185/84).

Article 19 (1)

Everyone shall have the right to hold opinions without interference.

This provision guarantees a right to which the Covenant permits no exception or restriction. General Comment No.: 10. The term *opinion* circumscribes a passive conduct that is protected from every interference. An "ideology conversion system" or "oath of law-abidance system" is incompatible with Article 19 (1). A State Party that wants to alter the political opinion of inmates by offering inducements of preferential treatment within prison and improved possibilities of parole does not respect the right to hold opinions without interference. Kang v. Republic of Korea (878/99). Persecution of persons for holding political opinions violates Article 19 (1). Mpaka-Nsusu v. Zaire (157/83). Mpandanjila et al. v. Zaire (138/83). Muteba v. Zaire (124/82).

Article 19 (2)

Everyone shall have the right to freedom of expression; this right shall include freedom to seek, receive and impart information and ideas of all kinds, regardless of frontiers, either orally, in writing or in print, in the form of art, or through any other media of his choice.

The right to freedom of expression is the manifestation of one's opinion. It is the cornerstone in any free and democratic society. Laptsevich v. Belarus (780/97). It is in the essence of such societies that its citizens must be allowed to inform themselves about alternatives to the political system or parties in power, and that they may criticize or openly and publicly evaluate their governments without fear of interference or punishment. Aduayom et al. v. Togo (422-424/90). Persecution for advocacy of multi-party democracy and an expression of opinions inimical to a State Party's government violates this right. Mukong v. Cameroon (458/91). Arrest and detention solely or primarily because of membership in, or activities for, a political party or a trade union, Burgos v. Uruguay (52/79), are not compatible with the right to freedom of expression. Miha v. Equatorial Guinea (414/90). Kalenga v. Zambia (326/88). Bwalya v. Zambia (314/88). A State Party that does not explain the scope and meaning of the term "subversive activities", which constitute a criminal offence under the legislation of the State Party, violates Article 19 (2) if a person is prosecuted solely for his opinion. Carballal v. Uruguay (33/78).

In view of the importance of access to information about the democratic process a person's exclusion from the publicly funded media facilities of Parliament constitutes a restriction of his right to have access to information. Gauthier v. Canada (633/95).

The Committee interprets the right to freedom of expression as encompassing every form of subjective idea and opinion capable of transmission to others. A person who joins others in issuing a statement supporting a strike and criticizing the government is exercising his right to impart information and ideas. Sohn v. Republic of Korea (518/92). An individual can express his political opinions by raising a banner, Kivenmaa v. Finland (412/90), or carrying a poster. Dergachev v. Belarus (921/00). A hunger strike is subsumed under the right to freedom of expression, Baban et al. v. Australia (1014/01), the defacing of road signs, however, is not. G. B. v. France (348/89). S. G. v. France (347/88). The fact that a person is not able to speak the language of his choice before a court raised no issues under Article 19 (2). Cadoret et al. v. France (323/88, 221/87, 219/86).

Freedom of expression is not confined to means of political, cultural or artistic expression. The commercial element in an expression taking the form of

outdoor advertising does not have the effect of removing this expression from the scope of the protected freedom. Ballantyne et al. v. Canada (359, 385/89).
A State Party may choose one or more official languages, but it may not exclude, outside the spheres of public life, the freedom to express oneself in a language of one's choice. Singer v. Canada (455/91). Ballantyne et al. v. Canada (359, 385/89).
Article 19 (2) protects the freedom of teachers to teach their subjects in accordance with their own views, without interference. Páez v. Colombia (195/85). But it does not include a right to exercise a specific teaching activity. R. T. v. France (262/87) - tenure as a teacher of a certain language. That applicants for the post of religious teacher must present to State authorities a certificates of suitability for teaching religion issued by the competent religious authority and that they have to teach religion in a certain way does not violate Article 19 (2). Páez v. Colombia (195/85).
Although the right to freedom of expression extends to the choice of medium, it does not amount to an unfettered right of any individual or group. Individuals or groups have no right to hold press conferences within the Parliamentary precincts, or to have such press conferences broadcasted by others. Therefore, a motion passed unanimously by the Parliament to exclude a person's access to the Parliamentary precincts fell outside the scope of the right to freedom of expression. The person remained at liberty to hold a press conference elsewhere. Zündel v. Canada (953/00). On the other hand the right of the producers of a television program under Article 19 (2) was violated when the program, produced for transmission within the framework of a broadcasting organization with the general approval of the responsible authorities, was censored. Hertzberg et al. v. Finland (61/79). Also, an Act that required publishers of periodicals to include certain publication data, including index and registration numbers, which could only be obtained from the administrative authorities, on a leaflet with a print run as low as 200 restricted the freedom to impart information. Laptsevich v. Belarus (780/97). The right to write and publish textbooks intended for use at school falls under the protection of Article 19. However, this Article does not entitle a person to have his textbook scrutinized and approved or rejected by the authorities for use as textbook in public schools. Nam v. Republic of Korea (693/96).

Article 19 (3)

The exercise of the rights provided for in paragraph 2 of this article carries with it special duties and responsibilities. It may therefore be subject to certain restrictions, but these shall only be such as are provided by law and are necessary:

This provision expressly stresses that the exercise of the right to freedom of expression carries with it *special duties* and *responsibilities*. Certain restrictions on the right to freedom of expression are permitted which may relate either to the interests of other persons or to those of the community as a whole. But a State Party may not, by imposing restrictions on the exercise of freedom of expression, jeopardize the right itself. General Comment No.: 10. Licensing of television and radio stations has to be done within reasonable and objective criteria. The licensing process may not have the effect of restricting media pluralism and freedom of expression. Concluding Comments on Lebanon (1997) UN doc. CCPR/C/79/Add. 78. State Parties have to provide guidelines for the granting or refusal of the registration of newspapers. Concluding Comments on Lesotho (1999) CCPR/C/79/Add. 106. State monopolization of media undermines the principle of freedom of expression. Concluding Comments on Sri Lanka (2003) UN doc. CCPR/CO/79/LKA. In order to avoid the inherent risks in the excessive concentration of control of the mass information media in a small group of people, State Parties have to adopt anti-trust legislation regulating mass media. Concluding Comments on Italy (1994) CCPR/C/79/Add. 37.

Any restriction on the right to freedom of expression must cumulatively meet the following conditions: It must address one of the aims set out in this Article. It must be necessary to achieve a legitimate purpose. Finally, it must be provided by law. Ross v. Canada (736/97). A restrictive law itself must meet these conditions. Faurisson v. France (550/93). The words *provided by law* include a statutory law, a law as read, interpreted and applied by a court, Faurisson v. France (550/93), a vague legal framework applied by a court, Ross v. Canada (736/97), and the law of parliamentary privilege. Gauthier v. Canada (633/95). Article 19 (3) does not permit restrictions on the expression of ideas merely because they coincide with those held by an enemy or may be considered to create sympathy for that entity. Concluding Comments on the Republic of Korea (1999) UN doc. CCPR/C/79/Add. 114.

Article 19 (3) a

The exercise of the rights provided for in paragraph 2 of this article carries with it special duties and responsibilities. It may therefore be subject to certain restrictions, but these shall only be such as are provided by law and are necessary:

For respect of the rights or reputations of others;

Restrictions on outdoor advertising in a language other than the one of the minority living in the area are not *necessary* for the respect of the *rights of*

others (minority). The right of a minority to use the own language is not jeopardized by the freedom of others to advertise in another language. Therefore, a State may choose one or more official languages, but it may not exclude, outside the spheres of public life, the freedom to express oneself in a language of one's choice. Ballantyne et al. v. Canada (359, 385/89).
An Act, which, in its effect, makes it a criminal offence to challenge the conclusions and the verdict of the International Military Tribunal at Nuremberg, is not incompatible with the right to freedom of expression if it does not encroach upon the right to hold and express an opinion in general and the restriction of the freedom of expression relates to the *interests of other persons* or to those of a community as a whole. Acts that serve the struggle against racism and anti-Semitism may restrict statements of a nature that raise or strengthen anti-Semitic feelings. Faurisson v. France (550/93). The transfer of a person from his teaching position to a non-teaching position because of his off-duty comments is, in effect, a restriction on his freedom of expression. Such a restriction has to be justified. It is justified if public statements are discriminatory against persons of a certain faith and ancestry, denigrate the faith and beliefs of those persons, and call upon true Christians to not merely question the validity of this beliefs and teachings, but to hold those of this faith and ancestry in contempt as undermining freedom, democracy and Christian beliefs and values. Such statements violate the rights or reputations of other persons, including the right to have an education in the public school system *free from bias, prejudice and intolerance*. Ross v. Canada (736/97). The Committee did not deem it *necessary* that leaflets (200 pieces) have to be registered with the administrative authorities prior to their publication and dissemination for the respect of the rights or reputations of others. Laptsevich v. Belarus (780/97).

Article 19 (3) b

The exercise of the rights provided for in paragraph 2 of this article carries with it special duties and responsibilities. It may therefore be subject to certain restrictions, but these shall only be such as are provided by law and are necessary.
For the protection of national security or of public order (ordre public), or of public health or morals.

None of the forms of expression can be subjected to varying degrees of limitation. Therefore, none of them should suffer broader restrictions than the others. Ballantyne et al. v. Canada (359, 385/89). Any restrictions to the exercise of the right to freedom of expression must meet a strict *test of justification*. Kim v. the Republic of Korea (574/94). The information that a person is charged with subversive association is not in itself sufficient to justify a restriction of the freedom of expression. Lanza et al. v. Uruguay (8/77). Also, the legitimate objective of safeguarding and strengthening national unity under difficult political circumstances cannot be achieved by attempting to muzzle advocacy of multi-party democracy, democratic tenets and human rights. Such measures never meet the "necessity" test. Mukong v. Cameroon (458/91). A State Party that invokes *national security* by reference to the general situation in the country and the threat posed by certain elements has to specify the precise nature of the threat which it deems posed by a person's exercise of freedom of expression. A reference to activities as a member of an enemy benefiting organization that endorses the policies of a certain government cannot justify a restriction of the peaceful exercise of the right of freedom of expression. Park v. Republic of Korea (628/95). If it is plain that the policies of another government are well known within the territory of a State Party, the State Party has to show how the reading and distributing of policy statements of that government can create a risk to national security. Kim v. Republic of Korea (574/94).

A statement supporting a strike and condemning a government's threat to send troops to break the strike does not threaten national security or *public order*. Sohn v. Republic of Korea (518/92). The protection of parliamentary procedure is a legitimate goal of public order. An accreditation system can thus be a justified means of achieving this goal. However, when an accreditation system operates as a restriction of Article 19 rights, its operation and application must be shown as *necessary and proportionate* to the goal in question and *not arbitrary*. Therefore, the relevant criteria for the accreditation scheme have to be specific, fair and reasonable, and their application has to be transparent. A State Party that allows a private organization to control access to parliamentary press facilities has to ensure that there will be no arbitrary exclusion from access to those facilities. The denial of access to the press facilities of Parliament for not being a member of the private organization that controls the access to those facilities is not necessary and proportionate in order to ensure the effective operation of Parliament and the safety of its members. Gauthier v. Canada (633/95). The Committee did not deem necessary, for the protection of public order: The requirement that, prior to publishing and disseminating a leaflet with a print run of 200, a person has to register his publication with the administrative authorities to obtain index and registration numbers and the measure that the breach of the requirement leads not only to pecuniary sanctions, but also to the confiscation of the leaflets still in the person's possession. Laptsevich v. Belarus (780/97).

Steps lawfully taken under regulations governing the operation of centres and supervision of detainees to remove hunger strikers, including young children, from a location because of *health* and *safety* concerns (namely to respect the rights of other detainees, to maintain the good order and security of the facility, to protect the safety and security of visitors) fall within the legitimate restrictions provided for in Article 19 (3). Baban et al. v. Australia (1014/01).
The exercise of the rights provided for in Article 19 (2) may be restricted for the protection of *public morals*. There is, according to the Committee, no universally applicable common standard of the content of the term *public morals*. Consequently, in this respect, a certain margin of discretion is accorded to the responsible national authorities. Hence, it is up to the responsible organs of a State Party to decide if radio and TV are the appropriate forums to discuss issues related to homosexuality. The state authorities have to bear in mind that the audience cannot be controlled. Also, harmful effects on minors have to be considered. Hertzberg et al. v. Finland (61/79). But a reference to an attempt to undermine the morale of the armed forces of a State Party is not in itself sufficient, without details of the alleged charges, to justify a restriction to the freedom of expression. Motta v. Uruguay (11/77).

ARTICLE 20

1. Any propaganda for war shall be prohibited by law.
2. Any advocacy of national, racial or religious hatred that constitutes incitement to discrimination, hostility or violence shall be prohibited by law.

Although this provision is not listed in Article 4 (2) as non-derogable, there are, according to the Committee, elements in it that cannot be made subject to a lawful derogation under Article 4. No declaration of a state of emergency made pursuant to Article 4 (1) may be invoked as justification for a State Party to engage itself in, contrary to this provision, propaganda for war, or advocacy of national, racial or religious hatred that constitutes incitement to discrimination, hostility or violence. General Comment No.: 29. The required prohibitions of this Article are fully compatible with the right of freedom of expression as contained in Article 19, the exercise of which carries with it special duties and responsibilities. General Comment No.: 11. Restrictions on expression which fall within the scope of Article 20 must also be permissible under Article 19 (3), which lays down requirements for determining whether restrictions on expression are permissible. Ross v. Canada (736/97).

Article 20 (1)

Any propaganda for war shall be prohibited by law.

The prohibition under this provision extends to all forms of propaganda threatening or resulting in an act of aggression or breach of the peace contrary to the Charter of the United Nations. Advocacy of the sovereign right of self-defence or the right of peoples to self-determination and independence, in accordance with the Charter, is not prohibited. General Comment No. 11.

Article 20 (2)

Any advocacy of national, racial or religious hatred that constitutes incitement to discrimination, hostility or violence shall be prohibited by law.

This Article is directed against any advocacy of national, racial or religious hatred that constitutes incitement to discrimination, hostility or violence, whether such propaganda or advocacy has aims, which are internal or external to the State concerned. General Comment No.: 11. Article 20 (2) reflects principles of the Covenant. Ross v. Canada (736/97). It obliges a State Party to prohibit the dissemination of opinions that clearly advocate racial or religious hatred through the telephone system. J. R. T. v. Canada (104/81).

ARTICLE 21

The right of peaceful assembly shall be recognized. No restrictions may be placed on the exercise of this right other than those imposed in conformity with the law and which are necessary in a democratic society in the interests of national security or public safety, public order (ordre public), the protection of public health or morals or the protection of the rights and freedoms of others.

A right of assembly also guarantees Article 18. Article 17 and 22 entail a right of assembly as the terms family and association are inseparable connected with the notion of different persons united under these terms. Article 21 guarantees the right of assembly to all the persons who are not protected by a more specific right. The restriction that a father, as a non-custodial parent, can exercise his right to access to his son only under supervision does not raise issues under the right of assembly. P. S. v. Denmark (397/90).
The right of assembly is only guaranteed to *peaceful assemblies*. Restrictions may be placed on the exercise of it. State Parties have the requirement of prior notification for assemblies to restrict to outdoor assemblies. Concluding

Comments on Morocco (1999) UN doc. CCPR/C/79/Add. 113. The regulation that prior notification be made **seven days**, Concluding Comments on Mauritius (1996) UN doc. CCPR/C/79/Add. 60, before any public meeting is held is a matter of concern for the Committee. A requirement of 15 days, Concluding Comments on Belarus (1997) UN doc. CCPR/C/79/Add. 86, unduly circumscribes legitimate forms of assembly. Concluding Comments on Republic of Moldova (2002) UN doc. CCPR/CO/75/MDA. A requirement to notify the police of an intended demonstration in a public place **six hours** before its commencement is compatible with the permitted limitations laid down in Article 21. Kivenmaa v. Finland (412/90).

The Committee did not regard the gathering of several individuals at the site of the welcoming ceremonies for a foreign head of State on an official visit, publicly announced in advance by the authorities, as a demonstration. Also, the displaying of a banner did not turn such a gathering into a demonstration. Hence, the application of a State Party's legislation on demonstrations to such a gathering cannot be considered as an application of a restriction permitted by Article 21. Kivenmaa v. Finland (412/90).

The right of peaceful assembly obliges State Parties to train their police forces in methods of crowd control so that offenders can be handled and participants of an assembly or bystanders are not injured. Concluding Comments on Denmark (1996) UN doc. CCPR/C/79/Add. 68. Particular attention has to be given to the rules and practices on the use of police dogs in crowd control. Concluding Comments on Denmark (2000) UN doc. CCPR/CO/70/DNK.

ARTICLE 22

1. Everyone shall have the right to freedom of association with others, including the right to form and join trade unions for the protection of his interests.

2. No restrictions may be placed on the exercise of this right other than those which are prescribed by law and which are necessary in a democratic society in the interests of national security or public safety, public order (ordre public), the protection of public health or morals or the protection of the rights and freedoms of others. This article shall not prevent the imposition of lawful restrictions on members of the armed forces and of the police in their exercise of this right.

3. Nothing in this article shall authorize States Parties to the International Labour Organization Convention of 1948 concerning Freedom of Association and Protection of the Right to Organize to take legislative measures which would prejudice, or to apply the law in such a manner as to prejudice, the guarantees provided for in that Convention.

Article 22 (1)

Everyone shall have the right to freedom of association with others, including the right to form and join trade unions for the protection of his interests.

Freedom of association gives people the right to join together for the pursuance of common interests. The right to form and join *trade unions* is particularly mentioned. Trade unions are, according to the Committee, associations of employees designed to further the common interest of their members. A State Party that persecutes a person for his trade union activities violates Article 22 (1). Burgos v. Uruguay (52/79). The Committee does not consider *the right to strike* as an implicit component of the right to form and join trade unions. J. B. et al. v. Canada (118/82). Issues under Article 22 (1) are raised if membership in an association is a condition for access to public facilities. Gauthier v. Canada (633/95) - press facilities of Parliament.

Article 22 (2)

No restrictions may be placed on the exercise of this right other than those which are prescribed by law and which are necessary in a democratic society in the interests of national security or public safety, public order (ordre public), the protection of public health or morals or the protection of the rights and freedoms of others. This article shall not prevent the imposition of lawful restrictions on members of the armed forces and of the police in their exercise of this right.

Non-governmental organizations and trade unions may not be subjected to difficult registration procedures. Their free functioning is essential for the protection of human rights and the dissemination of information in regard to human rights among the people. Concluding Comments on Belarus (1997) UN doc. CCPR/C/79/Add. 86. It is not incompatible with Article 22 that State Parties establish chambers with compulsory membership as organizations under public law. These organizations are not precluded by Article 22 of the Covenant from imposing annual membership fees on its members, unless such an establishment under public law aims at circumventing the guarantees contained in Article 22. Wallmann et al. v. Austria (1002/01).
State Parties have to allow foreign workers to hold official positions in trade unions and to provide guarantees and legal redress to trade unions against dissolution by administrative measures. Concluding Comments on Senegal (1997) UN doc. CCPR/C/79/Add. 82. A general prohibition imposed on the right of civil servants to organize a trade union and bargain collectively is

incompatible with Article 22. Concluding Comments on Chile (1999) UN doc. CCPR/C/79/Add. 104.
Civil servants may also not be unduly restricted with respect to the right to strike. Concluding Comments on Ireland (1993) UN doc. CCPR/C/79/Add. 21. An absolute ban on strikes by public servants who are not exercising authority in the name of the State and are not engaged in essential services violates Article 22. Concluding Comments on Germany (1996) UN doc. CCPR/C/79/Add. 73. Also, the requirement of a two-thirds majority to call a strike is incompatible with this Article. Concluding Comments on Lithuania (2004) UN doc. CCPR/CO/80/LTU.
Acts that lead to a conviction for involvement in reorganizing a fascist party that was dissolved by the authorities of a State Party are of a kind removed from the protection of the Covenant by Article 5. M. A. v. Italy (117/81). The restriction that a father, as a non-custodial parent, can exercise his right to access to his son only under supervision does not raise issues under the right of peaceful association. P. S. v. Denmark (397/90).

Article 22 (3)

Nothing in this article shall authorize States Parties to the International Labour Organization Convention of 1948 concerning Freedom of Association and Protection of the Right to Organize to take legislative measures which would prejudice, or to apply the law in such a manner as to prejudice, the guarantees provided for in that Convention.

Article 22 (3) underlines the freedom of association and the right to organize for workers and employers.

ARTICLE 23

1. The family is the natural and fundamental group unit of society and is entitled to protection by society and the State.
2. The right of men and women of marriageable age to marry and to found a family shall be recognized.
3. No marriage shall be entered into without the free and full consent of the intending spouses.
4. States Parties to the present Covenant shall take appropriate steps to ensure equality of rights and responsibilities of spouses as to marriage, during marriage and at its dissolution. In the case of dissolution, provision shall be made for the necessary protection of any children.

Different provisions of the Covenant guarantee, directly or indirectly, the protection of the family and its members. The guarantee of privacy in Article 17 establishes a prohibition on arbitrary or unlawful interference with the family. Additionally, Article 24 specifically addresses the protection of the rights of the child as such or as a member of a family. General Comment No.: 19.

Article 23 (1)

The family is the natural and fundamental group unit of society and is entitled to protection by society and the State.

The concept of *family* differs in some respects from State to State, and even from region to region within a State. Therefore, the Committee does not give the concept a standard definition. It derives from the objectives of the Covenant that the term family must be given a broad interpretation so as to include all those comprising the family as understood in the society in question. Ngambi et al. v. France (1179/03). When a group of persons is regarded as a family under the legislation and practice of a State Party, it must be given the protection referred to in Article 23. General Comment No.: 19.
The term "family" refers to the family home as it exists during marriage or cohabitation and also to the relations in general between parents and child. Minimal requirements for the existence of a family are such as life together, economic ties or a regular and intense relationship. Santacana et al. v. Spain (417/90). Article 23 (1) is not applicable when a mother and her adopted daughter have, except for a brief period of 2 years some 17 years ago, not lived together as a family. A. S. v. Canada (68/80). Cultural traditions have to be taken into account when defining the term family in a specific situation. Because of these traditions, the relationship to ancestors can be an essential element of identity and play an important role in family life. A State Party that did not consider such traditions and allowed the construction of a hotel complex on ancestral burial grounds violated Article 23 (1). Hopu et al. v. France (549/93).
Article 23 does not act as a barrier to protect a family from *legitimate interference*. But the decision to separate mother and children is, according to the Committee, of a weighty nature. A State Party has to act with the *best interests of the children* in mind so as not to violate the duty under Article 23 to protect the family. Buckle v. New Zealand (858/99). A Court that denied a father contact with his children on the ground of his conviction for sexual abuse of two of his children did not violate Article 23 (1). Maloney v. Germany (755/97).

State Parties have to give full consideration to Article 23 in relation to expulsion of long-term alien residents. Concluding Comments on Canada (1999) UN doc. CCPR/C/79/Add. 105. The interference with family relations is the inevitable outcome of a *deportation.* The Committee does not regard it as either unlawful or arbitrary when the deportation order is made under law in furtherance of a legitimate state interest and due consideration are given in the deportation proceedings to the deportee's family connections. The removal of a divorced individual who had been residing from age seven until his deportation with age thirty in the territory of a State Party was not seen as a violation of Article 23 (1). Stewart v. Canada (538/93) - leaving behind: his two children and his entire family apart from one brother who lived in the country where his was deported to. The separation of a mother and her children, arriving in a State where her spouse validly resided, from the husband and father gave rise to issues under Article 23. Removing the mother and her children without awaiting the final determination of the husband's and father's immigration proceedings constituted arbitrary interference in the family of these persons. Bakhtiyari v. Australia (1069/02). If a parent is removed from the territory of a State Party, Article 23 (1) is not violated if their children, because of their youth, also have to leave the territory. Rajan v. New Zealand (820/98). The mere fact that one member of a family is entitled to remain in the territory of a State Party does not necessarily mean that requiring other members of the family to leave involves arbitrary interference in family life contrary to Article 23 (1). But the Committee considered as arbitrary interference: The decision of a State Party to deport two parents and to compel the family to choose whether the 13-year old child, who had attained citizenship of the State Party after living there 10 years, either to remain alone in the country or accompany his parents. A State Party has to justify such a decision with additional factors that go beyond a simple enforcement of immigration law. Winata et al. v. Australia (930/00). The Committee saw no arbitrary interference in the removal of a grandfather from the territory of a State Party that left his grandson with his mother and her husband in the State, in the absence of exceptional factors. Sahid v. New Zealand (893/99). It also saw no arbitrary interference in the deportation of a person who had his wife, the mother and two brothers still in the State of his origin. Truong v. Canada (743/97).

The legal protection or measures a society or a State can afford to the families vary from country to country and depend on different social, economic, political and cultural conditions and traditions. Where the Covenant requires a substantial protection as in Article 23, it follows that such protection may not be discriminatory. The protection of a family may not vary with the sex of the one or the other spouse. State Parties may restrict the access of aliens to their territory and may expel them for security reasons. However, a legislation, which only subjects foreign spouses of a State Party's women to restrictions, but not foreign spouses of a State Party's men, is discriminatory with respect to women. Aumeeruddy-Cziffra et al. v. Mauritius (35/78).

Article 23 (2)

The right of men and women of marriageable age to marry and to found a family shall be recognized.

This provision affirms the right of men and women of marriageable age to marry and to found a family. The Committee considers, because of the existence of a specific provision in the Covenant on the *right to marriage*, any claim that this right has been violated in the light of this provision. Article 23 (2) is the only substantive provision in the Covenant which defines a right by using the term "men and women", rather than every human being (Article 6), everyone (Article 9) and all persons (Article 26). The use of the term "men and women", rather than the general terms used elsewhere of the Covenant, indicates to the Committee that State Parties are only obliged to recognize as marriage only the union between a man and a woman wishing to marry each other. Therefore, the mere refusal to provide for marriage between homosexual couples by a State Party does not violate this Article. Joslin et al. v. New Zealand (902/99).
Legal provisions that regulate marriages must, according to the Committee, be compatible with the full exercise of the other rights guaranteed by the Covenant. The right to freedom of thought, conscience and religion implies that the legislation of each State has to provide for the possibility of both religious and civil marriages. But it is not incompatible with Article 23 (2) that a marriage that is celebrated in accordance with religious rites be conducted, affirmed or registered also under civil law. The *right to found a family* implies, according to the Committee, the possibility to procreate and live together. Family planning policies by a State Party have not to be discriminatory or compulsory. A State Party has to ensure the unity or reunification of families, particularly when their members are separated for political, economic or similar reasons. General Comment No.: 19. Foreign workers who settle on the territory of a State Party have a right to be reunified with their families. **18 months** is too long a period for foreign workers to be separated from their families. Concluding Comments on Switzerland (1996) UN doc. CCPR/C/79/Add. 70. An amendment to the constitution, the effect of which is to deprive both women and men of the right to have their spouses registered as citizens, who as a consequence may not be allowed to reside in or enter the territory of the State Party, is incompatible with

Article 23. Concluding Comments on Zimbabwe (1998) UN doc. CCPR/C/79/Add. 89.

Article 23 (3)

No marriage shall be entered into without the free and full consent of the intending spouses.

This Article does not establish a specific marriageable age either for men or for women. However, that age has to be such as to enable each of the intending spouses to give his or her free and full personal consent in a form and under conditions prescribed by law. General Comment No.: 19. Practices of forced marriage violate Article 23 (3). Concluding Comments on Nigeria (1996) CCPR/C/79/Add. 65. A provision in a legislation that determines the minimum age for marriage at 13 years for female and 15 years for male persons for "arranged marriages" is incompatible with the condition of the free and full consent of the intending spouses. Concluding Comments on Suriname (2004) UN doc. CCPR/CO/80/SUR.

Article 23 (4)

States Parties to the present Covenant shall take appropriate steps to ensure equality of rights and responsibilities of spouses as to marriage, during marriage and at its dissolution. In the case of dissolution, provision shall be made for the necessary protection of any children.

Article 23 (4) provides that State Parties *have to take appropriate steps* to ensure equality of rights and responsibilities of spouses as to marriage, during marriage and at its dissolution. Such steps may take the form of legislative, administrative or other measures. General Comment No.: 18. No sex-based discrimination may, according to the Committee, occur in respect of the acquisition or loss of nationality by reason of marriage. Likewise, the right of each spouse to retain the use of his or her original family name or to participate on an equal basis in the choice of a new family name has to be safeguarded by the State Parties. During marriage the spouses have *equal rights and responsibilities* in the family. This equality extends to all matters arising from their relationship, such as choice of residence, running of the household, education of the children and administration of assets. And such equality the Committee applies also to arrangements regarding legal separation or dissolution of the marriage. Therefore, State Parties have to prohibit any discriminatory treatment in regard to the grounds and procedures for separation

or divorce, child custody, maintenance or alimony, visiting rights or the loss or recovery of parental authority. General Comment No.: 19. A prohibition for women to remarry within six months following the date of the dissolution or annulment of their marriage is incompatible with Article 23 (4). Concluding Comments on Japan (1998) UN doc. CCPR/C/79/Add. 102.
Although *divorce* legally ends a marriage, it cannot dissolve the bond uniting father, mother and child. This bond does not depend on the continuation of the parents′ marriage. Hendriks v. The Netherlands (201/85). Article 23 (4) grants, barring exceptional circumstances, a right to regular contact between children and both of their parents upon dissolution of a marriage. State Parties have to bear in mind the interest of the children. General Comment No.: 19. In the absence of exceptional circumstances, the Committee does not deem it to be in the best interest of children virtually to eliminate one parent's access to them. Fei v. Colombia (514/92). The unilateral opposition of one of the parents cannot be considered as an exceptional circumstance. Hendriks v. The Netherlands (201/85). The term *children* in Article 23 (4) refers only to the children of a marriage that is being dissolved. Santacana et al. v. Spain (417/90).

ARTICLE 24

1. Every child shall have, without any discrimination as to race, colour, sex, language, religion, national or social origin, property or birth, the right to such measures of protection as are required by his status as a minor, on the part of his family, society and the State.
2. Every child shall be registered immediately after birth and shall have a name.
3. Every child has the right to acquire a nationality.

As individuals, children benefit from all of the *civil rights* enunciated in the Covenant. Thus, as far as the right to life is concerned (Article 6 (5)), the death penalty cannot be imposed for crimes committed by persons less than 18 years of age. Similarly, if lawfully deprived of their liberty, accused juvenile persons have to be separated from adults, Thomas v. Jamaica (800/98), and are entitled to be brought as speedily as possible for adjudication (Article 10 (2) b). Convicted juvenile offenders have to be subject to a penitentiary system that involves segregation from adults and is appropriate to their age and legal status. The aim must be to foster reformation and social rehabilitation (Article 10 (3)). Children are also protected by the possibility of the restriction of a right recognized by the Covenant, such as the right to publicize a judgment in a suit at law or a criminal case, from which an exception may be made when the interest of the minor so requires (Article 14 (1)). The Article does not indicate the *age* at which a minor attains his majority. This is, according to the Committee, to be determined by each State Party in the light of relevant social and cultural conditions. A State Party cannot absolve itself from its obligations under the Covenant regarding persons under the age of 18, notwithstanding that they have reached the age of majority under domestic law. General Comment No.: 17. State Parties that let criminal responsibility begin with at age **seven** violate Article 24. Concluding Comments on Cyprus (1998) UN doc. CCPR/C/79/Add. 88. Persons between **sixteen** and **eighteen** years of age have to be considered as child or youthful offenders. They may not be subject to penal sanction. Concluding Comments on Cyprus (1994) UN doc. CCPR/C/79/Add. 39. It is incompatible with Article 24 to hold a child above **eight** years of age and under **twelve** years of age criminally responsible on the determination by a judge of the child's maturity of understanding as to the nature and consequence of his or her conduct. Concluding Comments on Sri Lanka (1995) UN doc. CCPR/C/79/Add. 39.

Responsibility for guaranteeing children the necessary protection lies, according to the Committee, with the family, society and the State. Although Article 24 does not indicate how such responsibility is to be apportioned, it is, in the opinion of the Committee, primarily incumbent on the family, which is interpreted broadly to include all persons composing it in the society of the State Party concerned, particularly the parents, to create conditions to promote the harmonious development of the child's personality and his enjoyment of the rights recognized in the Covenant. Parents can only fulfil their obligations if State Parties adopt the economic, social and cultural measures that make it possible for parents to foster the development of their children. Concluding Comments on Georgia (1997) UN doc. CCPR/C/79/Add. 75. Children have to be protected from sexual and physical abuse, which have to be subject to penal sanctions. Effective measures to end the use of children in domestic service, Concluding Comments on Sri Lanka (1995) UN doc. CCPR/C/79/Add. 56, prostitution, Concluding Comments on Japan (1998) UN doc. CCPR/C/79/Add. 102, and production of paedo-pornography, Concluding Comments on Belgium (1998), have to be taken. Child labour in both the industrial and rural sector must be eliminated. Concluding Comments on India (1997) UN doc. CCPR/C/79/Add. 81. The State Parties have to take adequate measures to protect children from employment below the legal minimum age and from forced recruitment by guerrilla and paramilitary groups. Concluding Comments on Colombia (1997) UN doc. CCPR/C/79/Add. 76.

In cases where the parents and the family seriously fail in their duties, ill-treat or neglect the child, the State, according to the Committee, has to intervene and restrict parental authority. The child may be separated from his family when circumstances so require. If a marriage is dissolved, steps have to be taken, keeping in view the paramount interest of the children to give them necessary protection and, as far as is possible, to guarantee personal relations with both parents. General Comment No.: 17

Article 24 (1)

Every child shall have, without any discrimination as to race, colour, sex, language, religion, national or social origin, property or birth, the right to such measures of protection as are required by his status as a minor, on the part of his family, society and the State.

This Article recognizes the rights of every child, without any discrimination, to receive from his family, society and the State the protection required by his status as a minor. The implementation of this provision entails the adoption of special measures to protect children, and in addition to the measures that States are required to take under Article 2 to ensure that everyone enjoys the rights provided for in the Covenant. General Comment No.: 17. Discrimination in law and practice against children born out of wedlock is incompatible with Article 24. Concluding Comments on Iceland (1998) UN doc. CCPR/C/79/Add. 98. Concluding Comments on Libyan Arab Jamahiriya (1998) UN doc. CCPR/C/79/Add. 101. Concluding Comments on France (1997) UN doc. CCPR/C/79/Add. 80 - succession rights.

The *principle* that in all decisions affecting a child, his *best interests* have to be the primary consideration forms an integral part of every child's right. State Parties that permit the marriage of a girl at the **age of 12**, Concluding Comments on Sri Lanka (1995) UN doc. CCPR/C/79/Add. 56, Concluding Comments on France (1997) CCPR/C/79/Add. 80 - **15 years**, or of a boy at the **age of 14**, Concluding Comments on Chile (1999) CCPR/C/79/Add. 104, violate this principle.

The *detention* of a minor is, according to the Committee, not a violation of Article 24 (1) per se. Doubts about a minor's identity, attempts by him to evade expulsion, reasonable prospects for his expulsion or an identity investigation that is still ongoing justify detention. Jalloh v. The Netherlands (794/98) - **three and a half months**. *Immigration detention* of children for almost **two years**, Baban et al. v. Australia (1014/01), or **two years and eight months**, without taking into account less intrusive measures that can achieve the same end of compliance with a State Party's immigration policies by, for example, imposition of reporting obligations, sureties or other conditions, which have to take into account a family's particular circumstances, is arbitrary. The Committee also does not consider it in the best interests of children. Bakhtiyari et al. v. Australia (1069/02).

In relation to the expulsion of long-term alien residents, State Parties have to give full consideration in all cases to the protection of Article 24. Concluding Comments on Canada (1999) UN doc. CCPR/C/79/Add. 105. The Committee considered as arbitrary the decision of a State Party to deport the parents and to compel the family to choose whether the 13-year old child, who had attained citizenship of the State Party after living there 10 years, either to remain alone in the country or accompany his parents. Additional factors that go beyond a simple enforcement of immigration law have to justify the removal of both parents in such a case. Winata et al. v. Australia (930/00). A State Party that moves with reasonable dispatch to enforce its immigration laws against criminal conduct and revocates the residence permits of a parent because of fraudulent actions to obtain residency does not violate Article 24 (1). This is the case even if their children, who as citizens have a right to stay in the territory, have to leave the territory with their parents because of their youth. Rajan et al. v. New Zealand (820/98). A State Party that does not adopt any particular measures to *investigate* allegations of illegal adoption of a child, Concluding Comments on Argentina (1995) UN doc. CCPR/C/79/Add. 46, the disappearance of a minor or does not locate her whereabouts to ensure her security and welfare, withholds the benefit and special measures of protection a minor is entitled to on account of her status as a minor. Laureano v. Peru (540/93). A grandchild, whose parents are dead, is without adequate *representation*, if her grandmother is denied a standing to represent her granddaughter in the proceedings about the child's guardianship. The denial deprives the child of the protection to which she is entitled as a minor. Gallicchio et al. v. Argentina (400/90).

Article 24 (2)

Every child shall be registered immediately after birth and shall have a name.

The Committee interprets this provision as being closely linked to Article 24 (1). Article 24 (2) is designed to promote the recognition of a child's legal personality. Providing for the right to have a name is, according to the Committee, of special importance in the case of children born out of wedlock. The main purpose of the obligation to register children after birth is to reduce the danger of abduction, sale of or traffic in children, or of other types of treatment that are incompatible with the enjoyment of the rights provided for in the Covenant. General Comment No.: 17. A delay by a State Party in legally establishing a child's real name and issuing identity papers entails a violation of Article 24 (2). Gallicchio et al. v. Argentina (400/90). State Parties have to ensure that all births are duly registered and that a name is guaranteed street children and abandoned children. Concluding Comments on Romania (1999) UN doc. CCPR/C/79/Add. 111.

Article 24 (3)

Every child has the right to acquire a nationality.

The purpose of this provision is, according to the Committee, to prevent a child from being afforded less protection by society and the State because he or she is stateless. It does not necessarily make it an obligation for States to give their nationality to every child born in their territory. However, States have to ensure that every child has a nationality when he or she is born. Concluding Comments on Colombia (1997) UN doc. CCPR/C/79/Add. 76. No discrimination is admissible between legitimate children, children born out of wedlock, children of stateless parents or based on the nationality status of one or both of the parents with regard to the acquisition of nationality under internal law. General Comment No.: 17. It is incompatible with Article 24 (3) that children who are born abroad may not acquire the citizenship of their parents. Concluding Comments on Zimbabwe (1998) UN doc. CCPR/C/79/Add. 89. The revocation of the citizenship of a child that renders him or her stateless raises an issue under this Article. Rajan et al. v. New Zealand (820/98).

ARTICLE 25

Every citizen shall have the right and the opportunity, without any of the distinctions mentioned in article 2 and without unreasonable restrictions:
(a) To take part in the conduct of public affairs, directly or through freely chosen representatives;
(b) To vote and to be elected at genuine periodic elections, which shall be by universal and equal suffrage and shall be held by secret ballot, guaranteeing the free expression of the will of the electors;
(c) To have access, on general terms of equality, to public service in his country.

This Article recognizes and protects the rights of every citizen to take part in the conduct of public affairs, the right to vote, to be elected and the right to have access to public service. It is only applicable to citizens and protects the rights of them. *Non-citizens* are not protected by Article 25. However, State Parties are not prohibited from conferring the rights of Article 25 to other groups than citizens. The Committee refers to permanent residents. General Comment No.: 25. State Parties that confer rights to groups other than citizens have to do it on a non-discriminatory basis. No distinctions are permitted in the enjoyment of these rights on the grounds of race, colour, sex, language, religion, political or other opinion, national or social origin, property, birth or other status. General Comment No.: 18. Distinctions between those who are entitled to citizenship by birth and those who acquire it by naturalization are incompatible with Article 25. Any conditions which apply to the exercise of the rights protected by Article 25 have to be based on objective and reasonable criteria. It is reasonable, according to the Committee, to require a higher age for election or appointment to particular offices than for exercising the right to vote, which has to be available to every adult citizen. General Comment No.: 25.

Article 25 (a)

Every citizen shall have the right and the opportunity, without any of the distinctions mentioned in article 2 and without unreasonable restrictions:
To take part in the conduct of public affairs, directly or through freely chosen representatives;

Article 25 (a) deals with the right of citizens to participate in the determination of their political status and the enjoyment of the right to choose the form of their constitution or government. These processes constitute, for the Committee, the *conduct of public affairs*. The conduct of public affairs is, according to the Committee, a broad concept, which relates to the exercise of political power, in particular the exercise of legislative, executive and administrative powers. It covers all aspects of public administration, as well as the formulation and implementation of policy at international, national, regional and local levels. Article 25 (a) does not, according to the Committee, presuppose any particular system of government. Whatever form of constitution or government is in force, this provision requires States to adopt such legislative and other measures as may be necessary to ensure that citizens have an effective opportunity to enjoy the rights it protects. General Comment No.: 25. Enclaves of power retained by members of a former regime that impede legal reform and the State Party to comply fully with its Covenant obligations are incompatible with Article 25. Concluding Comments on Chile (1999) UN doc. CCPR/C/79/Add. 104. Article 25 (a) lies at the core of every democratic government based on the consent of the people. It recognizes and protects the rights of every citizen to take part in the conduct of public affairs. This right is an individual right. Diergaardt et al. v. Namibia (760/96). It does not cover private employment matters such as the election of an employee to a private company's work-council. Karakurt v. Austria (965/00). The allocation of powers and the means by which citizens exercise the right to participate in the conduct of public affairs has to be established by the constitution and other laws. Citizens participate directly in the conduct of public affairs when they exercise power as members of legislative bodies or by holding executive office, when they choose or change their constitution or decide public issues through a referendum or other electoral process, when they take part in popular assemblies which have the power to make decisions about local issues or about the affairs of a particular community and in bodies established to represent citizens in consultation with government. Restrictions on political activity outside the only recognized political party are incompatible with Article 25 (a). Bwalya v. Zambia (314/88). Citizens also take part in the conduct of public affairs by exerting influence through public debate and dialogue with their representatives or through their capacity to organize themselves. This participation is, according to the Committee, supported by ensuring freedom of expression, assembly and association. General Comment No.: 25. Acts that lead to a conviction for involvement in reorganizing a fascist party that was dissolved by the authorities of a State Party are out of the scope of Article 25 (a). M. A. v. Italy (117/81).

In order to ensure the full enjoyment of Article 25 (a), the free communication of information and ideas about public and political issues between citizens, candidates and elected representatives is essential. This implies a free press and other media that are able to comment on public issues without censorship or restraint and to inform public opinion. Read together with Article 19, this also implies that citizens, in particular through the media, should have wide access to information and the opportunity to disseminate information and opinions about the activities of elected bodies and their members. Gauthier v. Canada (633/95).

The conduct of public affairs in a democratic State is, according to the Committee, the task of representatives of the people elected for that purpose and public officials appointed in accordance with the law. Where citizens participate in the conduct of public affairs through *freely chosen representatives*, it is implicit in Article 25 (a) that those representatives do, in fact, exercise governmental power and that they are accountable through the electoral process for their exercise of that power. It is also implicit that the representatives exercise only those powers that are allocated to them in accordance with constitutional provisions. The decisions of the freely chosen representatives or the appointed officials can affect the interest of specific groups of the society, large segments of the population or even the population as a whole. General Comment No.: 23. Therefore, prior consultations, such as public hearings or consultations with the most interested groups are often envisaged by law or have evolved as public policy in the conduct of public affairs. The Committee does not give Article 25 (a) the meaning that any directly affected group, large or small, has the unconditional right to choose the modalities of participation in the conduct of public affairs. Marshall et al. v. Canada (205/86). Minorities or indigenous groups, however, have the right that measures are taken to ensure the effective participation of members in decisions which affect them. Länsman Jouni et al. v. Finland (671/95). Länsman Ilmari et al. v. Finland (511/92).

Article 25 (b)

Every citizen shall have the right and the opportunity, without any of the distinctions mentioned in article 2 and without unreasonable restrictions:
To vote and to be elected at genuine periodic elections, which shall be by universal and equal suffrage and shall be held by secret ballot, guaranteeing the free expression of the will of the electors;

Article 25 (b) obliges State Parties to educate voters and conduct registration campaigns to ensure the effective exercise of the right by an informed community. For the "Travelling Community", Concluding Comments on Ireland (1994) UN doc. CCPR/C/79/Add 21, or internally displaced persons, Concluding Comments on Colombia (2004) UN doc. CCPR/CO/80/COL, participation in political and public life has to be facilitated.
The *right to vote* is not an absolute right. Restrictions may be imposed on the right to vote provided they are not discriminatory or unreasonable. Debreczeny v. Netherlands (500/92). Zapala v. Uruguay (44/79). It is, according to the Committee, reasonable to require a higher age for election or appointment to particular offices than for exercising the right to vote, which has to be available to every adult citizen. It is unreasonable to restrict the right to vote on the ground of physical disability or to impose literacy, educational or property requirements. Established mental incapacity may be a ground for denying a person the right to vote or to hold office. Party membership may neither be a condition of eligibility to vote, nor a ground of disqualification. The restriction for students of military schools to vote is an unreasonable restriction. Concluding Comments on Paraguay (1995) UN doc. CCPR/C/79/Add. 48. Depriving convicted persons of their voting rights for periods of up to 10 years is also a disproportionate restriction. Concluding Comments on United Kingdom of Great Britain and Northern Ireland (Hong Kong) (1995) UN doc. CCPR/C/79/Add. 57. The Committee determines the evaluation of any restrictions to the right to vote on a case-by-case basis. The purpose of the restrictions and the principle of proportionality are of importance. Where local ballots are conducted in the context of a process of self-determination of the population of a territory, they must, by virtue of their purpose, provide means of determining the opinion of not the whole of the national population but the persons *concerned* by the future of the territory. Criteria governing the right to vote in such a referendum have the effect of establishing a restricted electorate.

They have to take into account the specific factors attesting to the strength of the links to the territory and must make it possible to treat differently persons in objectively different situations. Criteria based on such objective elements are, in the framework of a self-determination process, in conformity with the purpose and nature of Article 25 (b). Gillot et al. v. France (932/00).
Article 25 (b) secures to every citizen the right and the opportunity *to be elected.* Considerable financial costs can adversely affect the right of persons to be candidates at elections. Concluding Comments on the United States of America (1995) UN doc. CCPR/C/79/Add. 50. Article 25 (b) guarantees genuine periodic elections without any of the distinctions mentioned in Article 2, including language. Therefore, the annulment of a person's candidacy pursuant to a review of the required proficiency in the official language that was not based on objective criteria was incompatible with a State Party's obligations under this Article. Ignatane v. Latvia (884/99) - procedurally incorrect. A Law on Elections which prohibits the nomination of persons as candidates for Parliament raises issues under Article 25 (b). Dergachev v. Belarus (921/00) - administrative conviction in the year prior to the election. A State Party violates Article 25 (b) if a person, notwithstanding the entitlement to stand as an electee is not permitted to do so. Mpaka-Nsusu v. Zaire (157/83) - for the presidency.
Article 25 (b) does not prohibit the *reservation of positions in elected bodies* for members of scheduled castes and tribes or women. Concluding Comments on India (1997) UN doc. CCPR/C/79/Add. 81.
Restrictions on the right to be elected have to be regulated by law and based on objective criteria. Restrictions that guarantee the democratic decision-making process by avoiding conflicts of interest are reasonable and do not violate Article 25 (b). A conflict of interest that endangers the democratic decision making process arises if a police officer in the national police force, who is as such for matters of public order subordinated to the mayor of a city, and who himself is accountable to the city council for measures taken in that regard, is not prevented from taking his seat in the municipal council of his city. Debreczeny v. The Netherlands (500/92).
In no case may a person be subjected to the deprivation of political rights solely because of his or her political opinion. The principle of proportionality requires that a measure as harsh as the deprivation of all political rights is specifically justified. Zapala v. Uruguay (44/79). In the situation of an emergency, a State Party has to show that the interdiction of any kind of political dissent is required in order to deal with the emergency situation and pave the way to political freedom. A measure that deprives all citizens who, as members of certain political groups, have been candidates in previous elections, of any political right for a period as long as 15 years, without distinction as to whether a person

sought to promote his political opinions by peaceful means or by resorting to, or advocating the use of, violent means, is incompatible with Article 25 (b). Silva et al. v. Uruguay (34/78). Touron v. Uruguay (32/78). Weinberger v. Uruguay (28/78). Altesor v. Uruguay (10/77). Bazzano et al. v. Uruguay (5/77).

Genuine periodic elections arc, according to the Committee, essential to ensure the accountability of representatives for the exercise of the legislative or executive powers vested in them. Such elections must be held at intervals that are not unduly long, and which ensure that the authority of government continues to be based on the free expression of the will of the electors. An independent electoral authority has to be established to supervise the electoral process and to ensure that it is conducted fairly, impartially and in accordance with established laws which are compatible with the Covenant. General Comment No.: 25. Balloting has to be free from fraud and take place in an atmosphere of calm. The willingness of the authorities to accept international observers during the balloting contributes to the transparency of elections. Concluding Comments on Mexico (1994) UN doc. CCPR/C/79/Add. 32.

The *equality* of election rights requires that election districts are proportional to the number of inhabitants. Mátyus v. Slovakia (923/00). The Covenant does not, according to the Committee, impose any particular electoral system. But any system operating in a State Party must be compatible with the rights protected by Article 25 and must guarantee and give effect to the free expression of the will of the electors. The principle of "one person one vote" must be applied within the framework of each State's electoral system. The vote of one elector has to be equal to the vote of another, and the drawing of electoral boundaries and the method of allocating votes may not distort the distribution of voters. The concept of functional constituencies, which gives undue weight to the views of the business community, discriminates among voters on the basis of property and functions. It constitutes a violation of Article 25 (b). Concluding Comments on United Kingdom of Great Britain and Northern Ireland (Hong Kong) (1995) UN doc. CCPR/C/79/Add. 57. According to the Committee, States have to take measures to guarantee the requirement of the *secrecy of the vote* during elections including absentee voting, where such a system exists. This implies that voters have to be protected from any form of coercion or compulsion to disclose how they intend to vote or how they voted, and from any unlawful or arbitrary interference with the voting process. Assistance provided to the disabled, blind or illiterate has to be independent. It is also essential that the security of the ballot boxes is guaranteed and votes are counted in the presence of the candidates or their representatives. Independent scrutiny of the voting and counting process must therefore exist and access to judicial review or other equivalent process must be possible. In order to ensure the *free expression of the will of the electors*, the free communication of information and ideas about public and political issues between citizens, candidates and elected representatives is also important. This implies a free press and other media able to comment on public issues without censorship or restraint and to inform public opinion. Strict governmental control over electronic media results in serious limitations to the exercise of the rights guaranteed in Article 25 (b). Concluding Comments on Armenia (1998) UN doc. CCPR/C/79/Add. 100. The free expression of the will of the electors requires the *freedom to engage in political activity* individually or through political parties and other organizations, the freedom to debate public affairs, to hold peaceful demonstrations and meetings, to criticize and oppose, to publish political material, to campaign for election and to advertise political ideas. General Comment No.: 25.

Article 25 (c)

Every citizen shall have the right and the opportunity, without any of the distinctions mentioned in article 2 and without unreasonable restrictions:
To have access, on general terms of equality, to public service in his country.

Article 25 (c) deals with the right and the opportunity of citizens to have *access on general terms of equality* to public service positions. The criteria and processes for appointment, promotion, suspension and dismissal must be objective and reasonable. Automatic exclusion of persons unable to satisfy requirements gives rise to an unreasonable restriction on the right of access to public service without discrimination. Concluding Comments on Estonia (1995) UN doc. CCPR/C/79/Add. 59.

Affirmative measures may be taken in appropriate cases to ensure that there is equal access to public service for all citizens. The implementation of an Act that gives more rights to former public employees than to other individuals does not violate Article 25 (c) if this Act seeks to restore the rights of those citizens who were wrongfully treated by a former government. Costa v. Uruguay (198/85) - dismissal on ideological, political or trade-union grounds.

Article 25 (c) does not define the term *public service.* Decided cases indicate that it encompasses legislation, jurisdiction and executive. Access, on general terms of equality, to public service in a country entails that election districts have to be proportional to the number of inhabitants, Mátyus v. Slovakia (923/00), and includes the right to the execution of decisions and judgments. Vargas-Machuca v. Peru (906/00). Mazou v. Cameroon (630/95). It encompasses the duty, for a State Party, to ensure that there is no discrimination on the ground of political opinion or expression. The freedom to engage in political activity individually or through political parties, the freedom to debate public affairs, to criticize a government and to publish material with political content is part of the right enshrined in Article 25 (c). Aduayom et al. v. Togo (422-424/90). Public service has to be based on equal opportunity and the general principles of merit, and has to provide secure tenure to ensure that persons holding public service positions are free from political interference or pressure. General Comment No.: 25.

The right under Article 25(c) is an individual right, Diergaardt et al. v. Namibia (760/96), that with, the phrase "on general terms of equality", implies the duty of the State Parties not to discriminate against anyone. It is a matter of concern for the Committee if the adherence to certain religious organizations or beliefs constitutes one of the main grounds for disqualifying individuals from obtaining employment in the public service. Concluding Comments on Germany (2004) UN doc. CCPR/CO/80/DEU. Article 25 (c) provides every citizen with the right and the opportunity, without any distinctions based on race, colour, sex, language, religion, political or other opinion, national or social origin, property, birth or other status, and without unreasonable restrictions *to have access*, on general terms of equality, *to public service* in his country. However, Article 25 (c) does not entitle every citizen to obtain guaranteed employment in the public service. Kall v. Poland (552/93).

Article 25 (c) is applicable to persons employed in the public service and to those who have been dismissed. The criteria for dismissing public servants have to be precise so that no public servant will be dismissed on the ground of political opinion held or expressed by him or her. Concluding Comments on Germany (1996) UN doc. CCPR/C/79/Add. 73. Constant harassment and threats against a person, in respect of which a State Party fails to provide protection and that make the person's continuation in public service impossible, violate Article 25 (c), Paez v. Colombia (195/85). Also, the dismissal of a person by an act of a government that does not respect the established procedures and guarantees is incompatible with this Article. Busyo et al. v. Democratic Republic of the Congo (933/00). Gedumbe v. Democratic Republic of the Congo (641/95). Hence, the Committee also saw in the dismissal of a person from the position as a judge of a constitutional court several years before the expiry of the term for which he was appointed, by a presidential decree that as sole reason stated the expiry of the term, a violation of Article 25 (c). Pastukhov v. Belarus (814/98).

ARTICLE 26

All persons are equal before the law and are entitled without any discrimination to the equal protection of the law. In this respect, the law shall prohibit any discrimination and guarantee to all persons equal and effective protection against discrimination on any ground such as race, colour, sex, language, religion, political or other opinion, national or social origin, property, birth or other status.

Article 26 does not merely duplicate the guarantees already provided for in Article 2 or 3 but provides in itself an autonomous right. Non-discrimination, together with equality before the law and equal protection of the law without any discrimination, constitutes a basic and general principle relating to the protection of human rights. General Comment No.: 18. The acquittal of one accused and the conviction of another raise no issue of *equality before the law* as long as each criminal case has been examined on its own merits. Werenbeck v. Australia (579/94). Article 26 does also not provide a right to see another person prosecuted, nor does the absence of prosecution against one person render the prosecution of another person involved in the same offence necessarily discriminatory, in the absence of specific circumstances revealing a deliberate policy of unequal treatment before the law. M. S. v. The Netherlands (396/90). H. C. M. A. v. The Netherlands (213/86). Groot v. The Netherlands (578/94). The decision to try a person before a Special Criminal Court has to be based upon reasonable and objective grounds. Accordingly, a State Party that fails to do this violates the right to equality before the law and to the equal protection of the law. Kavanagh v. Ireland (819/98).
The enjoyment of rights and freedoms on an equal footing, does not mean, however, according to the Committee, identical treatment in every instance. The Committee mentions: Article 6 (5), which prohibits the death sentence from being imposed on persons below 18 years of age. The same paragraph prohibits that sentence from being carried out on pregnant women. Article 10 (3), which requires the segregation of juvenile offenders from adults. Furthermore, Article 25, which guarantees certain political rights, differentiating on grounds of citizenship. *Affirmative action* is also mentioned. It requires State Parties to take measures, in order to diminish or eliminate conditions which cause or help to perpetuate discrimination prohibited by the Covenant. General Comment No.: 18. In a State where the general conditions of a certain part of the population prevent or impair their enjoyment of human rights and educational measures do not overcome obstacles to equality, such as outdated attitudes concerning the role and status of women, Concluding Comments on Mauritius (1996) UN doc. CCPR/C/79/Add. 60, the State Party has to take specific action to correct those conditions. Such action may involve granting certain preferential treatment, for a period of time, to the part of the population concerned in specific matters, as compared with the rest of the population. Concluding Comments on India (1997) UN doc. CCPR/C/79/Add. 81 - reservation of seats in elected bodies. As long as such action is needed to correct discrimination in fact, it is a case of

legitimate differentiation under the Covenant. Thus, the implementation of an act by a government that had to be seen as a remedy for public officials who had been dismissed by the old government on ideological, political or trade-union grounds in violation of Article 26 did not violate Article 26. Costa v. Uruguay (198/85). In the course of a *self-determination* process of a territory the *residence* criterion for participation in the referendum which will decide the future of the territory is in accordance with the nature and purpose of such a referendum. It is not discriminatory because in such a process, persons must be able to prove sufficiently strong ties to the territory whose future will be decided. Those who, over and above their ethnic origin or political affiliation, have helped, and continue to help, build the territory through their sufficiently strong ties to the territory have to decide the future of it. Gillot et al. v. France (932/00).

A different treatment based on one of the specific grounds enumerated in Article 26, however, places a heavy *burden on a State Party* to explain the reason for the differentiation. In view of the importance of the principle of equality between men and women, State Parties have to counteract all forms of gender inequality. Concluding Comments on Poland (1999) UN doc. CCPR/C/79/Add. 110 - employment sector. The application of a law that only husbands entitles to represent matrimonial property in court denies women equality before courts. Avellanal v. Peru (202/86). The argument of a long-standing tradition cannot be maintained as a general justification for different treatment of men and women. Courts may not consider domestic violence, including forced sexual intercourse, as a normal incident of married life. Concluding Comments on Japan (1998) UN doc. CCPR/C/79/Add. 102. In addition, traditional customs may not inhibit complaints. Concluding Comments on the United Republic of Tanzania (1998) UN doc. CCPR/C/79/Add. 97 - female genital mutilation. It is not reasonable to subject the possibility of choosing the wife's surname as family name to stricter and much more cumbersome conditions than the alternative choice of the husband's surname. Such distinction has no sufficient importance in order to outweigh the generally excluded gender-based approach. Engelhard v. Namibia (919/00). Legislation that gives the right of free access to the territory of a State Party and *immunity from deportation* only to foreign spouses of men, but not foreign spouses of women, is discriminatory with respect to the women. Aumeeruddy - Cziffra et al. v. Mauritius (35/78).

The *principle of non-discrimination* is so basic that Article 4 (1) requires that measures derogating from certain obligations under the Covenant in time of public emergency may not involve discrimination solely on the ground of race, colour, sex, language, religion or social origin. General Comment No.: 29. Even when the Covenant neither defines the term *discrimination* nor indicates what constitutes *discrimination*, the Committee understands it as implying any distinction, exclusion, restriction or preference based on any grounds such as race, colour, sex, language, religion, political or other opinion, national or social origin, property, birth or other status, and which has the purpose or effect of nullifying or impairing the recognition, enjoyment or exercise by all persons, on an equal footing, of all rights and freedoms. Hence, a *politically* motivated denial of severance pay to a long-standing civil servant who was dismissed by the government constituted a violation of Article 26. Valenzuela v. Peru (309/88). A State Party that politically persecuted its citizens so that many of them sought refuge in other countries where they applied for and obtained new citizenship, violates Article 26 if it demands as a prerequisite for the restitution of their property, or, alternatively, for the payment of compensation, to obtain again their original citizenship. The Committee did not consider such a demand reasonable in the light of the fact that the loss of the original citizenship was a function of their presence in a State in which they were able to obtain refuge. Blazek v. Czech Republic (857/99). Also, the coercive nature of an "ideology conversion system" or "oath of law-abidance system" which a State Party applied with the view to alter the political opinion of inmates by offering inducements of preferential treatment within prison and improved possibilities of parole was incompatible with Articles 26. Kang v. Republic of Korea (878/99).

Article 26 prohibits discrimination in any field regulated and protected by public authorities in law or in fact. Therefore, legislation adopted by the State Parties must comply with the requirements of Article 26. State Parties have to introduce comprehensive anti-discrimination laws to cover all spheres, public or private, protected by the Covenant. Concluding Comments on Mauritius (1997) UN doc. CCPR/C/79/Add. 60. Concluding Comments on Chile (1999) CCPR/C/79/Add. 104 - employment and housing. The courts of the State Parties are under an obligation to protect individuals against discrimination, whether this occurs within the public sphere or among private parties in the quasi-public sector of employment. Nahlik v. Austria (608/95).

A State Party also must not instruct its civil servants not to reply to a person's written or oral communications, when the civil servants are perfectly capable of doing so, in the language this person writes or speaks. Diergaardt et al. v. Namibia (760/96).

While age as such is not mentioned as one of the enumerated grounds of prohibited discrimination in the second sentence of Article 26, a distinction related to age which is not based on reasonable and objective criteria may, according to the Committee, amount to discrimination on the ground of *other status*, or to a denial of the equal protection of the law. In general, a mandatory

retirement age that includes a dimension of workers' protection by limiting the life-long working time, in particular when there are comprehensive social security schemes that secure the subsistence of persons who have reached such an age, does not constitute age discrimination. Furthermore, the Committee also recognizes reasons related to employment policy which may be behind legislation or policy on mandatory retirement age. And also the aim of maximizing safety to passengers, crew and persons otherwise affected by flight travel is a legitimate aim under the Covenant. Love et al. v. Australia (983/01). Discrimination between retirement ages for men and women has to be eliminated. Concluding Comments on Poland (1999) CCPR/C/79/Add. 110. The age limitation of allowing only partners who have reached the age of 60 years to obtain an entitlement to various rate reductions as a partner to a pensioner above the age of 65 years is an objective criterion of differentiation. The application of this differentiation is not unreasonable. Schmitz-de-Jong v. The Netherlands (855/99).
The prohibition against discrimination under Article 26 also comprises discrimination based on sexual orientation. Therefore, the reference to *sex* in Article 26 has to be taken as including *sexual orientation.* Toonen v. Australia (488/92). The mere refusal to provide for marriage between homosexual couples by a State Party does not violate Article 26. Joslin et al. v. New Zealand (902/99). But the distinction between same-sex partners, who are excluded from pension benefits under law, and unmarried heterosexual partners, who are granted such benefits, discriminates same sex partners because of their sex or sexual orientation if they have neither the possibility of entering into marriage, nor of recognition as cohabiting partners for the purpose of receiving pension benefits. Young v. Australia (941/00). An Act that provides for full pension benefits to widowers only if they have no other source of income while the income requirement does not apply to widows treats men and women, whose social circumstances are similar, differently, merely on the basis of sex. Such a differentiation is not reasonable. Pauger v. Austria (415/90).
The application of the principle of non-discrimination is not limited to those rights that are provided for in the Covenant. The Committee demonstrated this when it examined the function of a member of a *work-council*. The members of work councils have to promote staff interests and to supervise compliance with work conditions. In view of this, it was not reasonable for the Committee to base a distinction between aliens concerning their capacity to stand for election for a work council solely on their different nationality. Althammer et al. v. Austria (998/01). Karakurt v. Austria (965/00). The Committee also did not consider the exemption of only one group of *conscientious objectors* from military as reasonable. When a State Party recognizes a right of conscientious

objection to military service, no differentiation must be made among conscientious objectors on the basis of the nature of their particular beliefs. Brinkhof v. The Netherlands (402/90). The law and practice may establish differences between *military and national alternative service.* Such differences may justify a longer period of alternative service, provided that the differentiation is based on reasonable and objective criteria, such as the nature of the specific service concerned or the need for a special training in order to accomplish that service. The argument that doubling the length of service was the only way to test the sincerity of an individual's convictions did not satisfy the Committee. Differences in treatment have to be based on other arguments. Venier et al. v. France (690/96). Maille v. France (689/96). Foin v. France (666/95). The Committee considers, when it determines whether the prolongation of the term for alternative service by an act is based on reasonable and objective criteria, the ratio legis of the act. Arrangements that prolong an alternative service from twelve to sixteen months and remove, at the same time, from conscientious objectors the often difficult task of convincing the examination board of the genuineness of their beliefs and allow so a broader range of individuals potentially to opt for the possibility of alternative service, were not deemed as unreasonable by the Committee. Jarvinen v. Finland (295/88). The duration of an alternative service up to twice that of a military service appeared to the Committee to be discriminatory. Concluding Comments on Latvia (2003) UN doc. CCPR/CO/79/LVA.

Article 26 is concerned with the obligations imposed on State Parties in regard to their legislation and the application thereof. General Comment No.: 18. No State Party is relieved of its obligations under Article 26 by delegating some of its functions to autonomous organs or municipalities. B. d. B. et al. v. The Netherlands (273/88). Administrative faults of the authorities of a State Party that result in the deprivation of equal treatment violate Article 26. Fábryová v. Czech Republic (765/97) - restitution of confiscated property. This Article is also violated if a State Party denies non-citizens access to public archives and relevant documents which can prove their claims. Pezoldova v. Czech Republic (757/97) - restitution of confiscated property.

The scope of Article 26 does not extend to *differences of results* in the application of common rules in the *allocation of benefits.* Vos v. The Netherlands (218/86). P. P. C. v. The Netherlands (212/86). Hence, where compulsory military or alternative service entails certain modest pecuniary payments, there is nevertheless no entitlement to be paid as if one were still in private civilian life. H. A. E. d. J. v. The Netherlands (297/88). When a State Party equals pensions for married men and women, it has to prevent a difference in calculation of pensions for married men and married women who enjoy equal

rights to the pension. If a State Party fails to do so and, as a result, a married man has a higher percentage of deduction from his pension than a married woman in the same position, Article 26 is violated. Vos v. The Netherlands (786/97). Also, lump sums have to be paid to men and women on equal footing. Pauger v. Austria (716/96). An Unemployment Benefits Act that forces a married woman to prove that she is a breadwinner in order to receive benefits - a condition that does not apply to married men - places women at a disadvantage compared with married men. Such a differentiation is not reasonable. Zwaan-de Vries v. The Netherlands (182/84). A State Party that wants to justify unequal treatment cannot invoke mere administrative inconvenience or the possibility of some abuse of rights. Hence, if the services rendered by a person for a State Party and not the nationality determined the granting of a pension, the Committee did not consider the change of nationality as a sufficient justification for different treatment of these who kept the nationality and those who changed it. Gueye et al. v. France (196/85). But separately negotiated *bilateral treaties* which reflect agreements based on reciprocity can justify a differentiation. Hendrika van Oord v. The Netherlands (658/95).
The corollary of the fact that the Covenant does not protect the right to property is that there is no right, as such, to have (expropriated or nationalized) property restituted. Somers v. Hungary (566/93). Therefore, legislation adopted after the fall of a regime by a State Party to compensate victims of that regime is not, prima facie, discriminatory within the meaning of Article 26 merely because it does not compensate the victims of injustices committed in the period before that regime. Schlosser v. The Czech Republic (670/95). Malik v. The Czech Republic (669/95). Drobek v. Slovakia (643/95). However, laws that provide restitution or compensation to victims of confiscation may not discriminate among the victims to which they apply, since, according to the Committee, all victims are entitled to redress without arbitrary distinctions. It is irrespective whether the arbitrariness is inherent in a law itself or whether it results from the application of the law by the courts of a State Party. The exclusion of persons from the benefit of a restitution law because the State Party nationalized their property earlier than the property of others discloses a discriminatory treatment of the persons, compared to those individuals whose property was later confiscated. Brok v. Czech Republic (774/97). The requirement in a law for citizenship or continued citizenship as a necessary condition for restitution of property previously confiscated by the authorities makes an arbitrary, and, consequently, a discriminatory distinction between individuals who are equally victims of prior confiscations. Blazek et al. v. The Czech Republic (857/99). Walderode et al. v. The Czech Republic (747/97). Adam v. The Czech Republic (586/94). Simunek et al. v. The Czech Republic (516/93). If restitution is

provided, it is, according to the Committee, not unreasonable to give the current tenants of former State-owned property in the privatization sale of such property priority. They often already occupy a property for years and have contributed to the maintenance of the property through improvements of their own. Those whose property was expropriated or nationalized can be compensated with vouchers that can be redeemed in the open market or used for buying offered State-owned property. Somers v. Hungary (566/93).

Distinctions that are justified on *reasonable and objective grounds* are not inconsistent with Article 26. Balani v. Spain (1021/01). Kavanagh v Ireland (819/98). Sprenger v. The Netherlands (395/90). Broeks v. The Neherlands (172/84). The Committee regards legislation requiring that workers in federal employment be protected from injury and electric shock by the wearing of hard hats as reasonable and directed towards objective purposes that are compatible with the Covenant. Bhinder v. Canada (208/86) - Sikh. Federal Unions that permit differences among the federal units in respect of jury trial do not violate Article 26. Cheban et al. v. The Russian Federation (790/97). Differences in the statute of limitations in different parts of a federal state did not raise an issue. Hesse v. Australia (1087/02). A system that provided for various types of remedy depending on the seriousness of the offence did not necessarily constitute discrimination. Fernández v. Spain (1007/01). Vázquez v. Spain (701/96). The distinction between a person who holds a university degree and one who does not is compatible with Article 26. González v. Spain (1005/01).

The requirement for representation by a procurator reflects the need for a person with legal training to assume responsibility for proceedings in connection with appeals to a constitutional court. Therefore, the Committee did not see discrimination in the fact that persons with a law degree had not to be represented before such a court by a procurator whereas persons without a law degree were required to be so represented. Hruska v. Czech Republic (1191/03). González v. Spain (1005/01). Lafuente et al. v. Spain (866/99). The Committee also did not equal the representation of a person presenting a civil claim in a criminal case to representing the accused. Hence, the difference in remuneration between legal aid services performed by a counsel for the civil claimant and those performed by a counsel for the defendant did not constitute discrimination. Lestourneaud v. France (861/99).

Married and unmarried couples can be subject to different sets of laws and regulations. The decision to enter into a legal status by marriage, which provides under law for certain benefits and for certain duties and responsibilities, lies entirely with the cohabitating persons. A person has not, by choosing not to enter into marriage in law, assumed the full extent of the duties and responsibilities incumbent on married persons. Consequently, the person does not receive the full benefits provided for by law to married persons. Hoofdman v. The Netherlands (602/94). Danning v. The Netherlands (180/84). Differences in the receipt of benefits between married couples and heterosexual unmarried couples are reasonable and objective, as long as the unmarried couples have the choice to marry with all the entailing consequences. Danning v. The Netherlands (180/84).

A ban on dwarf tossing ordered by a State Party applies only to dwarves. These persons are covered to the exclusion of others. The reason is, according to the Committee, that they are the only persons capable of being thrown. Thus, the differentiation between the persons covered by the ban, namely dwarves, and those to whom it does not apply, namely persons not suffering from dwarfism, is based on an objective reason (physical reason) and not discriminatory in its purpose. The ban brings into play considerations of *human dignity*. Measures that protect the human dignity are compatible with the objectives of the Covenant. Wackenheim v. France (854/99). Polygamy violates the human dignity. It constitutes a discrimination against women. Therefore, the State Parties have the duty to abolish it. Concluding Comments on Mali (2003) UN doc. CCPR/CO/77/MLI.

The Committee saw no discrimination in the prohibition of the use of commercial advertising outdoors in a *language* other than the one specified because this prohibition applied to the speakers of this language as well as to speakers of any other language. Ballantyne et al. v. Canada (385, 359/89).

Article 26 does not of itself require State Parties either to provide *social security benefits* or to provide them retroactively, in respect of the date of application. However, when law regulates such benefits, then such a law must comply with Article 26. J. A. M. B. - R. v. The Netherlands (477/91). Sprenger v. The Netherlands (395/90). Zwaan-de Vries v. The Netherlands (182/84). The requirement of being unemployed at the time of application as a prerequisite for entitlement to benefit is, in view of the purposes of such legislation, namely to provide assistance to persons who are unemployed, not discriminatory. A. P. L. - v. d. M. v. The Netherlands (478/91). Araujo-Jongen v. The Netherlands (418/90). The Committee also did not deem as arbitrary or unreasonable a distinction between unemployed substitute judges who were civil servants on leave and those who were not. Pons v. Spain (454/91). In addition, the presumption that close family-members living in one and the same house or apartment share a household on a non-commercial basis was deemed neither unreasonable nor arbitrary. Neefs v. The Netherlands (425/90). The Committee sees objective differences between one's own children and foster children which justify different treatment. A foster parent has to be involved in the upbringing of the foster children, as a precondition to the granting of benefits. Oulajin v.

The Netherlands (426, 406/90). Personal contributions to an insurance scheme which covers the costs of residential care have to be calculated objectively and without arbitrariness. A distinction in the contribution has to be based upon factual differences or factual circumstances of life. Snijders et al. v. The Netherlands (651/95).

The Committee does not deem a State Party to be under an obligation to provide *benefits to private schools*. The preferential treatment given to public sector schooling is reasonable and based on objective criteria because it makes public sector schooling available to all children. The parents of children are free to take advantage of the public sector schooling or to choose private schooling for their children. The decision to choose private education reflects, according to the Committee, a free choice recognized and respected by a State Party. Such free decision, however, entails certain consequences, notably payment of tuition, transport, textbooks and school meals. A State Party that gives preferential treatment to public sector schooling does therefore not discriminate against parents who freely choose not to avail themselves of benefits, which are generally open to all. Lindgren et al. v. Sweden (298, 299/88). Where a State Party provides subsidies for the private educational system, it can make the private system subject to State supervision. Blom v. Sweden (191/85).

The Covenant does not oblige State Parties to fund *schools* that are established *on a religious basis*. However, if a State Party chooses to provide public funding to religious schools, it has to make this funding available without discrimination. This means that providing funding for the schools of one religious group and not for another must be based on reasonable and objective criteria. A distinction that is enshrined in the Constitution does not render it reasonable and objective. It is also unreasonable to differentiate in the allocation of public funds between private and public schools, if it is not possible for members of religious denominations other than a certain denomination to have their religious schools incorporated within the public school system. Waldman v. Canada (694/96). However, persons who only seek the removal of the public funding of religious separate schools and no publicly funded religious schools for their own children, have to substantiate how the public funding given to the religious separate schools causes them any disadvantage or affects them adversely. Tadman et al. v. Canada (816/98).

ARTICLE 27

In those States in which ethnic, religious or linguistic minorities exist, persons belonging to such minorities shall not be denied the right, in community with the other members of their group, to enjoy their own culture, to profess and practice their own religion, or to use their own language.

The right protected under Article 27 may not, according to the Committee, be confused with the right of peoples to self-determination as proclaimed in Article 1. The latter is expressed to be a right belonging to peoples and is dealt with in a separate part (Part I) of the Covenant. Self-determination is not a right cognizable under the Optional Protocol. Article 27 relates to rights conferred on *individuals* as such. It is cognizable under the Optional Protocol. Lubicon Lake Band v. Canada (167/84).
The Covenant distinguishes the rights protected under Article 27 from the guarantees under Articles 2(1) and 26. The entitlement, under Article 2(1), to enjoy the rights under the Covenant without discrimination applies, according to the Committee, to all individuals within the territory or under the jurisdiction of the State whether or not those persons belong to a minority. In addition, there is a distinct right provided under Article 26 for equality before the law, equal protection of the law, and non-discrimination in respect of rights granted and obligations imposed by the States. General Comment No.: 23. Article 26 governs the exercise of all rights, whether protected under the Covenant or not, which a State Party confers by law on individuals within its territory or under its jurisdiction, irrespective of whether they belong to the minorities specified in Article 27 or not. Zwaan-de Vries v. The Netherlands (182/84). Danning v. The Netherlands (180/84). The mere fact that equal rights are granted to all individuals and all individuals are equal before the law does not exclude the existence in fact of minorities in a country, their entitlement to the enjoyment of their culture, the practice of their religion or the use of their language in community with other members of their group. Concluding Comments on France (1997) UN doc. CCPR/C/79/Add. 80. Article 27 establishes and recognizes a right, which is distinct from and an additional to all the other rights which, minorities, as individuals in common with everyone else, are already entitled to enjoy under the Covenant. General Comment No.: 23.
The existence of an ethnic, religious or linguistic minority in a given State Party does not depend upon a decision by that State Party. Concluding Comments on Austria (1998) UN doc. CCPR/C/79/Add. 103 - legally recognized groups. The Committee examines the question by objective criteria. Therefore, a group may constitute a majority in a province but still be a minority in a State and thus be entitled to the benefits of Article 27. Ballantyne (359, 385/89). The terms used in Article 27 indicate to the Committee that the persons designed to be protected are those who belong to a group who shares in common a culture, a religion and/or a language. The Committee includes the term *indigenous peoples* in the term *minority* as it is used in Article 27. Concluding Comments on Brazil (1996) UN doc. CCPR/C/79/Add. 66.

A restriction upon the right of an individual member of a minority must be shown to have a reasonable and objective justification and to be necessary for the continued viability and welfare of the minority as a whole. Kitok v. Sweden (197/85). The Committee considers persons who are born and brought up on a reserve, who have kept ties with their community and wish to maintain these ties as belonging to that minority. The right to live on a reserve is not, as such, guaranteed by Article 27. Its denial can be reasonable and necessary to preserve the identity of a tribe. However, State Parties have to keep in mind that, to members of a tribe, the right of access to the native culture and language in community with other members of the group is guaranteed. Therefore, if there is no place outside the reserve where such a community exists, the denial of the legal right to reside on the reserve interferes with Article 27. Lovelace v. Canada (24/77).

The rights in this Article are guaranteed to persons belonging to minorities who *exist* in a State Party. It is not relevant to the Committee, given the nature and scope of the rights envisaged under Article 27, to determine the degree of permanence that the term *exist* connotes. Individuals belonging to minorities may not be denied the right, in community with members of their group, to enjoy their own culture, to practice their religion and speak their language. Concluding Comments on Slovenia (1994) UN doc. CCPR/C/79/Add. 40. In addition, they need not, according to the Committee, be nationals, citizens or permanent residents. Thus, migrant workers or even visitors in a State Party constituting such minorities are entitled to exercise those rights. As any other individual in the territory of the State Party, they are protected by Article 27. General Comment No.: 15. Therefore, legislation in the State Parties concerning the rights of persons belonging to minorities has to give protection to all persons referred to in Article 27. Concluding Comments on Ukraine (2001) UN doc. CCPR/CO/73/UKR.

The rights of individuals belonging to a *linguistic minority* to use their language among themselves, in private or in public, is, according to the Committee, distinct from other language rights protected under the Covenant. In particular, the Committee distinguishes it from the general right to freedom of expression protected under Article 19. The latter right is available to all persons, irrespective of whether they belong to minorities or not. Furthermore, the Committee distinguishes it from the particular right which Article 14 (3) (f) confers on accused persons to interpretation where they cannot understand or speak the language used in the courts. H. K. v. France (222/87). T. K. v. France (220/87). And if the introduction by law of the compulsory, immediate and exclusive use of a national language in all areas of public activity impedes a large section of the population in the enjoyment of the rights guaranteed in

Article 27, the law has to be reviewed by the State Party so as to remove the negative consequences that it produces. Concluding Comments on Algeria (1998) UN doc. CCPR/C/79/Add. 95. State Parties have to recognize in law the right to use local languages in official communications or administrative or court proceedings. Concluding Comments on Sudan (1997) UN doc. CCPR/C/79/Add. 85.

Although the rights protected under Article 27 are individual rights, they depend in turn on the ability of a minority group to maintain its culture, language or religion. Where historical iniquities and recent developments threaten the way of life of a tribe, Article 27 is violated. Ominayak et al. v. Canada (167/87). Accordingly, positive measures by States may also be necessary to protect the identity of a minority and the rights of its members to enjoy and develop the culture and language and to practice their religion, in community with the other members of the group. Concluding Comments on Brazil (1996) UN doc. CCPR/C/79/Add. 66 - demarcation of indigenous lands. Such positive measures must respect the provisions of Articles 2(1) and 26 of the Covenant both with regard to the treatment between different minorities and the treatment between the persons belonging to them and the remaining part of the population. As long as those measures are aimed at correcting conditions, which prevent or impair the enjoyment of the rights guaranteed under Article 27, they constitute, according to the Committee, a legitimate differentiation under the Covenant, provided that they are based on reasonable and objective criteria. The legislation of a State Party that discusses whether *affirmative action* programs for minorities should be withdrawn, has to bear in mind the obligation to provide the Covenant's rights in fact as well as in law. Concluding Comments on the United States of America (1995) UN doc. CCPR/C/79/Add. 50. When planning actions that affect members of indigenous communities, the State Party must pay primary attention to the sustainability of the indigenous culture and way of life and to the *effective participation* of members of indigenous communities in decisions that affect them. Concluding Comments on Chile (1999) UN doc. CCPR/C/79/Add. 104. The Committee demands positive measures of protection not only against the acts of the State Parties themselves, but also against the acts of other persons within the State Parties. General Comment No.: 23.

The acceptability of measures that affect or interfere with the culturally significant economic activities of a minority depends on, according to the Committee, whether the members of the minority in question have had the opportunity to participate in the decision-making process in relation to these measures and whether they will continue to benefit from their traditional economy. In circumstances where the right of individuals to enjoy their own culture is in conflict with the exercise of parallel rights by other members of the

minority group, or of the minority as a whole, a State Party has to consider whether the limitation in issue is in the interests of all members of the minority and whether there is reasonable and objective justification for its application to the individuals who claim to be adversely affected. Mahuika et al. v. New Zealand (547/93).
With regard to the exercise of the cultural rights protected under Article 27, the Committee observes that *culture* manifests itself in many forms and traditional activities. The Committee does not determine the right to enjoy one's culture in abstracto. It places the right in its context. The recognition of community rights by a treaty confirmes to the Committee that the exercise of these rights is a significant part of the culture of this community. Moreover, Article 27 does not only protect traditional means of livelihood of minorities, but allows also for *adaptation* of those means to the modern way of life and ensuing technology. Mahuika et al. v. New Zealand (547/93). The right of members of a minority to enjoy their culture under Article 27 includes also the protection of a particular way of life associated with the use of land resources through economic activities, such as hunting and fishing, especially in the case of indigenous peoples. Länsman et al. v. Finland (511/92, 671/95). It does not prejudice the sovereignty and territorial integrity of a State Party. This is the case even when some aspects of the rights of individuals protected under that Article may consist in a way of life which is closely associated with a certain territory and the use of its resources. Kitok v. Sweden (197/85). The link of a community to a land that dates back many years must not result in a relationship that gives rise to a distinctive culture. Therefore, even when a community bears distinctive properties as historical forms of self-government, it has to demonstrate to the Committee how these factors are based on their link to a land. Diergaardt et al. v. Namibia (760/96) - 125 years.

PART IV (ARTICLE 28 – 45)

Article 28

1. There shall be established a Human Rights Committee (hereafter referred to in the present Covenant as the Committee). It shall consist of eighteen members and shall carry out the functions hereinafter provided.
2. The Committee shall be composed of nationals of the States Parties to the present Covenant who shall be persons of high moral character and recognized competence in the field of human rights, consideration being given to the usefulness of the participation of some persons having legal experience.
3. The members of the Committee shall be elected and shall serve in their personal capacity.

Article 29

1. The members of the Committee shall be elected by secret ballot from a list of persons possessing the qualifications prescribed in article 28 and nominated for the purpose by the States Parties to the present Covenant.

2. Each State Party to the present Covenant may nominate not more than two persons. These persons shall be nationals of the nominating State.

3. A person shall be eligible for renomination.

Article 30

1. The initial election shall be held no later than six months after the date of the entry into force of the present Covenant.

2. At least four months before the date of each election to the Committee, other than an election to fill a vacancy declared in accordance with article 34, the Secretary-General of the United Nations shall address a written invitation to the States Parties to the present Covenant to submit their nominations for membership of the Committee within three months.

3. The Secretary-General of the United Nations shall prepare a list in alphabetical order of all the persons thus nominated, with an indication of the States Parties which have nominated them, and shall submit it to the States Parties to the present Covenant no later than one month before the date of each election.

4. Elections of the members of the Committee shall be held at a meeting of the States Parties to the present Covenant convened by the Secretary General of the United Nations at the Headquarters of the United Nations. At that meeting, for which two thirds of the States Parties to the present Covenant shall constitute a quorum, the persons elected to the Committee shall be those nominees who obtain the largest number of votes and an absolute majority of the votes of the representatives of States Parties present and voting.

Article 31

1. The Committee may not include more than one national of the same State.

2. In the election of the Committee, consideration shall be given to equitable geographical distribution of membership and to the representation of the different forms of civilization and of the principal legal systems.

Article 32

1. The members of the Committee shall be elected for a term of four years. They shall be eligible for re-election if renominated. However, the terms of nine of the members elected at the first election shall expire at the end of two years; immediately after the first election, the names of these nine members shall be chosen by lot by the Chairman of the meeting referred to in article 30, paragraph 4.

2. Elections at the expiry of office shall be held in accordance with the preceding articles of this part of the present Covenant.

Article 33

1. If, in the unanimous opinion of the other members, a member of the Committee has ceased to carry out his functions for any cause other than absence of a temporary character, the Chairman of the Committee shall notify the Secretary-General of the United Nations, who shall then declare the seat of that member to be vacant.

2. In the event of the death or the resignation of a member of the Committee, the Chairman shall immediately notify the Secretary-General of the United Nations, who shall declare the seat vacant from the date of death or the date on which the resignation takes effect.

Article 34

1. When a vacancy is declared in accordance with article 33 and if the term of office of the member to be replaced does not expire within six months of the declaration of the vacancy, the Secretary-General of the United Nations shall notify each of the States Parties to the present Covenant, which may within two months submit nominations in accordance with article 29 for the purpose of filling the vacancy.

2. The Secretary-General of the United Nations shall prepare a list in alphabetical order of the persons thus nominated and shall submit it to the States Parties to the present Covenant. The election to fill the vacancy shall then take place in accordance with the relevant provisions of this part of the present Covenant.

3. A member of the Committee elected to fill a vacancy declared in accordance with article 33 shall hold office for the remainder of the term of the member who vacated the seat on the Committee under the provisions of that article.

Article 35

The members of the Committee shall, with the approval of the General Assembly of the United Nations, receive emoluments from United Nations resources on such terms and conditions as the General Assembly may decide, having regard to the importance of the Committee's responsibilities.

Article 36

The Secretary-General of the United Nations shall provide the necessary staff and facilities for the effective performance of the functions of the Committee under the present Covenant.

Article 37

1. The Secretary-General of the United Nations shall convene the initial meeting of the Committee at the Headquarters of the United Nations.

2. After its initial meeting, the Committee shall meet at such times as shall be provided in its rules of procedure.
3. The Committee shall normally meet at the Headquarters of the United Nations or at the United Nations Office at Geneva.

Article 38

Every member of the Committee shall, before taking up his duties, make a solemn declaration in open committee that he will perform his functions impartially and conscientiously.

Article 39

1. The Committee shall elect its officers for a term of two years. They may be re-elected.
2. The Committee shall establish its own rules of procedure, but these rules shall provide, inter alia, that:
(a) Twelve members shall constitute a quorum;
(b) Decisions of the Committee shall be made by a majority vote of the members present.

ARTICLE 40

1. The States Parties to the present Covenant undertake to submit reports on the measures they have adopted which give effect to the rights recognized herein and on the progress made in the enjoyment of those rights:
(a) Within one year of the entry into force of the present Covenant for the States Parties concerned;
(b) Thereafter whenever the Committee so requests.
2. All reports shall be submitted to the Secretary-General of the United Nations, who shall transmit them to the Committee for consideration. Reports shall indicate the factors and difficulties, if any, affecting the implementation of the present Covenant.
3. The Secretary-General of the United Nations may, after consultation with the Committee, transmit to the specialized agencies concerned copies of such parts of the reports as may fall within their field of competence.
4. The Committee shall study the reports submitted by the States Parties to the present Covenant. It shall transmit its reports, and such general comments as it may consider appropriate, to the States Parties. The Committee may also transmit to the Economic and Social Council these comments along with the copies of the reports it has received from States Parties to the present Covenant.
5. The States Parties to the present Covenant may submit to the Committee observations on any comments that may be made in accordance with paragraph 4 of this article.

Article 40

A small number of States have submitted their reports on time. Most of them have been submitted with delays ranging from a few months to several years. General Comment No.: 1. Some of the reports submitted initially were so brief and general that the Committee found it necessary to elaborate general guidelines regarding the form and content of reports. The Committee considers that the reporting obligation embraces not only the relevant laws and other norms relating to the obligations under the Covenant but also the practices and decisions of courts and other organs of the State Party as well as further relevant facts which are likely to show the degree of the actual implementation and enjoyment of the rights recognized in the Covenant, the progress achieved and factors and difficulties in implementing the obligations under the Covenant. It is the practice of the Committee, in accordance with rule 68 of its Rules of Procedure, to examine reports in the presence of representatives of the reporting States. General Comment No.: 2.

Article 41

1. A State Party to the present Covenant may at any time declare under this article that it recognizes the competence of the Committee to receive and consider communications to the effect that a State Party claims that another State Party is not fulfilling its obligations under the present Covenant. Communications under this article may be received and considered only if submitted by a State Party which has made a declaration recognizing in regard to itself the competence of the Committee. No communication shall be received by the Committee if it concerns a State Party which has not made such a declaration. Communications received under this article shall be dealt with in accordance with the following procedure:

(a) If a State Party to the present Covenant considers that another State Party is not giving effect to the provisions of the present Covenant, it may, by written communication, bring the matter to the attention of that State Party. Within three months after the receipt of the communication the receiving State shall afford the State which sent the communication an explanation, or any other statement in writing clarifying the matter which should include, to the extent possible and pertinent, reference to domestic procedures and remedies taken, pending, or available in the matter;

(b) If the matter is not adjusted to the satisfaction of both States Parties concerned within six months after the receipt by the receiving State of the initial communication, either State shall have the right to refer the matter to the Committee, by notice given to the Committee and to the other State;

(c) The Committee shall deal with a matter referred to it only after it has ascertained that all available domestic remedies have been invoked and

exhausted in the matter, in conformity with the generally recognized principles of international law. This shall not be the rule where the application of the remedies is unreasonably prolonged;
(d) The Committee shall hold closed meetings when examining communications under this article;
(e) Subject to the provisions of subparagraph (c), the Committee shall make available its good offices to the States Parties concerned with a view to a friendly solution of the matter on the basis of respect for human rights and fundamental freedoms as recognized in the present Covenant;
(f) In any matter referred to it, the Committee may call upon the States Parties concerned, referred to in subparagraph (b), to supply any relevant information;
(g) The States Parties concerned, referred to in subparagraph (b), shall have the right to be represented when the matter is being considered in the Committee and to make submissions orally and/or in writing;
(h) The Committee shall, within twelve months after the date of receipt of notice under subparagraph (b), submit a report:
(i) If a solution within the terms of subparagraph (e) is reached, the Committee shall confine its report to a brief statement of the facts and of the solution reached;
(ii) If a solution within the terms of subparagraph (e) is not reached, the Committee shall confine its report to a brief statement of the facts; the written submissions and record of the oral submissions made by the States Parties concerned shall be attached to the report. In every matter, the report shall be communicated to the States Parties concerned.
2. The provisions of this article shall come into force when ten States Parties to the present Covenant have made declarations under paragraph I of this article. Such declarations shall be deposited by the States Parties with the Secretary-General of the United Nations, who shall transmit copies thereof to the other States Parties. A declaration may be withdrawn at any time by notification to the Secretary-General. Such a withdrawal shall not prejudice the consideration of any matter which is the subject of a communication already transmitted under this article; no further communication by any State Party shall be received after the notification of withdrawal of the declaration has been received by the Secretary-General, unless the State Party concerned has made a new declaration.

Article 42

1. (a) If a matter referred to the Committee in accordance with article 41 is not resolved to the satisfaction of the States Parties concerned, the Committee may, with the prior consent of the States Parties concerned, appoint an ad hoc Conciliation Commission (hereinafter referred to as the Commission). The good

offices of the Commission shall be made available to the States Parties concerned with a view to an amicable solution of the matter on the basis of respect for the present Covenant;
(b) The Commission shall consist of five persons acceptable to the States Parties concerned. If the States Parties concerned fail to reach agreement within three months on all or part of the composition of the Commission, the members of the Commission concerning whom no agreement has been reached shall be elected by secret ballot by a two-thirds majority vote of the Committee from among its members.
2. The members of the Commission shall serve in their personal capacity. They shall not be nationals of the States Parties concerned, or of a State not Party to the present Covenant, or of a State Party which has not made a declaration under article 41.
3. The Commission shall elect its own Chairman and adopt its own rules of procedure.
4. The meetings of the Commission shall normally be held at the Headquarters of the United Nations or at the United Nations Office at Geneva. However, they may be held at such other convenient places as the Commission may determine in consultation with the Secretary-General of the United Nations and the States Parties concerned.
5. The secretariat provided in accordance with article 36 shall also service the commissions appointed under this article.
6. The information received and collated by the Committee shall be made available to the Commission and the Commission may call upon the States Parties concerned to supply any other relevant information.
7. When the Commission has fully considered the matter, but in any event not later than twelve months after having been seized of the matter, it shall submit to the Chairman of the Committee a report for communication to the States Parties concerned:
(a) If the Commission is unable to complete its consideration of the matter within twelve months, it shall confine its report to a brief statement of the status of its consideration of the matter;
(b) If an amicable solution to the matter on tie basis of respect for human rights as recognized in the present Covenant is reached, the Commission shall confine its report to a brief statement of the facts and of the solution reached;
(c) If a solution within the terms of subparagraph (b) is not reached, the Commission's report shall embody its findings on all questions of fact relevant to the issues between the States Parties concerned, and its views on the possibilities of an amicable solution of the matter. This report shall also contain

the written submissions and a record of the oral submissions made by the States Parties concerned;
(d) If the Commission's report is submitted under subparagraph (c), the States Parties concerned shall, within three months of the receipt of the report, notify the Chairman of the Committee whether or not they accept the contents of the report of the Commission.
8. The provisions of this article are without prejudice to the responsibilities of the Committee under article 41.
9. The States Parties concerned shall share equally all the expenses of the members of the Commission in accordance with estimates to be provided by the Secretary-General of the United Nations.
10. The Secretary-General of the United Nations shall be empowered to pay the expenses of the members of the Commission, if necessary, before reimbursement by the States Parties concerned, in accordance with paragraph 9 of this article.

Article 43

The members of the Committee, and of the ad hoc conciliation commissions which may be appointed under article 42, shall be entitled to the facilities, privileges and immunities of experts on mission for the United Nations as laid down in the relevant sections of the Convention on the Privileges and Immunities of the United Nations.

Article 44

The provisions for the implementation of the present Covenant shall apply without prejudice to the procedures prescribed in the field of human rights by or under the constituent instruments and the conventions of the United Nations and of the specialized agencies and shall not prevent the States Parties to the present Covenant from having recourse to other procedures for settling a dispute in accordance with general or special international agreements in force between them.

Article 45

The Committee shall submit to the General Assembly of the United Nations, through the Economic and Social Council, an annual report on its activities.

PART V (ARTICLE 46 – 47)

Article 46

Nothing in the present Covenant shall be interpreted as impairing the provisions of the Charter of the United Nations and of the constitutions of the specialized agencies which define the respective responsibilities of the various organs of the United Nations and of the specialized agencies in regard to the matters dealt with in the present Covenant.

Article 47

Nothing in the present Covenant shall be interpreted as impairing the inherent right of all peoples to enjoy and utilize fully and freely their natural wealth and resources.

PART VI (ARTICLE 48 – 53)

Article 48

1. The present Covenant is open for signature by any State Member of the United Nations or member of any of its specialized agencies, by any State Party to the Statute of the International Court of Justice, and by any other State which has been invited by the General Assembly of the United Nations to become a Party to the present Covenant.

2. The present Covenant is subject to ratification. Instruments of ratification shall be deposited with the Secretary-General of the United Nations.

3. The present Covenant shall be open to accession by any State referred to in paragraph 1 of this article.

4. Accession shall be effected by the deposit of an instrument of accession with the Secretary-General of the United Nations.

5. The Secretary-General of the United Nations shall inform all States which have signed this Covenant or acceded to it of the deposit of each instrument of ratification or accession.

Article 49

1. The present Covenant shall enter into force three months after the date of the deposit with the Secretary-General of the United Nations of the thirty-fifth instrument of ratification or instrument of accession.

2. For each State ratifying the present Covenant or acceding to it after the deposit of the thirty-fifth instrument of ratification or instrument of accession, the present Covenant shall enter into force three months after the date of the deposit of its own instrument of ratification or instrument of accession.

Article 50

The provisions of the present Covenant shall extend to all parts of federal States without any limitations or exceptions.

Article 51

1. Any State Party to the present Covenant may propose an amendment and file it with the Secretary-General of the United Nations. The Secretary-General of the United Nations shall thereupon communicate any proposed amendments to the States Parties to the present Covenant with a request that they notify him whether they favour a conference of States Parties for the purpose of considering and voting upon the proposals. In the event that at least one third of the States Parties favours such a conference, the Secretary-General shall convene the conference under the auspices of the United Nations. Any amendment adopted by a majority of the States Parties present and voting at the conference shall be submitted to the General Assembly of the United Nations for approval.

2. Amendments shall come into force when they have been approved by the General Assembly of the United Nations and accepted by a two-thirds majority of the States Parties to the present Covenant in accordance with their respective constitutional processes.

3. When amendments come into force, they shall be binding on those States Parties which have accepted them, other States Parties still being bound by the provisions of the present Covenant and any earlier amendment which they have accepted.

Article 52

Irrespective of the notifications made under article 48, paragraph 5, the Secretary-General of the United Nations shall inform all States referred to in paragraph I of the same article of the following particulars:

(a) Signatures, ratifications and accessions under article 48;

(b) The date of the entry into force of the present Covenant under article 49 and the date of the entry into force of any amendments under article 51.

Article 53

1. The present Covenant, of which the Chinese, English, French, Russian and Spanish texts are equally authentic, shall be deposited in the archives of the United Nations.

2. The Secretary-General of the United Nations shall transmit certified copies of the present Covenant to all States referred to in article 48.

Optional Protocol to the International Covenant on Civil and Political Rights

G.A. res. 2200A (XXI), 21 U.N. GAOR Supp. (No. 16) at 59, U.N. Doc. A/6316 (1966), 999 U.N.T.S. 302, entered into force March 23, 1976.

PREAMBLE

The States Parties to the present Protocol,

Considering that in order further to achieve the purposes of the International Covenant on Civil and Political Rights (hereinafter referred to as the Covenant) and the implemenation of its provisions it would be appropriate to enable the Human Rights Committee set up in part IV of the Covenant (hereinafter referred to as the Committee) to receive and consider, as provided in the present Protocol, communications from individuals claiming to be victims of violations of any of the rights set forth in the Covenant.

Have agreed as follows:

It is for the Committee, as the treaty body to the International Covenant on Civil and Political Rights and its Optional Protocols, to interpret and determine the validity of *reservations* made to these treaties. The Optional Protocol itself does not govern the permissibility of reservations to its provisions. The Committee is of the opinion that, in accordance with Article 19 of the Vienna Convention on the Law of Treaties, 1155 U. N. T. S. 331, entered into force on January 27, 1980, and principles of customary international law, reservations can be made, as long as they are compatible with the object and purpose of the treaty in question. A reservation aimed at excluding the competence of the Committee under the Optional Protocol with regard to certain provisions of the Covenant is incompatible with the object and purpose of the Protocol. Its object and purpose is it to allow claims in respect of the Covenant's rights to be tested before the Committee. Also, a reservation to an obligation of a State to respect and ensure a right contained in the Covenant, made under the (First) Optional Protocol, when it has not previously been made in respect of the same rights under the Covenant, does not affect the State's duty to comply with its substantive obligation. A reservation cannot be made to the Covenant through the vehicle of the Optional Protocol. General Comment No.: 24. A reservation which singles out a certain group of individuals for lesser procedural protection than that which is enjoyed by the rest of the population constitutes a discrimination which runs counter to some of the basic principles embodied in the Covenant and its Protocols. The Committee does not deem, for this reason, such a reservation compatible with the object and purpose of the Optional Protocol. Kennedy v. Trinidad and Tobago (845/99).

ARTICLE 1

A State Party to the Covenant that becomes a Party to the present Protocol recognizes the competence of the Committee to receive and consider communications from individuals subject to its jurisdiction who claim to be victims of a violation by that State Party of any of the rights set forth in the Covenant. No communication shall be received by the Committee if it concerns a State Party to the Covenant which is not a Party to the present Protocol.

The procedure laid down in the Optional Protocol is not, according to the Committee, designed for conducting *public debate* over matters of public policy, such as support for disarmament and issues concerning nuclear and other weapons of mass destruction. E. C. W. v. The Netherlands (524/92). The Committee does not ascertain the validity or correctness of contentions that are highly controversial even in concerned scientific circles, Bordes et al. v. France (645/95), and, under the Optional Protocol procedure, it does also not examine *in abstracto* whether a State Party has complied with its obligations under the Covenant, Canepa v. Canada (558/93), or review, *in abstracto*, national legislation or practices as to their compliance with obligations imposed by the Covenant. J. H. v. Canada (187/85). The Committee also does not examine *hypothetical* violations of Covenant rights which might occur in the future. V. R. M. B. v. Canada (236/87). The possibility of a cancellation of a remission after release for a prisoner who has not yet served the two thirds of his sentence for which he is not entitled to remission and who, in addition to his release, depends on his good conduct up to that date, is hypothetical. A. R. S. v. Canada (91/81). On the other hand, claims based on the threat of removal of a State Party's territory are not of a hypothetical nature. Bakhtiyari et al. v. Australia (1069/02).
By ratifying the Covenant and the Optional Protocol, a State Party undertakes to fulfil its obligations and has recognized the Committee's competence to receive and consider communications from individuals subject to its jurisdiction who claim to be victims of a violation by the State Party of any of the rights set forth in the Covenant. Governments have therefore, according to the Committee, no right to erect obstacles to contacts between victims and the Committee. The Committee sees as a prerequisite for the effective application of the Optional

Protocol that detainees are able to communicate directly with the Committee. The contention that the Covenant and the Protocol apply only to States, as subjects of international law, and that, consequently, these instruments are not directly applicable to individuals is, according to the Committee, devoid of legal foundation in cases where a State has recognized the competence of the Committee to receive and consider communications from individuals under the Protocol. Denying individuals who are victims of an alleged violation their rights to bring the matter before the Committee is tantamount to denying the mandatory nature of the Optional Protocol. Antonaccio v. Uruguay (63/79).
Where the Covenant is not part of the domestic law of a State Party which can be applied directly by the courts, the State Party has nevertheless, according to the Committee, accepted the legal obligation to make the provisions of the Covenant effective. To this extent, it is an obligation for the State Party to adopt appropriate measures to give legal effect to the Views of the Committee as to the interpretation and application of the Covenant in particular cases arising under the Optional Protocol. This includes the Committee's Views under rule 86 of the Rules of Procedure on the desirability of *interim measures* of protection, to avoid irreparable damage to the victim of the alleged violation. Roberts v. Barbados (504/92). Bradshaw v. Barbados (489/92). A State Party commits a grave breach of its obligations under the Protocol by putting a person to death before the Committee has concluded its consideration of the communication. Piandiong et al. v. The Philippines (869/99). Also the extradition of a person before the Committee can address whether the person will thereby suffer irreparable harm does not conform to the obligations of the State Parties. Weiss v. Austria (1086/02). A State Party of the Covenant is always required to ensure that it carries out all its legal commitments in a manner consistent with the Covenant. Therefore, a State Party itself violates the Covenant that extradites a person within its jurisdiction without considering that there is a real risk that his or her rights under the Covenant will be violated in another jurisdiction. Kindler v. Canada (470/91).
The Optional Protocol provides a procedure under which *individuals* can claim that their individual rights have been violated. Mohamed v. Barbados (502/92). A company which has its own legal personality has no standing within the meaning of Article 1, Lamagna v. Australia (737/97), S. M. v. Barbados (502/92), regardless of whether its allegations appear to raise issues under the Covenant. A publication and a printing company v. Trinidad and Tobago (361/89). Also an association cannot as such submit a communication to the Committee under the Optional Protocol. J. R. T. et al. v. Canada (104/81).
No claim for self-determination may be brought under the Optional Protocol. A. B. et al. v. Italy (413/90). E. P. et al. v. Colombia (318/88). Kitok v. Sweden

(197/85). The Committee does not, however, object to a group of individuals, who claim to be similarly affected, collectively submitting a communication about alleged breaches of their rights. Diergaardt et al. v. Namibia (760/96). Lubicon Lake Band v. Canada (167/84).

A claim that refers to the right to property is inadmissible because this right is not protected by the Covenant. E. et al. v. Hungary (520/92). Ackla v. Togo (505/92). Blanco v. Nicaragua (328/88). Extradition as such is also outside the scope of application of the Covenant. There is no provision of the Covenant that makes it unlawful for a State Party to seek extradition of a person from another country. Cox v. Canada (539/93). In addition, the Covenant also does not provide that an alien convicted and sentenced for a crime has a right to serve his sentence in his own country. Maleki v. Italy (699/96).

Only a claim out of which follows that an author is *personally a victim* of acts of a State Party is admissible. Vlad v. Germany(1214/03). Claims in the nature of an *actio popularis*, relating to further actions taken by the State Party in respect of third parties rather than the author, Kavanagh v. Ireland (1114/02), or claims that discuss issues in the abstract without reference to any particular facts where the author has been prevented from exercising his rights, are inadmissible. Colchúin v. Ireland (1038/01). But the mere fact of large numbers of petitioners does not render their communication an *actio popularis*. E. W. et al. v. The Netherlands (429/90).

The Committee declares a communication admissible if the claims submitted are sufficiently substantiated and do not constitute an *abuse of the right of submission*. M. A. B. et al. v. Canada (570/93). Authors are not required, for purposes of the Optional Protocol, necessarily to invoke specific Articles of the Covenant. Hoofdman v. The Netherlands (602/94). But allegations of a sweeping nature justify doubts about the seriousness of claims. M. A. B. et al. v. Canada (570/93). An author, who, in violation of a State Party's law, does not serve his sentence because he is a fugitive from justice neither loses the right to lodge a complaint nor abuses the right of submission with his complaint. Vázquez v. Spain (701/96).

A person who claims to be a *victim* of a violation of a right protected by the Covenant must show either that an act, Riley et al. v. Canada (1048/02) - permission to wear religious symbols, Tadman et al. v. Canada (816/98) - publicly funded religious schools, or omission, Poongavanam v. Mauritius (567/93) - absence of women on a jury, of a State Party has already adversely affected his or her enjoyment of rights, or that there is a real threat of such a result. Young v. Australia (941/00). Bordes et al. v. France (645/95). The preparations for deployment of cruise missiles and the continuing deployment of other nuclear weapons in the territory of a State Party does not place persons in

the position to claim to be victims whose rights are violated or under imminent prospect of violation. E. W. et al. v. The Netherlands (429/90). An agreement with the authorities over the amount of the penalties which an author of a communication is ready to pay excludes any claim to be a victim. Gerritsen v. The Netherlands (714/96). Even if a law in question were to be considered inconsistent, prior to an enactment of an amendment, with a provision of the Covenant, a State Party, by amending the law retroactively, has corrected the alleged inconsistency of the law with the Covenant, thereby remedying the alleged violation. A. P. L. - v. d. M. v. The Netherlands (478/91). If a Supreme Court allows an appeal and substitutes a term of imprisonment in place of the sentence of death, the issues raised by an author concerning the alleged violations of Article 6 of the Covenant through imposition of the death penalty have become moot, in relation to Article 1 of the Protocol. Baroy v. The Philippines (1045/02). An author who does not apply under a law cannot claim to be a victim of a violation of the Covenant by the application of the law. This is the case even if the Committee finds the law to be discriminatory in respect of some of those applying under it. J. A. M. B. - R. v. The Netherlands (477/91). Also, a person who does not produce any arguments relating to any efforts he has made to claim his rights has not demonstrated that he is a victim of a violation of the Covenant. Bi v. Cote d'Ivoire (940/00) - either as a voter or as a candidate in a presidential election.
However, even if provisions have not been enforced for a decade, this does not amount to a guarantee that no actions will be brought against a person that violates the provisions in the future. Therefore, the existence of provisions alone can interfere with a person's rights and support a claim to be a victim of a violation of a right protected by the Covenant. Toonen v. Australia (488/92). But the burden of proving that under a law an author is a victim lies with the author. MacIsaac v. Canada (55/79). The Committee regarded as vicitim a person whose business activities (commercial signs outside the business premises) could be regarded as contrary to law, because of a legislation that allowed only the use of a certain language in public billposting and in commercial advertising. Ballantyne v. Canada (359, 385/89). Also a mother whose daughter disappeared after her arrest because of her anguish and stress and the continuing uncertainty concerning the fate and whereabouts of the daughter. Almeida v. Uruguay (107/81). The Committee deemed it as appropriate that a person who had been sentenced to a prison term and preventive detention (indefinite detention until release by a Parole Board) argued the compatibility of his sentence to preventive detention with the Covenant at an earlier point, rather than when the years of imprisonment have elapsed. Rameka et al. v. New Zealand (1090/02).

A State Party cannot be *held responsible* for the actions of private individuals. Keshavjee v. Canada (949/00) - Union of Taxation Employees. The contracting out of core State activities which involve the use of force and the detention of persons to the private commercial sector does not, however, absolve a State Party of its obligations under the Covenant. Consequently, the State Party is accountable under the Covenant and the Optional Protocol of the treatment of inmates in a prison facility run by a private enterprise. Cabal et al. v. Australia (1020/01). No State Party is relieved of its obligations under the Covenant by delegating some of its functions to autonomous organs or municipalities. Lindgren et al. v. Sweden (298, 299/88). However, a State Party cannot be held accountable for alleged errors made by the privately retained counsel, unless it has been manifest to the judge or the judicial authorities that the lawyer's behaviour is incompatible with the interests of justice. Henry et al. v. Jamaica (571/94). Lewis v. Jamaica (527/93). The execution of a person after the submission of the communication, but prior to its registration cannot be attributed to a State Party. Staselovich et al. v. Belarus (887/99). Schedko et al. v. Belarus (886/99). Also, the fact that the Human Rights Committee has not requested a stay of execution before the warrant of execution was read to an author does not amount to a violation of the Covenant attributable to the State Party. Simpson v. Jamaica (695/96).

The Committee only examines *individual petitions* presented by the alleged victims themselves or by duly authorized representatives. Krausser et al. v. Austria (890/99). There are no specific requirements for representation before the Human Rights Committee. Vázquez v. Spain (701/96). Standing under the Optional Protocol is determined independently of national regulations and legislation governing an individual's standing before a court of law. Santacana et al. v. Spain (417/90). The Committee has always taken a wide view of the right of alleged victims to be represented by a counsel in submitting communications under the Optional Protocol. However, a counsel acting on behalf of victims of alleged violations must show that he has real authorization from the victims (or their immediate family) to act on their behalf, that there were circumstances which prevented the counsel from receiving such authorization, or that given the close relationship in the past between the counsel and the alleged victim it is fair to assume that the victim did indeed authorize the counsel to proceed with a communication to the Human Rights Committee. Mr. Y v. Australia (772/97).

The relationship between father and son in cases where a State Party has awarded custody to the mother is deemed sufficient to justify representation before the Committee. P. S. v. Denmark (397/90). A non-custodial parent is therefore not necessarily excluded from possessing sufficient standing to bring a complaint on a child's behalf. Rogl v. Germany (808/98). It is, however, inappropriate for a grandfather to bring a claim on behalf of his grandson without expression of assent to such a course by a custodial parent. Sahid et al. v. New Zealand (893/99).

An individual must show compelling grounds for bringing a communication on behalf of another in the absence of authorization. R. et al. v. Italy (565/93). The Committee considers a communication submitted by a third party on behalf of an alleged victim only if the author justifies his authority to submit the communication. J. F. v. Uruguay (137/83). U. R. v. Uruguay (128/82). Hence, an author has to establish the grounds justifying his authority to act. Mbenge v. Zaire (16/77) - on behalf of the family driver or pharmacist. A person can submit a communication on behalf of another person if this person is unable himself or herself to submit the communication. Mojica v. Dominican Republic (449/91) - **father**. S. E. v. Argentina (275/88) - **mother**. Zapala v. Uruguay (44/79) - **daughter**. Altesor v. Uruguay (10/77) - **son**. El-Megreisi v. Libyan Arab Jamahiriya (440/90), Beguio v. Uruguay (88/81) - **brother**. Thompson v. Panama (438/90). Patino v. Panama (437/90), Fillastre et al. v. Bolivia (336/88), Romero v. Uruguay (85/81) - **wife**. M'Boissona v. Central African (428/90) - **sister**. A. M. v. Finland (398/90) - **husband**. Lanza et al. v. Uruguay (8/77) - **aunt** and **uncle**. Barbato et al. v. Uruguay (84/81) - **cousin**. Bazzano et al. v. Uruguay (5/77) - **stepfather**. R. A. V. N. et al. v. Argentina (343 - 345/88) - **relatives**. However, if the alleged victim is in the position to authorize the representation before the Committee, it has to do so, or else the person has no more standing before the Committee within the meaning of Article 1. Palma v. Panama (436/90). An *authorization* duly provided in advance of the communication confers, in the ordinary course, sufficient authority on a counsel to see a communication through to its conclusion. The length of time before a communication is in fact filed and registered, or subsequent circumstances, cannot negate the inference as long as a counsel is, and remains, duly authorized. Baban et al. v. Australia (1014/01). A counsel can continue to represent a person after his death if he indicates that he has been instructed to do so. Burrell v. Jamaica (546/93) - local Council for Human Rights; family. A person who has no (more) power of attorney or other documented proof of the relationship that authorizes him or her to act on behalf of an alleged victim has no (more) standing under Article 1. R. et al. v. Italy (565/93).

The *obligations* that a State Party assumes when it signs the Covenant or the Protocoll *take effect* on the date on which the Covenant enters into force for the State Party. A et al. v. S (1/76). The Committee does not consider violations that took place before the Optional Protocol entered into force for a State Party, unless such violations persist after the entry into force of the Optional Protocol.

A *persistent violation* is understood to mean the continuation of violations which a State Party committed previously, either through actions or implicitly. Kurowski v. Poland (872/99). General Comment No.: 24. It also includes the element of affirmation, by act or clear implication, of the previous violations of the State Party. Somers v. Hungary (566/93). Where effects of a violation continue after the Covenant and the Protocol entered into force for a State Party, the Committee considers those effects if they themselves constitute a violation of the Covenant. Kim v. Republic of Korea (574/94). A term of imprisonment without the involvement of additional factors does not amount to a continuing effect per se, in violation of the Covenant, sufficient to bring the original circumstances giving rise to the imprisonment within the Committee's jurisdiction *ratione temporis*. Kang v. Republic of Korea (878/99). Also, claims that relate to the death of a person that occurred prior to the entry into force of the Covenant, are inadmissible *ratione temporis*. A Supreme Court judgment after entry into force of the Covenant was not regarded as a new event that affected the rights of the person who was killed before the entry into force of the Covenant. Aceituno et al v. Chile (746/97). An author who has not made any specific claims based on continuing effects of alleged violations of the Covenant during his trial that would, on their own, constitute a violation of the Covenant, precludes the Committee *ratione temporis* from considering the communication. Baulin v. Russian Federation (771/97).

The Human Rights Committee receives and considers only communications in respect of claims that come under the *jurisdiction* of a State Party to the Covenant. The reference to the "individuals subject" to a State Party's "jurisdiction" does not only refer to the place where a violation occurs, but also the relationship between the individual and the State in relation to a violation of any of the rights set forth in the Covenant, wherever they occur. Casariego v. Uruguay (56/79). Burgos v. Uruguay (52/79). The issuing of a passport by a State Party to the State Party's national is a matter within the jurisdiction of the State Party's authorities. The national is subject to the jurisdiction of the State Party for that purpose wherever he resides. M. M. Q. v. Uruguay (125/82). Nunez v. Uruguay (108/81). Montero v. Uruguay (106/81). Lichtensztejn v. Uruguay (77/80). Therefore, the fact that he resides abroad does not affect the competence of the Committee to receive and consider his communication under Article 1. Martins v. Uruguay (57/79).

Grievances concerning the recruitment policies of an international organization do not come within the jurisdiction of any State Party to the Covenant and the Optional Protocol thereto. H. v. d. P. v. The Netherlands (217/86).

ARTICLE 2

Subject to the provisions of article 1, individuals who claim that any of their rights enumerated in the Covenant have been violated and who have exhausted all available domestic remedies may submit a written communication to the Committee for consideration.

The Committee does not review the interpretation of domestic law or the evaluation of facts and evidences by domestic courts. Hom v. The Philippines (1169/03). Fernández v. Spain (1007/01). G. v. Canada (934/00). Tamihere v. New Zealand (891/99). Petkov v. Bulgaria (844/98). Singh v. Canada (761/97). Sahadeo v. Guyana (728/96). J. K. v. Canada (174/84). What *the Committee examines*, aside from the exhausting of domestic remedies, is whether a communication is sufficiently substantiated and does not constitute an abuse of the right of submission. H. J. H. v. The Netherlands (448/91). A claim that is not based on any new factual developments that go beyond what the Committee has already decided in an author's initial communication is inadmissible. Kavanagh v. Ireland (1114/02).

Notwithstanding any doubts an author may have as to the *effectiveness* of the remedies, it is incumbent on him to seek all available remedies. Veriter v. France (1088/02). Complaints that are not raised with the competent national courts in the period set by law are inadmissible. Clippele v. Belgium (1082/02).

As long as remedies under a domestic legal system are *available*, an individual who claims that his or her rights under the Covenant have been violated is not entitled to submit a communication to the Committee. Koi v. Portugal (925/00).

The Committee decides the question of *exhaustion of domestic remedies* at the point of its consideration of the communication. Bakhtiyari et al. v. Australia (1069/02). An author has to exhaust the domestic remedies available to him at the time of *submission* of the communication. Rameka et al. v. New Zealand (1090/02). A territory that becomes a special administrative region of another State after submission of a communication, while its legal system remains intact and the system of appeals unchanged, still has remedies that have to be pursued under the domestic legal system, irrespective of the State which exercises control over the territory. Koi v. Portugal (925/00).

A State Party can explicitly waive any challenge to the admissibility of a communication. Joslin et al. v New Zealand (902/99). Rajan et al. v. New Zealand (820/98). However, even if a State Party has not challenged the admissibility of a communication, the Committee has the right to ascertain whether all the admissibility criteria laid down in the Optional Protocol have been met. Whyte v. Jamaica (732/97).

ARTICLE 3

The Committee shall consider inadmissible any communication under the present Protocol which is anonymous, or which it considers to be an abuse of the right of submission of such communications or to be incompatible with the provisions of the Covenant.

The Optional Protocol does not fix *time limits* for submission of communications. The mere delay in submission does not of itself involve abuse of the rights of communication. However, in certain circumstances, a reasonable explanation justifying a delay is expected. A delay of **five years** before a communication is submitted has to be justified. In the absence of an explanation, such a time lapse is regarded as an *abuse of the right of submission.* Gobin v. Mauritius (787/97). A former judge with a great deal of experience renounces his right of appeal by insisting on being tried only by the Supreme Court. If he now insists on his right of appeal before the Committee, he abuses his right to submit a communication. Estevill v. Spain (1004/01). The Committee also sees an abuse of the right to submission if trial transcripts do not correspond with claims, Levy v. Jamaica (719/96), or allegations are of a sweeping nature without being substantiated. M. A. B. et al. v. Canada (570/93). J. J. C. v. Canada (367/89). Pinkney v. Canada (27/77). However, an author does not forfeit his right to submit a complaint under the Optional Protocol simply by leaving the jurisdiction of the State Party against which the complaint is made, in breach of the conditions of his release. Hill v. Spain (526/93).
The conditions for declaring a communication admissible include that the claims submitted be sufficiently substantiated and do not constitute an abuse of the right of submission. H. J. H. v. The Netherlands (448/91). C. W. v. Finland (379/89). A claim that does not show how the imposition of disciplinary measures relates to a criminal charge or a criminal offence in the meaning of Article 14 or 15 of the Covenant lies outside the scope of the Covenant. Strik v. The Netherlands (1001/01). Where the Covenant relates to *general undertakings* by State Parties, these undertakings cannot be invoked by individuals as a self-standing ground for a communication under the Optional Protocol. Wackenheim v. France (854/99).
The Committee exercises its decision-making power on the interpretation of the Covenant *independently* of the determination by any national bodies. Therefore, a claim that a direct obligation exists under the Covenant to implement the findings of domestic human rights bodies is incompatible *ratione materiae* with the Covenant. Love et al. v. Australia (983/01). There is also no provision in the

Covenant that makes it unlawful for a State Party to seek the extradition of a person from another country. M. A. v. Italy (117/81).

ARTICLE 4

1. Subject to the provisions of article 3, the Committee shall bring any communications submitted to it under the present Protocol to the attention of the State Party to the present Protocol alleged to be violating any provision of the Covenant.
2. Within six months, the receiving State shall submit to the Committee written explanations or statements clarifying the matter and the remedy, if any, that may have been taken by that State.

Article 4 (1)

Subject to the provisions of article 3, the Committee shall bring any communications submitted to it under the present Protocol to the attention of the State Party to the present Protocol alleged to be violating any provision of the Covenant.

The Committee has to bring any communications submitted to it under the Optional Protocol to the attention of the State Party to the Protocol alleged to be violating a provision of the Covenant. A State Party cannot claim that it was not apprised of an allegation when the allegation was reproduced in a resolution of the Inter-American Commission on Human Rights and a copy of the resolution was transmitted by the Committee to the State Party a year and a half before the Committee's decision on admissibility. Wright v. Jamaica (349/89). Where an author's allegations are sufficiently precise and substantiated so as to allow the State Party to address them, they are brought to the attention of the State Party, even when the Committee does not indicate to which Articles of the Covenant its admissibility decision relates. Gordon v. Jamaica (237/87).

Article 4 (2)

Within six months, the receiving State shall submit to the Committee written explanations or statements clarifying the matter and the remedy, if any, that may have been taken by that State.

It is incumbent upon the author of a complaint to substantiate his allegations properly. Wolf v. Panama (289/88). The Committee has to bring the communications submitted to it to the attention of the State Party. The State Party has to submit to the Committee its written observations on the admissibility and merits of the communication within **six months** of the transmittal of the communication to it for comments. This period may be shortened, in the interest of justice, if a State Party so wishes. Adams v. Jamaica (607/94). Sterling v. Jamaica (598/94). At the stage of the determination of the admissibility of a communication, a State Party has to provide *sufficiently detailed information* about remedies pursued by, as well as remedies still available, to an author. Wolf v. Panama (289/88). A State Party has to investigate allegations in accordance with its laws and its obligations under the Covenant and the Optional Protocol to clarify the matter. Ramirez v. Uruguay (4/77). Gordon v. Jamaica (237/87). It has to provide the Committee with all the information at its disposal. In no circumstances has a State Party to fail to investigate fully allegations of ill treatment if the author of a communication identifies the person or persons allegedly responsible for the ill treatment. Rubio et al. v. Colombia (161/83). A *refutation of allegations* in general terms is not sufficient for the Committee. Conteris v. Uruguay (139/83). The Committee did not regard a State Party's reference to a medical report as a sufficient refutation of the allegations of mistreatment and torture. In such a case a State Party has to furnish copies of court orders or decisions relevant to the matter under consideration for the determination of the nature of judicial proceedings. Burgos v. Uruguay (52/79).

Any author or counsel who wishes to substantiate his claims or comment on a State Party's submission has to do so in a *timely m*anner so as to enable the Committee to conclude its examination in an appropriately expeditious way. Douglas et al. v. Jamaica (352/89).

If a State Party fails *to cooperate* with the Committee on the matter before it, the Committee gives due weight to an author's allegations to the extent that they have been substantiated. Mansaraj et al. v. Sierra Leone (839 - 841/98). Burrell v. Jamaica (546/93). Aduayom et al. v. Togo (422 - 424/90). Barrett et al. v. Jamaica (270, 271/88). In cases where allegations are corroborated by evidence submitted by an author and where further clarification of the case depends on information exclusively in the hands of the State Party, the Committee considers an author's allegations as substantiated in the absence of satisfactory evidence and explanations to the contrary submitted by the State Party. Baboeram-Adhin et al. v. Suriname (146, 148 - 154/83). Romero v. Uruguay (85/81).

ARTICLE 5

1. The Committee shall consider communications received under the present Protocol in the light of all written information made available to it by the individual and by the State Party concerned.

2. The Committee shall not consider any communication from an individual unless it has ascertained that:
(a) The same matter is not being examined under another procedure of international investigation or settlement;
(b) The individual has exhausted all available domestic remedies. This shall not be the rule where the application of the remedies is unreasonably prolonged.

Article 5 (1)

The Committee shall consider communications received under the present Protocol in the light of all written information made available to it by the individual and by the State Party concerned.

Pursuant to Article 5 (1) of the Optional Protocol, the Committee considers communications on the basis of all written information made available to it by the individual and by the State Party concerned. Bahamonde v. Equatorial Guinea (468/91). Lanza et al. v. Uruguay (8/77). It adheres strictly to the principle of *audiatur et altera pars* (let the other side also be heard). Quinteros v. Uruguay (107/81). Bleier v. Uruguay (30/78).

Article 5 (2) a

The Committee shall not consider any communication from an individual unless it has ascertained that:
The same matter is not being examined under another procedure of international investigation or settlement;

The Committee understands the concept of the *same matter* as including the same claim concerning the same individual, submitted by him or someone else who has the standing to act on his behalf before another international body. Blom v. Sweden (191/85). Fanali v. Italy (75/80). Therefore, Article 5 (2) a cannot be interpreted as implying that an unrelated third party, acting without the knowledge and consent of the alleged victim, can preclude the latter from having access to the Human Rights Committee. Estrella v. Uruguay (74/80). The same matter concerns the same authors, the same facts and the same substantive rights. Karakurt v. Austria (965/00). López v. Spain (777/97). Blom v. Sweden (191/85). It refers to the facts and events which are at the basis of a complaint examined under another procedure of international investigation or settlement. Trebutien v. France (421/90). The mere fact that the wording of provisions varies is, according to the Committee, not enough, of itself, to conclude that an issue raised under a Covenant right has not been considered by

another procedure of international investigation or settlement. A material difference in the applicable provisions must be demonstrated. The Committee considers the provisions of Articles 6 (fair trial), 8 (private and family life) and 14 (prohibition of discrimination) of the European Convention for the Protection of Human Rights and Fundamental Freedoms, as interpreted by the Commission (until October 1998) or the Court, sufficiently proximate to the provisions of Articles 14 and 17 of the Covenant, Rogl v. Germany (808/98), and, despite certain differences in the interpretation of Article 6 (1) of the European Convention and Article 14 (1) of the Covenant by the competent organs, both the content and scope of these provisions to be largely converging. Kollar v. Austria (989/01). Linderholm v. Croatia (744/97). A. M. v. Denmark (121/82). But the independent right to equality and non-discrimination embedded in Article 26 of the Covenant provides, according to the Committee, a greater protection than the accessory right to non-discrimination contained in Article 14 of the European Convention. Althammer et al. v. Austria (998/01).
Article 5 (2) a precludes the Committee from considering a communication if the same matter *is being examined* under another procedure of international investigation or settlement. The Committee has therefore to ascertain that a case is, or has not, been under examination elsewhere. It has been found that there is a discrepancy between the Spanish text of Article 5 (2) a and the English and French versions (Article 5 (2)a: „El Comité no examinará ninguna comunicación de un individuo a menos que se haya cerciorado de que: El mismo asunto no ha sido sometido ya a otro procedimiento de examen o arreglo internacionales / Le Comité n'examinera aucune communication d'un particulier sans s'être assuré que: La même question n'est pas déjà en cours d'examen devant une autre instance internationale d'enquête ou de règlement. / The Committee shall not consider any communication from an individual unless it has ascertained that: The same matter is not being examined under another procedure of international investigation or settlement.“) which goes beyond a mere translation error and reveals fundamental differences in substance. Therefore, the Committee interprets the term “sometido” in the Spanish version in the light of the other versions and understands it as meaning “is being examined” by another procedure of international investigation or settlement. Semey v. Spain (986/01). Where an international body has based a declaration of inadmissibility solely on procedural grounds, the same matter has not been examined. Pauger v. Austria (716/96). Moreover, since many rights of the European Convention differ in substance, and in regard of their implementation procedures from the rights set forth in the Covenant, not every matter that has been declared inadmissible *ratione materiae* has been examined in such a way

that the Committee is considering itself as precluded from examining it. Casanovas v. France (441/90).

Where an international body has gone beyond making a procedural or technical decision on admissibility, and has made an assessment of the merits of the case, the complaint has been, according to the Committee, examined within the terms of the Optional Protocol, if the rights considered do not differ in substance. A decision that a case is not of sufficient importance to continue its examination after an applicant's action to withdraw the complaint does not amount to a real assessment of its substance. Accordingly, the Committee does not consider such a complaint to have been examined by an *international body*. Weiss v. Austria (1086/02) - European Court. The Committee is also not precluded, under Article 5 (2) a, from considering a case that has been registered by the Inter-American Commission on Human Rights if the Commission indicates that it has no plans to prepare a report on the case within the next 12 months. Campos v. Peru (577/94).

The Commission on Human Rights is not a body of international investigation or settlement within the meaning of Article 5 (2) a. Randolph v. Togo (910/00). Extra-conventional procedures or mechanisms established by the United Nations Commission on Human Rights or the Economic and Social Council, and whose mandates are to examine and publicly report on human rights situations in specific countries or territories or on major phenomena of human rights violations world wide, do not constitute a procedure of international investigation or settlement within the meaning of Article 5 (2) a. A study of human rights problems of a more global character, even if it refers to or draws on information concerning individuals, is not seen as being the same matter as the examination of individual cases. Laureano v. Peru (540/93). Baboeram-Adhin et al. v. Suriname (146, 148, 154/83). The examination of States reports, submitted under Article 16 of the International Covenant on Economic, Social and Cultural Rights, does not, within the meaning of Article 5 (2) a, constitute an examination of the same matter as a claim by an individual submitted to the Human Rights Committee under the Optional Protocol. Zwaan-de Vries v. The Netherlands (182/84). Danning v. The Netherlands (180/84). Broeks v. The Netherlands (172/84). Also, the general investigation, by regional and intergovernmental human rights organizations, of situations affecting a number of individuals, including the author of a communication under the Optional Protocol, does not constitute the same matter within the meaning of Article 5 (2) a. Blanco v. Nicaragua (328/88).

The competence of the Committee to consider a case that is being examined under another procedure of international investigation or settlement by an international body can be precluded by a State Party through a *reservation* to that effect. T. W. M. B. v. The Netherlands (403/90). L. E. S. K. v. The Netherlands (381/89). A reservation that a State Party has entered to Article 5 (2) a does not impede consideration of a communication by the Committee if the State Party does not invoke that reservation. Wackenheim v. France (854/99). A reservation that precludes the examination of the same matter if it had been *submitted* to, V. E. M. v. Spain (467/91), or *considered* by, an international body precludes the Committee from considering a communication, A. M. v. Denmark (121/82), even if the submitted case before the international body was summarily dismissed as inadmissible, V. E. M. v. Spain (467/91) - European Commission, or declared inadmissible as manifestly ill-founded. A. M. v. Denmark (121/82) - European Commission.

Article 5 (2) b

The Committee shall not consider any communication from an individual unless it has ascertained that:
The individual has exhausted all available domestic remedies. This shall not be the rule where the application of the remedies is unreasonably prolonged.

The Committee decides the question of *exhaustion* of domestic remedies in contested cases, at the point of its consideration of the communication. The reason being, according to the Committee, that a communication in respect of which domestic remedies had been exhausted after submission could be immediately re-submitted to the Committee, if declared inadmissible for that reason. Bakhtiyari et al. v. Australia (1069/02). As long as remedies under a domestic legal system are available, an individual who claims that his or her rights under the Covenant have been violated is not entitled to submit a communication to the Committee. A territory that becomes a special administrative region of another State after submission of a communication, while its legal system remains intact, and the system of appeals unchanged, still has remedies that have to be pursued under the domestic legal system, irrespective of the State which exercises control over the territory. Koi v. Portugal (925/00).
The Committee understands the term *domestic remedies* as referring primarily to judicial remedies. R. T. v. France (262/87). But for the purpose of Article 5 (2) b, an applicant must make use of all judicial or administrative avenues that offer him a reasonable prospect of redress. Jonassen et al. v. Norway (942/00). Pereira v. Panama (437/90). An author has to invoke, before the domestic instances, the substantive right he claims to be violated. However, it is not necessary that he invokes the specific Article of the Covenant in which the substantive right is embodied. Vos v. The Netherlands (786/97).

Domestic remedies need not be exhausted, if they objectively have no prospect of success, Semey v. Spain (986/01), where under applicable domestic laws the claim will inevitably be dismissed or where established jurisprudence of the highest domestic tribunals precludes a positive result. Young v. Australia (941/00). Müller et al. v. Namibia (919/00). Länsman Ilmari et al. v. Finland (511/92). Cadoret et al. v. France (221/87, 323/88). No chance for success exists if a court already repeatedly rejected similar applications. Vázquez v. Spain (701/96). Maille v. France (689/96) - 3 times. An author is not generally required to re-petition a body that has already pronounced itself in his or her case. Kazantzis v. Cyprus (972/01). A request to reopen a case on the basis of new evidence, once regular remedies have been exhausted, does not form part of the domestic remedies that must be exhausted in order to satisfy the admissibility requirement set forth in Article 5 (2) b. Perel v. Latvia (650/95). However, where an author has lodged renewed proceedings with the authorities that go to the substance of the claim before the Committee, the author has failed to exhaust domestic remedies. Benali v. The Netherlands (1272/04). If an author fails to file a normal appeal after conviction, but his case is nevertheless reviewed through extraordinary appeal by the Supreme Court and the State Party does not challenged the admissibility of the communication on this ground, he has met the requirements of Article 5 (2) b. Kurbanov v. Tajikistan (1096/02).

In addition to ordinary judicial and administrative appeals, an author must also make available all other judicial remedies, including constitutional complaints, insofar as such remedies appear to be *effective* in the given case and are, de facto, *available* to the author. That a counsel does not represent an author and that he is unaware of procedural requirements does not justify his failure to comply with the procedural prerequisites. P. L. v. Germany (1003/01). A. P. A. v. Spain (433/90). Notwithstanding any *doubts* an author has as to the effectiveness of the remedies, it is incumbent on him to seek all available remedies. Veriter v. France (1088/02). Mere doubts about the effectiveness of local remedies or the prospect of financial costs involved do not absolve an author from pursuing remedies. A v. Australia (560/93).

Article 5 (2) b does not preclude the Committee from considering a communication received under the Protocol where the allegations themselves raise issues concerning the *availability* or *effectiveness* of domestic remedies. Ramirez v. Uruguay (4/77). Specific information by a State Party concerning the available domestic remedies and the effectiveness of those remedies as enforced by the competent authorities have to be given to the Committee. A et al. v. S (1/76). A State Party has to demonstrate that the remedies it advances are both available and effective. Wilson v. The Philippines (868/99). Vaca v. Colombia

(859/99). The mere affirmation by the State Party that a remedy exists is not sufficient. Smart v. Trinidad and Tobago (672/95). A State Party that removes a person within hours of a decision from its territory renders an attempt to appeal this decision moot. Judge v. Canada (829/98). In the absence of legal aid, a constitutional motion is not an available remedy for a person who has no means of his own to pursue it. Osbourne v. Jamaica (759/97). Henry v. Trinidad and Tobago (752/97). Leslie v. Jamaica (564/93). Champagnie et al. v. Jamaica (445/91). Grant v. Jamaica (353/88). Gordon v. Jamaica (237/87). Remedies that take **several months** to reach a conclusion and whose exhaustion means that a person loses in this time his right are not effective. Ignatane v. Latvia (884/99 - election. A remedy that is said to exist after an event occurred, which interim measures by the Committee sought to prevent, is by definition ineffective. Weiss v. Austria (1086/02) - extradition. The effectiveness of a remedy also depends on the nature of the alleged violation. The Committee does not consider purely administrative and disciplinary remedies if the alleged offence is particularly serious, as in the case of violations of basic human rights, in particular the right to life, adequate and effective. Vicente et al. v. Colombia (612/95). A *habeas corpus* application that only tested whether an individual in fact possessed the status of an unlawful arrival, rather than whether the individual detention was justified, was not deemed an effective remedy for the purposes of the Optional Protocol. Bakhtiyari et al. v. Australia (1069/02). The Committee also did not regard the processing of an author's application for a visa, which required him to leave the territory of a State Party for an appreciable period of time, as an available domestic remedy against the removal order of a State Party. Winata et al. v. Australia (930/00). Randolph v. Togo (910/00).

If avenues are available to an author for submitting his case before the authorities of a State Party, he has to demonstrate that they are *unreasonably prolonged* or unlikely to bring him effective relief to justify his inaction. Mankarious v. Australia (1065/02). The Committee considered a remedy that had not led, after more than 4 **years**, to a final conclusion as unreasonably prolonged. Weinberger v. Uruguay (28/78). Sarma et al. v. Sri Lanka - **7 years**(950/00). L. P. v. Czech Republic (946/00) - **13 years**.

ARTICLE 6 - 14

Article 6

The Committee shall include in its annual report under article 45 of the Covenant a summary of its activities under the present Protocol.

Article 7

Pending the achievement of the objectives of resolution 1514(XV) adopted by the General Assembly of the United Nations on 14 December 1960 concerning the Declaration on the Granting of Independence to Colonial Countries and Peoples, the provisions of the present Protocol shall in no way limit the right of petition granted to these peoples by the Charter of the United Nations and other international conventions and instruments under the United Nations and its specialized agencies.

Article 8

1. The present Protocol is open for signature by any State which has signed the Covenant.

2. The present Protocol is subject to ratification by any State which has ratified or acceded to the Covenant. Instruments of ratification shall be deposited with the Secretary-General of the United Nations.

3. The present Protocol shall be open to accession by any State which has ratified or acceded to the Covenant.

4. Accession shall be effected by the deposit of an instrument of accession with the Secretary-General of the United Nations.

5. The Secretary-General of the United Nations shall inform all States which have signed the present Protocol or acceded to it of the deposit of each instrument of ratification or accession.

Article 9

1. Subject to the entry into force of the Covenant, the present Protocol shall enter into force three months after the date of the deposit with the Secretary-General of the United Nations of the tenth instrument of ratification or instrument of accession.

2. For each State ratifying the present Protocol or acceding to it after the deposit of the tenth instrument of ratification or instrument of accession, the present Protocol shall enter into force three months after the date of the deposit of its own instrument of ratification or instrument of accession.

Article 10

The provisions of the present Protocol shall extend to all parts of federal States without any limitations or exceptions.

Article 11

1. Any State Party to the present Protocol may propose an amendment and file it with the Secretary-General of the United Nations. The Secretary-General shall thereupon communicate any proposed amendments to the States Parties to the present Protocol with a request that they notify him whether they favour a conference of States Parties for the purpose of considering and voting upon the proposal. In the event that at least one third of the States Parties favours such a conference, the Secretary-General shall convene the conference under the auspices of the United Nations. Any amendment adopted by a majority of the

States Parties present and voting at the conference shall be submitted to the General Assembly of the United Nations for approval.
2. Amendments shall come into force when they have been approved by the General Assembly of the United Nations and accepted by a two-thirds majority of the States Parties to the present Protocol in accordance with their respective constitutional processes.
3. When amendments come into force, they shall be binding on those States Parties which have accepted them, other States Parties still being bound by the provisions of the present Protocol and any earlier amendment which they have accepted.

Article 12

1. Any State Party may denounce the present Protocol at any time by written notification addressed to the Secretary-General of the United Nations. Denunciation shall take effect three months after the date of receipt of the notification by the Secretary-General.
2. Denunciation shall be without prejudice to the continued application of the provisions of the present Protocol to any communication submitted under article 2 before the effective date of denunciation.

Article 13

Irrespective of the notifications made under article 8, paragraph 5, of the present Protocol, the Secretary-General of the United Nations shall inform all States referred to in article 48, paragraph I, of the Covenant of the following particulars:
(a) Signatures, ratifications and accessions under article 8;
(b) The date of the entry into force of the present Protocol under article 9 and the date of the entry into force of any amendments under article 11;
(c) Denunciations under article 12.

Article 14

1. The present Protocol, of which the Chinese, English, French, Russian and Spanish texts are equally authentic, shall be deposited in the archives of the United Nations.
2. The Secretary-General of the United Nations shall transmit certified copies of the present Protocol to all States referred to in article 48 of the Covenant.

Rules of Procedure of the Human Rights Committee.

(April 24, 2001. U. N. Doc. CCPR/C/3/Rev.6.)

Provisional rules of procedure were initially adopted by the Committee at its first and second sessions and subsequently amended at its 3rd, 7th and 36th sessions. At its 918th meeting on 26 July 1989, the Committee decided to make its rules of procedure definitive, eliminating the term "provisional" from the title. The rules of procedure were subsequently amended at the 47th, 49th, 50th, and 59th sessions. The current version of the rules was adopted at the Committee's 1924th meeting during its 71st session.

PART I. GENERAL RULES (RULE 1 – 65)

I. SESSIONS

Rule 1

The Human Rights Committee (hereinafter referred to as „the Committee") shall hold sessions as may be required for the satisfactory performance of its functions in accordance with the International Covenant on Civil and Political Rights (hereinafter referred to as "the Covenant").

Rule 2

1. The Committee shall normally hold three regular sessions each year.
2. Regular sessions of the Committee shall be convened at dates decided by the Committee in consultation with the Secretary-General of the United Nations (hereinafter referred to as „the Secretary-General"), taking into account the calendar of conferences as approved by the General Assembly.

Rule 3

1. Special sessions of the Committee shall be convened by decision of the Committee. When the Committee is not in session, the Chairperson may convene special sessions in consultation with the other officers of the Committee. The Chairperson of the Committee shall also convene special sessions:
(a) At the request of a majority of the members of the Committee;
(b) At the request of a State party to the Covenant.
2. Special sessions shall be convened as soon as possible at a date fixed by the Chairperson in consultation with the Secretary-General and with the other officers of the Committee, taking into account the calendar of conferences as approved by the General Assembly.

Rule 4

The Secretary-General shall notify the members of the Committee of the date and place of the first meeting of each session. Such notification shall be sent, in the case of a regular session, at least six weeks in advance and, in the case of a special session, at least 18 days in advance.

Rule 5

Sessions of the Committee shall normally be held at the Headquarters of the United Nations or at the United Nations Office at Geneva. Another place for a session may be designated by the Committee in consultation with the Secretary-General.

II. AGENDA

Rule 6

The provisional agenda for each regular session shall be prepared by the Secretary-General in consultation with the Chairperson of the Committee, in conformity with the relevant provisions of the Covenant and of the Optional Protocol to the International Covenant on Civil and Political Rights (hereinafter referred to as „the Protocol"), and shall include:

(a) Any item the inclusion of which has been ordered by the Committee at a previous session;

(b) Any item proposed by the Chairperson of the Committee;

(c) Any item proposed by a State party to the Covenant;

(d) Any item proposed by a member of the Committee;

(e) Any item proposed by the Secretary-General relating to functions of the Secretary-General under the Covenant, the Protocol or these rules.

Rule 7

The provisional agenda for a special session of the Committee shall consist only of those items which are proposed for consideration at that special session.

Rule 8

The first item on the provisional agenda for any session shall be the adoption of the agenda, except for the election of the officers when required under rule 17 of these rules.

Rule 9

During a session, the Committee may revise the agenda and may, as appropriate, defer or delete items; only urgent and important items may be added to the agenda.

Rule 10

The provisional agenda and the basic documents relating to each item appearing thereon shall be transmitted to the members of the Committee by the Secretary-General, who shall endeavour to have the documents transmitted to the members at least six weeks prior to the opening of the session.

III. MEMBERS OF THE COMMITTEE

Rule 11

The members of the Committee shall be the 18 persons elected in accordance with articles 28 to 34 of the Covenant.

Rule 12

The term of office of the members of the Committee elected at the first election shall begin on 1 January 1977. The term of office of members of the Committee elected at subsequent elections shall begin on the day after the date of expiry of the term of office of the members of the Committee whom they replace.

Rule 13

1. If, in the unanimous opinion of the other members, a member of the Committee has ceased to carry out the functions of the member for any cause other than absence of a temporary character, the Chairperson of the Committee shall notify the Secretary-General, who shall then declare the seat of that member to be vacant.

2. In the event of the death or the resignation of a member of the Committee, the Chairperson shall immediately notify the Secretary-General, who shall declare the seat vacant from the date of death or the date on which the resignation takes effect. The resignation of a member of the Committee shall be notified by that member

in writing directly to the Chairperson or to the Secretary-General and action shall be taken to declare the seat of that member vacant only after such notification has been received.

Rule 14

A vacancy declared in accordance with rule 13 of these rules shall be dealt with in accordance with article 34 of the Covenant.

Rule 15

Any member of the Committee elected to fill a vacancy declared in accordance with article 33 of the Covenant shall hold office for the remainder of the term of the member who vacated the seat on the Committee under the provisions of that article.

Rule 16

Before assuming duties as a member, each member of the Committee shall give the following solemn undertaking in open Committee: „I solemnly undertake to discharge my duties as a member of the Human Rights Committee impartially and conscientiously."

IV. OFFICERS

Rule 17

The Committee shall elect from among its members a Chairperson, three Vice-Chairpersons and a Rapporteur.

Rule 18

The officers of the Committee shall be elected for a term of two years. They shall be eligible for re-election. None of them, however, may hold office after ceasing to be a member of the Committee.

Rule 19

The Chairperson shall perform the functions conferred upon the Chairperson by the Covenant, the rules of procedure and the decisions of the Committee. In the exercise of those functions, the Chairperson shall remain under the authority of the Committee.

Rule 20

If during a session the Chairperson is unable to be present at a meeting or any part thereof, the Chairperson shall designate one of the Vice-Chairpersons to act as Chairperson.

Rule 21

A Vice-Chairperson acting as Chairperson shall have the same rights and duties as the Chairperson.

Rule 22

If any of the officers of the Committee ceases to serve or declares to be unable to continue serving as a member of the Committee or for any reason is no longer able to act as an officer, a new officer shall be elected for the unexpired term of the predecessor.

V. SECRETARIAT

Rule 23

1. The secretariat of the Committee and of such subsidiary bodies as may be established by the Committee (hereinafter referred to as „the Secretariat") shall be provided by the Secretary-General.

2. The Secretary-General shall provide the necessary staff and facilities for the effective performance of the functions of the Committee under the Covenant.

Rule 24

The Secretary-General or representative of the Secretary-General shall attend all meetings of the Committee. Subject to rule 38 of these rules, the Secretary-General or the representative may make oral or written statements at meetings of the Committee or its subsidiary bodies.

Rule 25

The Secretary-General shall be responsible for all the necessary arrangements for meetings of the Committee and its subsidiary bodies.

Rule 26

The Secretary-General shall be responsible for informing the members of the Committee without delay of any questions which may be brought before it for consideration.

Rule 27

Before any proposal which involves expenditure is approved by the Committee or by any of its subsidiary bodies, the Secretary-General shall prepare and circulate to the members of the Committee or subsidiary body, as early as possible, an estimate of the cost involved in the proposal. It shall be the duty of the Chairperson to draw the attention of members to this estimate and to invite discussion on it when the proposal is considered by the Committee or subsidiary body.

VI. LANGUAGES

Rule 28

Arabic, Chinese, English, French, Russian and Spanish shall be the official languages, and Arabic, English, French, Russian and Spanish the working languages of the Committee.

Rule 29

Speeches made in any of the working languages shall be interpreted into the other working languages. Speeches made in an official language shall be interpreted into the working languages.

Rule 30

Any speaker addressing the Committee and using a language other than one of the official languages shall normally provide for interpretation into one of the working languages. Interpretation into the other working languages by interpreters of the Secretariat may be based on the interpretation given in the first working language.

Rule 31

Summary records of the meetings of the Committee shall be drawn up in the working languages.

Rule 32

All formal decisions of the Committee shall be made available in the official languages. All other official documents of the Committee shall be issued in the working languages and any of them may, if the Committee so decides, be issued in all the official languages.

VII. PUBLIC AND PRIVATE MEETINGS

Rule 33

The meetings of the Committee and its subsidiary bodies shall be held in public unless the Committee decides otherwise or it appears from the relevant provisions of the Covenant or the Protocol that the meeting should be held in private. The adoption of concluding observations under article 40 shall take place in closed meetings.

Rule 34

At the close of each private meeting the Committee or its subsidiary body may issue a communiqué through the Secretary-General.

VIII. RECORDS

Rule 35

Summary records of the public and private meetings of the Committee and its subsidiary bodies shall be prepared by the Secretariat. They shall be distributed in provisional form as soon as possible to the members of the Committee and to any others participating in the meeting. All such participants may, within three working days after receipt of the provisional record of the meeting, submit corrections to the Secretariat. Any disagreement concerning such corrections shall be settled by the Chairperson of the Committee or the Chairperson of the subsidiary body to which the record relates or, in the case of continued disagreement, by decision of the Committee or of the subsidiary body.

Rule 36

1. The summary records of public meetings of the Committee in their final form shall be documents of general distribution unless, in exceptional circumstances, the Committee decides otherwise.

2. The summary records of private meetings shall be distributed to the members of the Committee and to other participants in the meetings. They may be made available to others upon decision of the Committee at such time and under such circumstances as the Committee may decide.

IX. CONDUCT OF BUSINESS

Rule 37

Twelve members of the Committee shall constitute a quorum.

Rule 38

The Chairperson shall declare the opening and closing of each meeting of the Committee, direct the discussion, ensure observance of these rules, accord the right to speak, put questions to the vote and announce decisions. The Chairperson, subject to these rules, shall have control over the proceedings of the Committee and over the maintenance of order at its meetings. The Chairperson may, in the course of the discussion of an item, propose to the Committee the limitation of the time to be allowed to speakers, the limitation of the number of times each speaker may speak on any question and the closure of the list of speakers. The Chairperson shall rule on points of order and shall have the power to propose adjournment or closure of the debate or adjournment or suspension of a meeting. Debate shall be confined to the question before the Committee, and the Chairperson may call a speaker to order if that speaker's remarks are not relevant to the subject under discussion.

Rule 39

During the discussion of any matter, a member may at any time raise a point of order, and the point of order shall immediately be decided by the Chairperson in accordance with the rules of procedure. Any appeal against the ruling of the Chairperson shall immediately be put to the vote, and the ruling of the Chairperson shall stand unless overruled by a majority of the members present. A member may not, in raising a point of order, speak on the substance of the matter under discussion.

Rule 40

During the discussion of any matter, a member may move the adjournment of the debate on the item under discussion. In addition to the proposer of the motion, one member may speak in favour of and one against the motion, after which the motion shall immediately be put to the vote.

Rule 41

The Committee may limit the time allowed to each speaker on any question. When debate is limited and a speaker exceeds his allotted time, the Chairperson shall call that speaker to order without delay.

Rule 42

When the debate on an item is concluded because there are no other speakers, the Chairperson shall declare the debate closed. Such closure shall have the same effect as closure by the consent of the Committee.

Rule 43

A member may at any time move the closure of the debate on the item under discussion, whether or not any other member or representative has signified a wish to speak. Permission to speak on the closure of the debate shall be accorded only to two speakers opposing the closure, after which the motion shall immediately be put to the vote.

Rule 44

During the discussion of any matter, a member may move the suspension or the adjournment of the meeting. No discussion on such motions shall be permitted, and they shall immediately be put to the vote.

Rule 45

Subject to rule 39 of these rules, the following motions shall have precedence in the following order over all other proposals or motions before the meeting:

(a) To suspend the meeting;

(b) To adjourn the meeting;

(c) To adjourn the debate on the item under discussion;

(d) For the closure of the debate on the item under discussion.

Rule 46

Unless otherwise decided by the Committee, proposals and substantive amendments or motions submitted by members shall be introduced in writing and handed to the Secretariat, and their consideration shall, if so requested by any member, be deferred until the next meeting on the following day.

Rule 47

Subject to rule 45 of these rules, any motion by a member calling for a decision on the competence of the Committee to adopt a proposal submitted to it shall be put to the vote immediately before a vote is taken on the proposal in question.

Rule 48

A motion may be withdrawn by its proposer at any time before voting on it has commenced, provided that the motion has not been amended. A motion which has thus been withdrawn may be reintroduced by another member.

Rule 49

When a proposal has been adopted or rejected, it may not be reconsidered at the same session unless the Committee so decides. Permission to speak on a motion to reconsider shall be accorded only to two speakers in favour of the motion and two speakers opposing the motion, after which it shall immediately be put to the vote.

X. VOTING

Rule 50

Each member of the Committee shall have one vote.

Rule 51

Except as otherwise provided in the Covenant or elsewhere in these rules, decisions of the Committee shall be made by a majority of the members present.

The Committee decided, at its first session, that, in a footnote to rule 51 of the provisional rules of procedure, attention should be drawn to the following: 1. The members of the Committee generally expressed the view that its method of work normally should allow for attempts to reach decisions by consensus before voting, provided that the Covenant and the rules of procedure were observed and that such attempts did not unduly delay the work of the Committee. 2. Bearing in mind paragraph 1 above, the Chairperson at any meeting may, and at the request of any member shall, put the proposal to a vote.

Rule 52

Subject to rule 58 of these rules, the Committee shall normally vote by show of hands, except that any member may request a roll-call, which shall then be taken in the alphabetical order of the names of the members of the Committee, beginning with the member whose name is drawn by lot by the Chairperson.

Rule 53

The vote of each member participating in a roll-call shall be inserted in the record.

Rule 54

After the voting has commenced, it shall not be interrupted unless a member raises a point of order in connection with the actual conduct of the voting. Brief statements by members consisting solely of explanations of their votes may be permitted by the Chairperson before the voting has commenced or after the voting has been completed.

Rule 55

Parts of a proposal shall be voted on separately if a member requests that the proposal be divided. Those parts of the proposal which have been approved shall then be put to the vote as a whole; if all the operative parts of a proposal have been rejected, the proposal shall be considered to have been rejected as a whole.

Rule 56

1. When an amendment to a proposal is moved, the amendment shall be voted on first. When two or more amendments to a proposal are moved, the Committee shall first vote on the amendment furthest removed in substance from the original proposal and then on the amendment next furthest removed therefrom and so on until all the amendments have been put to the vote. If one or more amendments are adopted, the amended proposal shall then be voted upon.

2. A motion is considered an amendment to a proposal if it merely adds to, deletes from or revises part of that proposal.

Rule 57

1. If two or more proposals relate to the same question, the Committee shall, unless it decides otherwise, vote on the proposals in the order in which they have been submitted.

2. The Committee may, after each vote on a proposal, decide whether to vote on the next proposal.

3. Any motions requiring that no decision be taken on the substance of such proposals shall, however, be considered as previous questions and shall be put to the vote before them.

Rule 58

Elections shall be held by secret ballot, unless the Committee decides otherwise in the case of an election to fill a place for which there is only one candidate.

Rule 59

1. When only one person or member is to be elected and no candidate obtains the required majority in the first ballot, a second ballot shall be taken, which shall be restricted to the two candidates who obtained the greatest number of votes.

2. If the second ballot is inconclusive and a majority vote of members present is required, a third ballot shall be taken in which votes may be cast for any eligible candidate. If the third ballot is inconclusive, the next ballot shall be restricted to the two candidates who obtained the greatest number of votes in the third ballot and so on, with unrestricted and restricted ballots alternating, until a person or member is elected.

3. If the second ballot is inconclusive and a two-thirds majority is required, the balloting shall be continued until one candidate secures the necessary two-thirds majority. In the next three ballots, votes may be cast for any eligible candidate. If three such unrestricted ballots are inconclusive, the next three ballots shall be restricted to the two candidates who obtained the greatest number of votes in the third such unrestricted ballot, and the following three ballots shall be unrestricted, and so on until a person or member is elected.

Rule 60

When two or more elective places are to be filled at one time under the same conditions, those candidates obtaining the required majority in the first ballot shall be elected. If the number of candidates obtaining such majority is less than the number of persons or members to be elected, there shall be additional ballots to fill the remaining places, the voting being restricted to the candidates obtaining the greatest number of votes in the previous ballot, to a number not more than twice the places remaining to be filled; provided that, after the third inconclusive ballot, votes may be cast for any eligible candidate. If three such unrestricted ballots are inconclusive, the next three ballots shall be restricted to the candidates who obtained the greatest number of votes in the third of the unrestricted ballots, to a number not more than twice the places remaining to be filled, and the following three ballots thereafter shall be unrestricted, and so on until all the places have been filled.

Rule 61

If a vote is equally divided on a matter other than an election, the proposal shall be regarded as rejected.

XI. SUBSIDIARY BODIES

Rule 62

1. The Committee may, taking into account the provisions of the Covenant and the Protocol, set up such subcommittees and other ad hoc subsidiary bodies as it deems necessary for the performance of its functions, and define their composition and powers.

2. Subject to the provisions of the Covenant and the Protocol and unless the Committee decides otherwise, each subsidiary body shall elect its own officers and may adopt its own rules of procedure. Failing such rules, the present rules of procedure shall apply mutatis mutandis.

XII. ANNUAL REPORT OF THE COMMITTEE

Rule 63

As prescribed in article 45 of the Covenant, the Committee shall submit to the General Assembly of the United Nations, through the Economic and Social Council, an annual report on its activities, including a summary of its activities under the Protocol as prescribed in article 6 thereof.

XIII. DISTRIBUTION OF REPORTS AND OTHER OFFICIAL DOCUMENTS OF THE COMMITTEE

Rule 64

1. Without prejudice to the provisions of rule 36 of these rules of procedure and subject to paragraphs 2 and 3 of the present rule, reports, formal decisions and all other official documents of the Committee and its subsidiary bodies shall be documents of general distribution unless the Committee decides otherwise.

2. All reports, formal decisions and other official documents of the Committee and its subsidiary bodies relating to articles 41 and 42 of the Covenant and to the Protocol shall be distributed by the Secretariat to all members of the Committee, to the States parties concerned and, as may be decided by the Committee, to members of its subsidiary bodies and to others concerned.

3. Reports and additional information submitted by States parties pursuant to article 40 of the Covenant shall be documents of general distribution. The same applies to other information provided by a State party unless the State party concerned requests otherwise.

XIV. AMENDMENTS

Rule 65

These rules of procedure may be amended by a decision of the Committee, without prejudice to the relevant provisions of the Covenant and the Protocol.

PART II. RULES RELATING TO THE FUNCTIONS OF THE COMMITTEE (RULE 66 – 98)

XV. REPORTS FROM STATES PARTIES UNDER ARTICLE 40 OF THE COVENANT

Rule 66

1. The States parties to the Covenant shall submit reports on the measures they have adopted which give effect to the rights recognized in the Covenant and on the progress made in the enjoyment of those rights. Reports shall indicate the factors and difficulties, if any, affecting the implementation of the Covenant.

2. Requests for submission of a report under article 40, paragraph 1 (b), of the Covenant may be made in accordance with the periodicity decided by the Committee or at any other time the Committee may deem appropriate. In the case of an exceptional situation when the Committee is not in session, a request may be made through the Chairperson, acting in consultation with the members of the Committee.

3. Whenever the Committee requests States parties to submit reports under article 40, paragraph 1 (b), of the Covenant, it shall determine the dates by which such reports shall be submitted.

4. The Committee may, through the Secretary-General, inform the States parties of its wishes regarding the form and content of the reports to be submitted under article 40 of the Covenant.

Rule 67

1. The Secretary-General may, after consultation with the Committee, transmit to the specialized agencies concerned copies of such parts of the reports from States members of those agencies as may fall within their field of competence.

2. The Committee may invite the specialized agencies to which the Secretary-General has transmitted parts of the reports to submit comments on those parts within such time-limits as it may specify.

Rule 68

1. The Committee shall, through the Secretary-General, notify the States parties as early as possible of the opening date, duration and place of the session at which their respective reports will be examined. Representatives of the States parties may be present at the meetings of the Committee when their reports are examined. The Committee may also inform a State party from which it decides to seek further information that it may authorize its representative to be present at a specified meeting. Such a representative should be able to answer questions which may be put to that representative by the Committee and make statements on reports already submitted by the State party concerned, and may also submit additional information from that State party.

2. If a State party has submitted a report but fails to send any representative, in accordance with rule 68.1, under article 40, paragraph 1, of the Covenant, to the session at which it has been notified that its report will be examined, the Committee may, at its discretion, take one of the following courses:

(a) notify the State party through the Secretary General that at a specified Session it intends to examine the report in accordance with rule 68.2 and thereafter act in accordance with rule 70.3; or

(b) proceed at the session originally specified to examine the report and thereafter make and submit to the State party its provisional concluding observations and determine the date on which the report shall be examined

under rule 68 or the date on which a new periodic report shall be submitted under rule 66.

3. Where the Committee acts under this rule, it shall so state in the annual report submitted under article 45 of the Covenant; provided that, where it acts under para. 2(b) above, the report shall not include the text of the provisional concluding observations.

Rule 69

1. At each session the Secretary-General shall notify the Committee of all cases of non-submission of reports or additional information requested under rules 66 and 70 of these rules. In such cases the Committee may transmit to the State party concerned, through the Secretary-General, a reminder concerning the submission of the report or additional information.

2. If, after the reminder referred to in paragraph 1 of this rule, the State party does not submit the report or additional information required under rules 66 and 70 of these rules, the Committee shall so state in the annual report which it submits to the General Assembly of the United Nations through the Economic and Social Council.

Rule 69 A

1. In cases where the Committee has been notified under Rule 69.1 of the failure of a State to submit under rule 66.3 any report, under article 40, para. 1(a) or (b) of the Covenant, and has sent reminders to the State party, the Committee may, at its discretion, notify the State party through the Secretary General that it intends, on a date or at a session specified in the notification, to examine in a private session the measures taken by the State party to give effect to the rights recognized in the Covenant, and to proceed by adopting provisional concluding observations which will be submitted to the State party.

2. Where the Committee acts under paragraph 1 of this rule, it shall transmit to the State party, well in advance of the date or session specified, information in its possession which it considers appropriate as to the matters to be examined.

3. Where the Committee acts under this rule, it shall proceed in accordance with rule 68.3 and may set a date when it proceeds to act under rule 68.1.

Rule 70

1. When considering a report submitted by a State party under article 40 of the Covenant, the Committee shall first satisfy itself that the report provides all the information required under rule 66 of these rules.

2. If a report of a State party to the Covenant, in the opinion of the Committee, does not contain sufficient information, the Committee may request that State to furnish the additional information which is required, indicating by what date the said information should be submitted.

3. On the basis of its examination of any report or information supplied by a State party, the Committee may make appropriate concluding observations which will be communicated to the State party, together with notification of the date by which the next report, under article 40, shall be submitted.
4. No member of the Committee shall participate in the examination of state reports or the discussion and adoption of concluding observations if they involve the State party in respect of which he or she was elected to the Committee.
5. The Committee may request the State party to give priority to such aspects of its concluding observations as it may specify.

Rule 70 A

Where the Committee has specified for priority, under rule 70.5, certain aspects of its concluding observations on a State party's report, it shall establish a procedure to consider replies by the State party on those aspects and to decide what consequent action, including the date set for the next periodic report, may be appropriate.

Rule 71

The Committee shall communicate, through the Secretary General, to States parties the General Comments which has adopted under article 40, paragraph 4, of the Covenant.

XVI. PROCEDURE FOR THE CONSIDERATION OF COMMUNICATIONS RECEIVED UNDER ARTICLE 41 OF THE COVENANT

Rule 72

1. A communication under article 41 of the Covenant may be referred to the Committee by either State party concerned by notice given in accordance with paragraph 1 (b) of that article.
2. The notice referred to in paragraph 1 of this rule shall contain or be accompanied by information regarding:
(a) Steps taken to seek adjustment of the matter in accordance with article 41, paragraphs 1 (a) and (b), of the Covenant, including the text of the initial communication and of any subsequent written explanations or statements by the States parties concerned which are pertinent to the matter;
(b) Steps taken to exhaust domestic remedies;
(c) Any other procedure of international investigation or settlement resorted to by the States parties concerned.

Rule 73

The Secretary-General shall maintain a permanent register of all communications received by the Committee under article 41 of the Covenant.

Rule 74

The Secretary-General shall inform the members of the Committee without delay of any notice given under rule 72 of these rules and shall transmit to them as soon as possible copies of the notice and relevant information.

Rule 75

1. The Committee shall examine communications under article 41 of the Covenant at closed meetings.

2. The Committee may, after consultation with the States parties concerned, issue communiques, through the Secretary-General, for the use of the information media and the general public regarding the activities of the Committee at its closed meetings.

Rule 76

A communication shall not be considered by the Committee unless:

(a) Both States parties concerned have made declarations under article 41, paragraph 1, of the Covenant which are applicable to the communication;

(b) The time-limit prescribed in article 41, paragraph 1 (b), of the Covenant has expired;

(c) The Committee has ascertained that all available domestic remedies have been invoked and exhausted in the matter in conformity with the generally recognized principles of international law, or that the application of the remedies is unreasonably prolonged.

Rule 77 A

Subject to the provisions of rule 76 of these rules, the Committee shall proceed to make its good offices available to the States parties concerned with a view to a friendly solution of the matter on the basis of respect for human rights and fundamental freedoms as recognized in the Covenant.

Rule 77 B

The Committee may, through the Secretary-General, request the States parties concerned or either of them to submit additional information or observations orally or in writing. The Committee shall indicate a time-limit for the submission of such written information or observations.

Rule 77 C

1. The States parties concerned shall have the right to be represented when the matter is being considered in the Committee and to make submissions orally and/or in writing.

2. The Committee shall, through the Secretary-General, notify the States parties concerned as early as possible of the opening date, duration and place of the session at which the matter will be examined.

3. The procedure for making oral and/or written submissions shall be decided by the Committee, after consultation with the States parties concerned.

Rule 77 D

1. Within 12 months after the date on which the Committee received the notice referred to in rule 72 of these rules, the Committee shall adopt a report in accordance
with article 41, paragraph 1 (h), of the Covenant.
2. The provisions of paragraph 1 of rule 77C of these rules shall not apply to the deliberations of the Committee concerning the adoption of the report.
3. The Committee's report shall be communicated, through the Secretary-General, to the States parties concerned.

Rule 77 E

If a matter referred to the Committee in accordance with article 41 of the Covenant is not resolved to the satisfaction of the States parties concerned, the Committee may, with their prior consent, proceed to apply the procedure prescribed in article 42 of the Covenant.

XVII. PROCEDURE FOR THE CONSIDERATION OF COMMUNICATIONS RECEIVED UNDER THE OPTIONAL PROTOCOL

A. Transmission of communications to the Committee

Rule 78

1. The Secretary-General shall bring to the attention of the Committee, in accordance with the present rules, communications which are or appear to be submitted for consideration by the Committee under article 1 of the Protocol.
2. The Secretary-General, when necessary, may request clarification from the author of a communication as to whether the author wishes to have the communication submitted to the Committee for consideration under the Protocol. In case there is still doubt as to the wish of the author, the Committee shall be seized of the communication.
3. No communication shall be received by the Committee or included in a list under rule 79 if it concerns a State which is not a party to the Protocol.

Rule 79

1. The Secretary-General shall prepare lists of the communications submitted to the Committee in accordance with rule 78 above, with a brief summary of their contents, and shall circulate such lists to the members of the Committee at regular intervals. The Secretary-General shall also maintain a permanent register of all such communications.
2. The full text of any communication brought to the attention of the Committee shall be made available to any member of the Committee upon request by that member.

Rule 80

1. The Secretary-General may request clarification from the author of a communication concerning the applicability of the Protocol to his communication, in particular regarding:

(a) The name, address, age and occupation of the author and the verification of the author's identity;

(b) The name of the State party against which the communication is directed;

(c) The object of the communication;

(d) The provision or provisions of the Covenant alleged to have been violated;

(e) The facts of the claim;

(f) Steps taken by the author to exhaust domestic remedies;

(g) The extent to which the same matter is being examined under another procedure of international investigation or settlement.

2. When requesting clarification or information, the Secretary-General shall indicate an appropriate time-limit to the author of the communication with a view to avoiding undue delays in the procedure under the Protocol.

3. The Committee may approve a questionnaire for the purpose of requesting the above-mentioned information from the author of the communication.

4. The request for clarification referred to in paragraph 1 of the present rule shall not preclude the inclusion of the communication in the list provided for in rule 79, paragraph 1, of these rules.

Rule 81

For each registered communication the Secretary-General shall as soon as possible prepare and circulate to the members of the Committee a summary of the relevant information obtained.

B. General provisions regarding the consideration of communications by the Committee or its subsidiary bodies

Rule 82

Meetings of the Committee or its subsidiary bodies during which communications under the Protocol will be examined shall be closed. Meetings during which the Committee may consider general issues such as procedures for the application of the Protocol may be public if the Committee so decides.

Rule 83

The Committee may issue communiques, through the Secretary-General, for the use of the information media and the general public regarding the activities of the Committee at its closed meetings.

Rule 84

1. A member shall not take part in the examination of a communication by the Committee:

(a) if the State party in respect of which he or she was elected to the Committee is a party to the case;
(b) if the member has any personal interest in the case; or
(c) if the member has participated in any capacity in the making of any decision on the case covered by the communication.
2. Any question which may arise under paragraph 1 above shall be decided by the Committee.

Rule 85

If, for any reason, a member considers that he or she should not take part or continue to take part in the examination of a communication, the member shall inform the Chairperson of his or her withdrawal.

Rule 86

The Committee may, prior to forwarding its views on the communication to the State party concerned, inform that State of its views as to whether interim measures may be desirable to avoid irreparable damage to the victim of the alleged violation. In doing so, the Committee shall inform the State party concerned that such expression of its views on interim measures does not imply a determination on the merits of the communication.

Interim measures pursuant to rule 86 of the Committee's rules adopted in conformity with Article 39 of the Covenant are essential to the Committee's role under the Protocol. Flouting of the Rule, especially by irreversible measures such as the execution of the alleged victim, Kandu-Bo et al. v. Sierra Leone (839 - 841/98), or his/her deportation from the country, Weiss v. Austria (1086/02), undermines the protection of Covenant rights through the Optional Protocol. By adhering to the Optional Protocol, a State Party of the Covenant recognizes the competence of the Human Rights Committee to receive and consider communications from individuals claiming to be victims of violations of any of the rights set forth in the Covenant. An undertaking to cooperate with the Committee in good faith so as to permit and enable it to consider such communications, and after examination to forward its Views to the State Party and to the individual is, according to the Committee, implicit in a State's adherence to the Protocol. It is incompatible with these obligations for a State Party to take any action that prevents or frustrates the Committee in its consideration and examination of the communication, and in the expression of its Views. A State Party commits grave breaches of its obligations under the Optional Protocol if it acts to prevent or frustrate consideration by the Committee of a communication alleging a violation of the Covenant, or to render examination by the Committee moot and the expression of its Views nugatory and futile. Piandiong et al. v. The Philippines (869/99).

C. Procedure to determine admissibility

Rule 87

1. The Committee shall decide as soon as possible and in accordance with the following rules whether the communication is admissible or is inadmissible under the Protocol.

2. A working group established under rule 89, paragraph 1, may also declare a communication admissible when it is composed of five members and all the members so decide.

Rule 88

1. Communications shall be dealt with in the order in which they are received by the Secretariat, unless the Committee or a working group established under rule 89, paragraph 1, decides otherwise.

2. Two or more communications may be dealt with jointly if deemed appropriate by the Committee or a working group established under rule 89, paragraph 1.

The Committee deals with communications that refer to closely related events together. R. A. V. N. et al. v. Argentina (343 - 345/88).

Rule 89

1. The Committee may establish one or more working groups to make recommendations to the Committee regarding the fulfilment of the conditions of admissibility laid down in articles 1, 2, 3 and 5 (2) of the Protocol.

2. The rules of procedure of the Committee shall apply as far as possible to the meetings of the working group.

3. The Committee may designate special rapporteurs from among its members to assist in the handling of communications.

Rule 90

With a view to reaching a decision on the admissibility of a communication, the Committee, or a working group established under rule 89, paragraph 1, shall ascertain:

(a) That the communication is not anonymous and that it emanates from an individual, or individuals, subject to the jurisdiction of a State party to the Protocol;

(b) That the individual claims, in a manner sufficiently substantiated, to be a victim of a violation by that State party of any of the rights set forth in the Covenant. Normally, the communication should be submitted by the individual personally or by that individual's representative; a communication submitted on behalf of an alleged victim may, however, be accepted when it appears that the individual in question is unable to submit the communication personally;

(c) That the communication does not constitute an abuse of the right of submission;
(d) That the communication is not incompatible with the provisions of the Covenant;
(e) That the same matter is not being examined under another procedure of international investigation or settlement;
(f) That the individual has exhausted all available domestic remedies.

Rule 91

1. As soon as possible after the communication has been received, the Committee, a working group established under rule 89, paragraph 1, or a special rapporteur designated under rule 89, paragraph 3, shall request the State party concerned to submit a written reply to the communication.
2. Within six months the State party concerned shall submit to the Committee written explanations or statements that shall relate both to the communication's admissibility and its merits as well as to any remedy that may have been provided in the matter, unless the Committee, working group or special rapporteur has decided, because of the exceptional nature of the case, to request a written reply that relates only to the question of admissibility. A State party that has been requested to submit a written reply that relates only to the question of admissibility is not precluded thereby from submitting, within six months of the request, a written reply that shall relate both to the communication's admissibility and its merits.
3. A State party that has received a request for a written reply under paragraph 1 both on admissibility and on the merits of the communication, may apply in writing, within two months, for the communication to be rejected as inadmissible, setting out the grounds for such inadmissibility. Submission of such an application shall not extend the period of six months given to the State party to submit its written reply to the communication, unless the Committee, a working group established under rule 89, paragraph 1, or a special rapporteur designated under rule 89, paragraph 3, decides to extend the time for submission of the reply, because of the special circumstances of the case, until the Committee has ruled on the question of admissibility.
4. The Committee, a working group established under rule 89, paragraph 1, or a special rapporteur designated under rule 89, paragraph 3, may request the State party or the author of the communication to submit, within specified time limits, additional written information or observations relevant to the question of admissibility of the communication or its merits.
5. A request addressed to a State party under paragraph 1 of this rule shall include a statement of the fact that such a request does not imply that any decision has been reached on the question of admissibility.

6. Within fixed time-limits, each party may be afforded an opportunity to comment on submissions made by the other party pursuant to this rule.

Rule 92

1. Where the Committee decides that a communication is inadmissible under the Protocol it shall as soon as possible communicate its decision, through the Secretary-General, to the author of the communication and, where the communication has been transmitted to a State party concerned, to that State party.

2. If the Committee has declared a communication inadmissible under article 5, paragraph 2, of the Protocol, this decision may be reviewed at a later date by the Committee upon a written request by or on behalf of the individual concerned containing information to the effect that the reasons for inadmissibility referred to in article 5, paragraph 2, no longer apply.

D. Procedure for the consideration of communications on the merits

Rule 93

1. In those cases in which the issue of admissibility is decided before receiving the State party's reply on the merits, if the Committee or a working group established under rule 89, paragraph 1, rules that the communication is admissible, that decision and all other relevant information shall be submitted, through the SecretarynGeneral, to the State party concerned. The author of the communication shall also be informed, through the Secretary-General, of the decision.

2. Within six months, the State party concerned shall submit to the Committee written explanations or statements clarifying the matter under consideration and the remedy, if any, that may have been taken by that State.

3. Any explanations or statements submitted by a State party pursuant to this rule shall be communicated, through the Secretary-General, to the author of the communication, who may submit any additional written information or observations within fixed time-limits.

4. Upon consideration of the merits, the Committee may review a decision that a communication is admissible in the light of any explanations or statements submitted by the State party pursuant to this rule.

A request for the review of an admissibility decision must not be addressed prior to, and separately from, consideration of communication on the merits. Sawyers et al. v. Jamaica (226, 256/87).

Rule 94

1. In those cases in which the parties have submitted information relating both to the questions of admissibility and the merits, or in which a decision on

admissibility has already been taken and the parties have submitted information on the merits, the Committee shall consider the communication in the light of all written information made available to it by the individual and the State party concerned and shall formulate its views thereon. Prior thereto the Committee may refer the communication to a working group or to a special rapporteur to make recommendations to the Committee.

2. The Committee shall not decide on the merits of the communication without having considered the applicability of all the admissibility grounds referred to in the Optional Protocol.

3. The views of the Committee shall be communicated to the individual and to the State party concerned.

Rule 95

1. The Committee shall designate a Special Rapporteur for follow up on views adopted under article 5, paragraph 4, of the Optional Protocol, for the purpose of ascertaining the measures taken by States parties to give effect to the Committee's views.

2. The Special Rapporteur may make such contacts and take such action as appropriate for the due performance of the follow up mandate. The Special Rapporteur shall make such recommendations for further action by the Committee as may be necessary.

3. The Special Rapporteur shall regularly report to the Committee on follow up activities.

4. The Committee shall include information on follow up activities in its annual report.

E. Rules concerning confidentiality

Rule 96

1. Communications under the Optional Protocol shall be examined by the Committee and its Working Group established pursuant to rule 89 in closed session. Oral deliberations and summary records shall remain confidential.

2. All working documents issued for the Committee, the Working Group established pursuant to rule 89 or the Special Rapporteur designated pursuant to rule 89 (3) by the Secretariat, including summaries of communications prepared prior to registration, the list of summaries of communications, and all drafts prepared for the Committee, its Working Group established pursuant to rule 89 or the Special Rapporteur designated pursuant to rule 89 (3) shall remain confidential, unless the Committee decides otherwise.

3. Paragraph 1 shall not affect the right of the author of a communication or the State party concerned to make public any submissions or information bearing on the proceedings. However, the Committee, the Working Group established pursuant to rule 89 or the Special Rapporteur designated pursuant to rule 89 (3)

may, as deemed appropriate, request the author of a communication or the State party concerned to keep confidential the whole or part of any such submissions or information.
4. When a decision has been taken on the confidentiality pursuant to paragraph 3 above, the Committee, the Working Group established pursuant to rule 89 or the Special Rapporteur designated pursuant to rule 89 (3) may decide that all or part of the submissions and other information, such as the identity of the author, may remain confidential after the Committee's decision on inadmissibility, merits or discontinuance has been adopted.
5. Subject to paragraph 4, the Committee's decisions on inadmissibility, merits and discontinuance shall be made public. The decisions of the Committee or the Special Rapporteur designated pursuant to rule 89 (3) under rule 86 shall be made public. No advance copies of any Committee decision shall be issued.
6. The Secretariat is responsible for the distribution of the Committee's final decisions. It shall not be responsible for the reproduction and the distribution of submissions concerning communications.

Rule 96, adopted at the 1585th meeting of the Committee on April 10, 1997.

Rule 97

Information furnished by the parties within the framework of follow-up to the Committee's views is not subject to confidentiality, unless the Committee decides otherwise. Decisions of the Committee relating to follow-up activities are equally not subject to confidentiality, unless the Committee decides otherwise.

F. Individual Opinions

Rule 98

Any member of the Committee who has participated in a decision may request that his her individual opinion be appended to the Committee's Views or decision.

APPENDIX: CASES QUOTED IN THE COMMENTARY

NAME OF CASE	CCPR /C/	COMM. NO.
A et al. v. S	2/D/	1/1976
William Torres Ramirez v. Uruguay	10/D/	4/1977
Moriana Hernandez Valentini de Bazzano, Luis Maria Bazzano Ambrosini, Martha Valentini de Massera, Jose Luis Massera v. Uruguay	7/D/	5/1977
Miguel A. Millán Sequeira v. Uruguay	10/D/	6/1977
Beatriz Weismann Lanza and Alcides Lanza Perdomo v. Uruguay	9/D/	8/1977
Edgardo Dante Santullo Valcada v. Uruguay	8/D/	9/1977
Alberto Altesor v. Uruguay	15/D/	10/1977
Alberto Grille Motta and other persons v. Uruguay	10/D/	11/1977
Daniel Monguya Mbenge, members of his family and persons in their employ v. Zaire	18/D/	16/1977
Sandra Lovelace v. Canada	13/D/	24/1977
Carmen Amendola Massiotti and Graciela Baritussio v. Uruguay	16/D/	25/1978
Larry James Pinkney v. Canada	14/D/	27/1977
Ismael Weinberger v. Uruguay	11/D/	28/1978
Eduardo Bleier v. Uruguay	15/D/	30/1978
Luis Touron v. Uruguay	12/D/	32/1978
Leopoldo Buffo Carballal v. Uruguay	12/D/	33/1978
Jorge Landinelli Silva et al. v. Uruguay	12/D/	34/1978
Shirin Aumeeruddy-Cziffra and 19 other Mauritian women v. Mauritius	12/D/	35/1978
Esther Soriano de Bouton v. Uruguay	12/D/	37/1978
Erkki Juhanni Hartikainen and other members of the Union of Free Thinkers v. Finland	12/D/	40/1978
Adolfo Drescher Caldas v. Uruguay	19/D/	43/1979
Rosario Pietraroia (also known as Rosario Pietraroia (or Roya) Zapala v. Uruguay	12/D/	44/1979
Maria Fanny Suarez de Guerrero v. Colombia	15/D/	45/1979
Orlando Borda, Maria Salazar de Fals Borda, Justo Bermudez, Martha Valderrama Becerra v. Colombia	16/D/	46/1979

NAME OF CASE	CCPR /C/	COMM. NO.
Dave Marais, Jr. v. Madagascar	18/D/	49/1979
Gordon C. van Duzen v. Canada	15/D/	50/1979
Sergio Ruben Lopez Burgos v. Uruguay	13/D/	52/1979
Alexander MacIsaac v. Canada	17/D/	55/1979
Lilian Celiberti de Casariego v. Uruguay	13/D/	56/1979
Sophie Vidal Martins v. Uruguay	15/D/	57/1979
Anna Maroufidou v. Sweden	12/D/	58/1979
Leo R- Hertzberg, Ulf Mansson, Astrid Nikula and Marko and Tuovi Putkonen v. Finland	15/D/	61/1979
Raul Sendic Antonaccio v. Uruguay	14/D/	63/1979
Consuelo Salgar de Montejo v. Colombia	15/D/	64/1979
David Alberto Campora Schweizer v. Uruguay	17/D/	66/1980
E.H.P. and others v. Canada	17/D/	67/1980
A.S. her daughter and grandson v. Canada	12/D/	68/1980
Mirta Cubas Simones v. Uruguay	15/D/	70/1981
Mario Alberto Teti Izquierdo v. Uruguay	15/D/	73/1981
Miguel Angel Estrella v. Uruguay	18/D/	74/1980
Duilio Fanali v. Italy	18/D/	75/1980
Samuel Lichtensztejn v. Uruguay	18/D/	77/1980
Elena Beatriz Vasilskis v. Uruguay	18/D/	80/1980
Raul Noel Martinez Machado v. Uruguay	20/D/	83/1981
Guillermo Ignacio Dermit Barbato and Hugo Haroldo Dermit Barbato v. Uruguay	17/D/	84/1981
Hector Alfredo Romero v. Uruguay	21/D/	85/1981
Gustavo Raul Larrosa Beguio v. Uruguay	18/D/	88/1981
Paavo Muhonen v. Finland	24/D/	89/1981
Luyeye Magana ex-Philibert v. Zaire	19/D/	90/1981
A.R.S. v. Canada	14/D/	91/1981
Battle Oxandabarat Scarrone v. Uruguay	20/D/	103/1981
J.R.T. and the W .G. Party v. Canada	18/D/	104/1981
Mabel Pereira Montero v. Uruguay	18/D/	106/1981
Maria del Carmen Almeida de Quinteros and Elena Quinteros Almeida v. Uruguay	19/D/	107/1981
Carlos Varela Nunez v. Uruguay	19/D/	108/1981
Antonio Viana v. Uruguay	21/D/	110/1981
Y.L. v. Canada	27/D/	112/1981
John Wight v. Madagascar	22/D/	115/1982

NAME OF CASE	CCPR /C/	COMM. NO.
M.A. v. Italy	21/D/	117/1981
J.B., P.D., L.S., T.M., D.P., D.S. v. Canada	28/D/	118/1982
A.M. v. Denmark	16/D/	121/1982
Jorge Manera Lluberas v. Uruguay	21/D/	123/1982
Tshitenge Muteba v. Zaire	22/D/	124/1982
M.M.Q. v. Uruguay	21/D/	125/1982
U.R. v. Uruguay	18/D/	128/1982
Monja Jaona v. Madagascar	24/D/	132/1982
J.F. v. Uruguay	19/D/	137/1983
Ngalula Mpandanjila et al. v. Zaire	27/D/	138/1983
Hiber Conteris v. Uruguay	25/D/	139/1983
John Kemraadi Baboeram, Andre Kamperveen, Cornelis Harold Riedewald, Gerald Leckie, Harry Sugrim Oemrawsingh, Somradj Robby Sohansingh, Lesley Paul Rahman, Edmund Alexander Hoost v. Suriname	24/D/	146, 148-154/1983
Lucia Arzuada Gilboa v. Uruguay	26/D/	147/1983
John Kemraadi Baboeram, Andre Kamperveen, Cornelis Harold Riedewald, Gerald Leckie, Harry Sugrim Oemrawsingh, Somradj Robby Sohansingh, Lesley Paul Rahman, Edmund Alexander Hoost v. Suriname	24/D/	148-154, 146/1983
Eric Hammel v. Madagascar	29/D/	155/1983
Luis Alberto Solorzano v. Venezuela	27/D/	156/1983
Andre Alphonse Mpaka Mpaka-Nsusu v. Zaire	27/D/	157/1983
O. F. v. Norway	23/D/	158/1983
Joaquin Herrera Rubio and his deceased parents, Jose Herrera and Emma Rubio de Herrera v. Colombia	31/D/	161/1983
Omar Berterretche Acosta v. Uruguay	34/D/	162/1983
G. F. Croes v. The Netherlands	34/D/	164/1984
Lubicon Lake Band v. Canada	38/D/	167/1984
E.H. v. Finland (A)	26/D/	170/1984
S.W M. Broeks v. The Netherlands	29/D/	172/1984
J.K. v. Canada	23/D/	174/1984
Walter Lafuente Penarrieta, Miguel Rodriguez Candia, Oscar Ruiz Caceres, and Julio Cear Toro Dorado v. Bolivia	31/D/	176/1984
L.G. Danning v. The Netherlands	29/D/	180/1984
Alfredo Rafael a. Samuel Sanjuán Arévalo v. Colombia	37/D/	181/1984

NAME OF CASE	CCPR /C/	COMM. NO.
F. H. Zwaan-de Vries v. The Netherlands	29/D/	182/1984
L.T.K. v. Finland	25/D/	185/1984
English speaking members of the Canadian Armed Forces v. Canada	24/D/	187/1985
Ramon B. Martinez Portorreal v. Dominican Republic	31/D/	188/1984
Carl Henrik Blom v. Sweden	32/D/	191/1985
Pierre Giry v. Dominican Republic	39/D/	193/1985
Jean Miango Muiyo v. Zaire	31/D/	194/1985
William Eduardo Delgado Páez v. Colombia	39/D/	195/1985
Ibrahima Gueye et al. v. France	35/D/	196/1983
Ivan Kitok v. Sweden	33/D/	197/1985
R.D. Stalla Costa v. Uruguay	30/D/	198/1985
Wim Hendricks Sr. v. The Netherlands	33/D/	201/1985
Graciela Ato del Avellanal v. Peru	34/D/	202/1986
Rubén Toribio Muñoz Hermoza v. Peru	34/D/	203/1986
A.P. v. Italy	31/D/	204/1986
Grand Chief Donald Marshall, Grand Captain Alexander Denny and Adviser Simon Marshall, as officers of the Grand Council of the Mikmaq tribal society and the Mikmaq tribal society v. Canada	43/D/	205/1986
Yves Morael v. France	36/D/	207/1986
Karnel Singh Bhinder v. Canada	37/D/	208/1986
Earl Pratt and Ivan Morgan v. Jamaica	35/D/	210, 225/1986
P.P.C. v. The Netherlands	32/D/	212/1986
H.C.M.A. v. The Netherlands	35/D/	213/1986
G.A.van Meurs v. The Netherlands	39/D/	215/1986
H.v.d.P. v. The Netherlands	29/D/	217/1986
Hendrika S. Vos v. The Netherlands	35/D/	218/1986
Dominique Guesdon v. France	39/D/	219/1986
T.K. v. France	37/D/	220/1987
Yves Cadoret, Hervé Le Bihan v. France	41/D/	221, 323/1988
H.K. v. France	37/D/	222/1987
Frank Robinson v. Jamaica	35/D/	223/1987
Earl Pratt and Ivan Morgan v. Jamaica	35/D/	225, 210/1987

NAME OF CASE	CCPR /C/	COMM. NO.
Michael Sawyers; Michael and Desmond McLean v. Jamaica	41/D/	226, 256/1987
Irvine Reynolds v. Jamaica	41/D/	229/1987
Raphael Henry v. Jamaica	43/D/	230/1987
Daniel Pinto v. Trinidad and Tobago	39/D/	232/1987
V.M.R.B. v. Canada	33/D/	236/1987
Denroy Gordon v. Jamaica	46/D/	237/1987
Floresmilo Bolaños v. Ecuador	36/D/	238/1987
Willard Collins v. Jamaica	43/D/	240/1987
F. Birindwa ci Bithashwiwa, E. Tshisekedi wa Mulumba v. Zaire	37/D/	241; 242/1987
Glenford Campbell v. Jamaica	44/D/	248/1987
Carlton Reid v. Jamaica	39/D/	250/1987
Paul Kelly v. Jamaica	41/D/	253/1987
Carlton Linton v. Jamaica	46/D/	255/1987
Michael Sawyers; Michael and Desmond McLean v. Jamaica	41/D/	256, 226/1987
R.T. v. France	35/D/	262/1987
Miguel González del Rio v. Peru	46/D/	263/1987
Antti Vuolanne v. Finland	35/D/	265/1987
M.G.B. and S.P. v. Trinidad and Tobago	37/D/	268/1987
Randolph Barrett and Clyde Sutcliffe v. Jamaica	44/D/	270, 271/1988
Alrick Thomas v. Jamaica	44/D/	272/1988
B.d. B. et al. v. The Netherlands	35/D/	273/1989
Loxley Griffiths v. Jamaica	47/D/	274/1988
S.E. and her disappeared children v. Argentina	38/D/	275/1988
Juan Fernando Terán Jijón v. Ecuador	44/D/	277/1988
Leaford Smith v. Jamaica	47/D/	282/1988
Aston Little v. Jamaica	43/D/	283/1988
Dieter Wolf v. Panama	44/D/	289/1988
Mario Inés Torres v. Finland	38/D/	291/1988
Aapo Järvinen v. Finland	39/D/	295/1988
J.R.C. v. Costa Rica	35/D/	296/1988
H.A.E. d. J. v. The Netherlands	37/D/	297/1988
G. and L. Lindgren and L. Holm A. and B. Hjord, E. and I. Lundquist, L. Radko and E. Stahl v. Sweden	40/D/	298, 299/1988

NAME OF CASE	CCPR /C/	COMM. NO.
R.M. v. Finland	35/D/	301/1998
Hugo van Alphen v. The Netherlands	39/D/	305/1988
John Campbell v. Jamaica	47/D/	307/1988
Carlos Orihuela Valenzuela and his family v. Peru	48/D/	309/1988
Peter Chiiko Bwalya v. Zambia	48/D/	314/1988
C.E.A. v. Finland	42/D/	316/1988
Howard Martin v. Jamaica	47/D/	317/1988
E.P. et al. v. Colombia	39/D/	318/1988
Edgar A. Cañón García v. Ecuador	43/D/	319/1988
Victor Francis v. Jamaica	47/D/	320/1988
Maurice Thomas v. Jamaica	49/D/	321/1988
Hugo Rodríguez v. Uruguay	51/D/	322/1988
Yves Cadoret, Hervé Le Bihan v. France	41/D/	323, 221/1988
Henry Kalenga v. Zambia	48/D/	326/1988
Hervé Barzhig v. France	41/D/	327/1988
Roberto Zelaya Blanco v. Nicaragua	51/D/	328/1988
Albert Berry v. Jamaica	50/D/	330/1988
Allen v. Jamaica (V)	50/D/	332/1988
Lenford Hamilton v. Jamaica	50/D/	333/1988
Michael Bailey v. Jamaica	47/D/	334/1988
Andre Fillastre and Pierre Bizouarn v. Bolivia	43/D/	336/1988
Leroy Simmonds v. Jamaica	46/D/	338/1988
Z.P. v. Canada	41/D/	341/1988
Relatives of the authors (R.A.V.N. et al.) v. Argentina	38/D/	343, 344, 345/1988
S.G. v. France	43/D/	347/1988
G.B. v. France	43/D/	348/1989
Clifton Wright v. Jamaica	45/D/	349/1989
Dennis Douglas, Errol Gentles and Lorenzo Kerr v. Jamaica	49/D/	352/ 1989
Lloyd Grant v. Jamaica	50/D/	353/1988
Georg Winston Reid v. Jamaica	51/D/	355/1989
Trevor Collins v. Jamaica	47/D/	356/1989
R.L. et al. v. Canada	43/D/	358/1989
John Ballantyne and Elizabeth Davidson, and Gordon McIntyre v. Canada	47/D/	359, 385/1989

NAME OF CASE	CCPR /C/	COMM. NO.
The company v. Trinidad and Tobago	36/D/	360/1989
The companies v. Trinidad and Tobago	36/D/	361/1989
Balkissoon Soogrim v. Trinidad and Tobago	47/D/	362/1989
R.L.M. v. France	44/D/	363/1989
Isidore Kanana Tshiongo a Minanga v. Zaire	49/D/	366/1989
J.J.C. v. Canada	43/D/	367/1989
Lennon Stephens v. Jamaica	55/D/	373/1989
Glenmore Compass v. Jamaica	49/D/	375/1989
Anthony Currie v. Jamaica	50/D/	377/1989
C.W. v. Finland	38/D/	379/1989
R.L.M. v. Trinidad and Tobago	48/D/	380/1989
L.E.S.K. v. The Netherlands	45/D/	381/1989
H.C. v. Jamaica	45/D/	383/1989
John Ballantyne and Elizabeth Davidson, and Gordon McIntyre v. Canada	47/D/	385, 359/1989
Famara Koné v. Senegal	52/D/	386/1989
Arvo O. Karttunen v. Finland	46/D/	387/1989
Bernard Lubuto v. Zambia	45/D/	390/1990
C.B.D. v. The Netherlands	45/D/	394/1990
M.Th. Sprenger v. The Netherlands	44/D/	395/1990
M.S. v. The Netherlands	45/D/	396/1990
P.S. and his son, T.S. v. Denmark	45/D/	397/1990
A.M. v. Finland	45/D/	398/1990
Darwinia Rosa Mónaco de Gallicchio and Ximena Vicario v. Argentina	53/D/	400/1990
J.P.K. v. The Netherlands	43/D/	401/1990
Henricus Antonius Godefriedus Maria Brinkhof v. The Netherlands	48/D/	402/1990
T.W.M.B. v. The Netherlands	43/D/	403/1990
Lahcen B.M. Oulajin and Mohamed Kaiss v. The Netherlands	46/D/	406, 426/1990
Dwayne Hylton v. Jamaica	51/D/	407/1990
W.J.H. v. The Netherlands	45/D/	408/1990
Csaba Párkányi v. Hungary	45/D/	410/1990
Auli Kivenmaa v. Finland	50/D/	412/1990
A.B. et al. v. Italy	40/D/	413/1990
Primo José Essono Mika Miha v. Equatorial Guinea	51/D/	414/1990

NAME OF CASE	CCPR /C/	COMM. NO.
Dietmar Pauger v. Austria	44/D/	415/1990
Manuel Balaguer Santacana and his daughter, María del Carmen Balaguer Montalvo v. Spain	51/D/	417/1990
C.H.J. Cavalcanti Araujo-Jongen v. The Netherlands	49/D/	418/1990
Thierry Trebutién v. France	51/D/	421/1990
Adimayo M. Aduayom; Sofianou T. Diasso; Yawo S. Dobou v. Togo	57/D/	422, 423, 424/1990
A.M.M. Doesburg Lannooij Neefs v. The Netherlands	51/D/	425/1990
Lahcen B.M. Oulajin and Mohamed Kaiss v. The Netherlands	46/D/	426, 406/1990
Francois Bozize v. Central African Republic	50/D/	428/1990
E.W. et al. v. The Netherlands	47/D/	429/1990
W.B.E. v. The Netherlands	46/D/	432/1990
A.P.A. v. Spain	50/D/	433/1990
Lal Seerattan v. Trinidad and Tobago	55/D/	434/1990
Manuel Solís Palma v. Panama	51/D/	436/1990
Benjamin Colamarco Patiño v. Panama	52/D/	437/1990
Enrique Thompson v. Panama	52/D/	438/1990
C.L.D. v. France	43/D/	439/1990
Mohammed Bashir El-Megreisi v. Libyan Arab Jamahiriya	50/D/	440/1990
Robert Casanovas v. France	51/D/	441/1990
Lynden Champagnie, Delroy Palmer, Oswald Chisholm et. al v. Jamaica	51/D/	445/1991
Dr. J. P. v. Canada	43/D/	446/1991
Leroy Shalto v. Trinidad and Tobago	53/D/	447/1991
H.J.H. v. The Netherlands	43/D/	448/1991
Rafael Mojica v. Dominican Republic	51/D/	449/1991
I.P.v. Finland	48/D/	450/1991
Barry Stephen Harward v. Norway	51/D/	451/1991
A.R. Coeriel and M.A.R. Aurik v. The Netherlands	52/D/	453/1991
Enrique García Pons v. Spain	55/D/	454/1991
Allan Singer v. Canada	51/D/	455/1991
Ismet Celepli v. Sweden	51/D/	456/1991
Albert Womah Mukong v. Cameroon	51/D/	458/1991
Osbourne Wright and Eric Harvey v. Jamaica	55/D/	459/1991
Terani Omar Simons v. Panama	52/D/	460/1991

NAME OF CASE	CCPR /C/	COMM. NO.
George Graham and Arthur Morrison v. Jamaica	56/D/	461/1991
Garfield Peart ; Andrew Peart v. Jamaica	54/D/	464, 482/1991
V.E.M. v. Spain	48/D/	467/1991
Angel N. Oló Bahamonde v. Equatorial Guinea	49/D/	468/1991
Charles Chitat Ng v. Canada	49/D/	469/1991
Joseph Kindler v. Canada	48/D/	470/1991
Mario Abel del Cid Gómez v. Panama	54/D/	473/1991
J.A.M.B.-R. v. The Netherlands	50/D/	477/1991
A.P.L.-v.d.M. v. The Netherlands	48/D/	478/1991
José Luis García Fuenzalida v. Ecuador	57/D/	480/1991
Jorge Villacrés Ortega v. Ecuador	59/D/	481/1991
Garfield Peart ; Andrew Peart v. Jamaica	54/D/	482, 464/1991
J.v.K. and C.M.G.v.K.-S. v. The Netherlands	45/D/	483/1991
Nicholas Toonen v. Australia	50/D/	488/1992
Peter Bradschaw v. Barbados	51/D/	489/1992
J.L. v. Australia	45/D/	491/1992
Lauri Peltonen v. Finland	51/D/	492/1992
Gerald John Griffin v. Spain	53/D/	493/1992
Joszef Debreczeny v. The Netherlands	53/D/	500/1992
S.M. v. Barbados	50/D/	502/1992
Denzil Roberts v. Barbados	51/D/	504/1992
Kéténguéré Ackla v. Togo	56/D/	505/1992
A.R.U. v. The Netherlands	49/D/	509/1992
Ilmari Länsman et al. v. Finland	52/D/	511/1992
Daniel Pinto v. Trinidad and Tobago	57/D/	512/1992
Sandra Fei v. Colombia	53/D/	514/1992
Alina Simunek, Jaroslav Simunek; Dagmar Hastings Tuzilova, Josef Prochazka et al. v. Czech Republic	54/D/	516/1992
Jong-Kyu Sohn v. Republic of Korea	54/D/	518/1992
E. and A.K. v. Hungary	50/D/	520/1992
Vladimir Kulomin v. Hungary	56/D/	521/1992
Clyde Neptune v. Trinidad and Tobago	57/D/	523/1992
E.C.W. v. The Netherlands	49/D/	524/1992
Michael and Brian Hill v. Spain	59/D/	526/1993
Uton Lewis v. Jamaica	57/D/	527/1993

NAME OF CASE	CCPR /C/	COMM. NO.
Michael Steadman v.Jamaica	59/D/	528/1993
Hervin Edwards v. Jamaica	60/D/	529/1993
Maurice Thomas v. Jamaica	61/D/	532/1993
Harold Elahie v. Trinidad and Tobago	60/D/	533/1993
H.T.B. v. Canada	49/D/	534/1993
Lloydell Richards v. Jamaica	59/D/	535/1993
Paul Anthony Kelly v. Jamaica	57/D/	537/1993
Charles E. Stewart v. Canada	58/D/	538/1993
Keith Cox v. Canada	52/D/	539/1993
Ana Rosario Celis Laureano v. Peru	56/D/	540/1993
Errol Simms v. Jamaica	53/D/	541/1993
Katombe L. Tshishimbi v. Zaire	56/D/	542/1993
Rickly Burrell v. Jamaica	57/D/	546/1993
Apirana Mahuika et al. v. New Zealand	70/D/	547/1993
Francis Hopu and Tepoaitu Bessert v. France	60/D/	549/1993
Robert Faurisson v. France	58/D/	550/1993
Wieslaw Kall v. Poland	60/D/	552/1993
Michael Bullock v. Trinidad and Tobago	54/D/	553/1993
Robinson LaVende v. Trinidad and Tobago	61/D/	554/1993
Ramcharan Bickaroo v. Trinidad and Tobago	61/D/	555/1993
Giosue Canepa v. Canada	59/D/	558/1993
A. v. Australia	59/D/	560/1993
Desmond Williams v. Jamaica	59/D/	561/1993
Nydia Erika Bautista de Arellana v. Colombia	55/D/	563/1993
Junior Leslie v. Jamaica	63/D/	564/1993
R. and M.H. v. Italy	50/D/	565/1993
Ivan Somers and his mother v. Hungary	57/D/	566/1993
Ponsamy Poongavanam v. Mauritius	51/D/	567/1993
K.V. and C.V. v. Germany	50/D/	568/1993
Patterson Matthews v. Trinidad and Tobago	62/D/	569/1993
M.A.B., W.A.T. and J.-A.Y.T. v. Canada	50/D/	570/1993
Eustace Henry and Everald Douglas v. Jamaica	57/D/	571/1994
Hezekiah Price v. Jamaica	58/D/	572/1994
Keun-Tae Kim v. Republic of Korea	64/D/	574/1994
Victor Alfredo Polay Campos v. Peru	61/D/	577/1994
Leonardus Johannes Maria de Groot v. The Netherlands	54/D/	578/1994

NAME OF CASE	CCPR /C/	COMM. NO.
Klaus Werenbeck v. Australia	59/D/	579/1994
Glenn Ashby v. Trinidad and Tobago	74/D/	580/1994
Ronald Herman van der Houwen v. The Netherlands	54/D/	583/1994
Tony Jones v. Jamaica	62/D/	585/1994
Joseph Frank Adam v. Czech Republic	57/D/	586/1994
Irvine Reynolds v. Jamaica	59/D/	587/1994
Errol Johnson v. Jamaica	56/D/	588/1994
Crafton Tomlin v. Jamaica	57/D/	589/1994
Trevor Bennett v. Jamaica	65/D/	590/1994
Ian Chung v. Jamaica	62/D/	591/1994
Clive Johnson v. Jamaica	64/D/	592/1994
Irving Phillip v. Trinidad and Tobago	64/D/	594/1992
Dennie Chaplin v. Jamaica	55/D/	596/1994
Peter Grant v. Jamaica	56/D/	597/1994
Carl Sterling v. Jamaica	57/D/	598/1994
Wayne Spence v. Jamaica	57/D/	599/1994
Dwayne Hylton v. Jamaica	57/D/	600/1994
Cornelis Hoofdman v. The Netherlands	64/D/	602/1994
Clement Francis v. Jamaica	54/D/	606/1994
Michael Adams v. Jamaica	58/D/	607/1994
Franz Nahlik v. Austria	57/D/	608/1995
Nathaniel Williams v. Jamaica	61/D/	609/1995
Nicholas Henry v. Jamaica	64/D/	610/1995
Hixford Morrison v. Jamaica	63/D/	611/1995
José Vicente and Amado Villafañe Chaparro, Luís Napoleón Torres Crespo, Angel María Torres Arroyo and Antonio Hugues Chaparro Torres v. Colombia	60/D/	612/1995
Anthony Leehong v. Jamaica	66/D/	613/1995
Samuel Thomas v. Jamaica	65/D/	614/1995
Byron Young v. Jamaica	61/D/	615/1995
Zephiniah Hamilton v. Jamaica	66/D/	616/1995
Anthony Finn v. Jamaica	63/D/	617/1995
Barrington Campbell v. Jamaica	64/D/	618/1995
Fray Deidrick v. Jamaica	62/D/	619/1995
Victor P. Domukovsky, Zaza Tsiklauri, Petre Gelbakhiani and Irakli Dokvadze v. Georgia	62/D/	623, 624, 626, 627/1995

NAME OF CASE	CCPR /C/	COMM. NO.
Michael Freemantle v. Jamaica	68/D/	625/1995
Victor P. Domukovsky, Zaza Tsiklauri, Petre Gelbakhiani and Irakli Dokvadze v. Georgia	62/D/	626, 627, 623, 624/1995
Tae Hoon Park v. Republic of Korea	64/D/	628/1995
Abdoulaye Mazou v. Cameroon	72/D/	630/1995
Aage Spakmo v. Norway	67/D/	631/1995
Herbert Thomas Potter v. New Zealand	60/D/	632/1995
Robert W. Gauthier v. Canada	65/D/	633/1995
Desmond Amore v. Jamaica	65/D/	634/1995
Everton Morrison v. Jamaica	63/D/	635/1995
Trevor Walker and Lawson Richards v. Jamaica	60/D/	639/1995
McIntosh v. Jamaica	61/D/	640/1995
Nyekuma Kopita Toro Gedumbe v. Democratic Republic of the Congo	75/D/	641/1995
Peter Drobek v. Slovakia	60/D/	643/1995
Vaihere Bordes and Mr. John Temeharo et al. v. Franve	57/D/	645/1995
Leonard John Lindon v. Australia	64/D/	646/1995
Wilfred Pennant v. Jamaica	64/D/	647/1995
Winston Forbes v. Jamaica	64/D/	649/1995
Meer and Shulamit Vaisman (on behalf of) their nephew Martin Perel v. Latvia	62/D/	650/1995
J. Snijders, A.A. Willemen and Ch. C. M. Van der Wouw v. The Netherlands	63/D/	651/1995
Colin Johnson v. Jamaica	64/D/	653/1995
Adu v. Canada	60/D/	654/1995
Jacob and Jantina Hendrika van Oord v. The Netherlands	60/D/	658/1995
Peter Lumley v. Jamaica	65/D/	662/1995
McCordie Morrison v. Jamaica	64/D/	663/1995
Gesina Kruyt-Amesz, Hendrik Gerrit Schraa, Hendrikus Gerardus Maria Karis and Maria Johanna Josephina Moors v. The Netherlands	64/D/	664/1995
Owen Brown and Burchell Parish v. Jamaica	66/D/	665/1995
Frédéric Foin v. France	67/D/	666/1995
Ricketts v. Jamaica	74/D/	667/1995
Errol Smith and Oval Stewart v. Jamaica	65/D/	668/1995

NAME OF CASE	CCPR /C/	COMM. NO.
Gerhard Malik v. Czech Republic	64/D/	669/1995
Jouni E. Länsman et al. v. Finland	58/D/	671/1995
Clive Smart v. Trinidad and Tobago	63/D/	672/1995
Franklyn Gonzales v. Trinidad andTobago	65/D/	673/1995
Simalae Toala et al. v. New Zealand	70/D/	675/1995
Abdool Saleem Yasseen and Noel Thomas v. Republic of Guyana	62/D/	676/1996
Kenneth Teesdale v. Trinidad and Tobago	74/D/	677/1996
José Luis Gutiérrez Gutiérrez Vicanco v. Peru	74/D/	678/1996
Lancy Gallimore v. Jamaica	66/D/	680/1996
Paul Westerman v. The Netherlands	67/D/	682/1996
Michael Wanza v. Trinidad and Tobago	74/D/	683/1996
R. S. v. Trinidad and Tobago	74/D/	684/1996
Rafael Armando Rojas García v. Colombia	71/D/	687/1996
María Sybila Arredondo v. Peru	69/D/	688/1996
Richard Maille v. France	69/D/	689/1996
Marc Venier, Paul Nicolas v. France	69/D/	690, 691/1996
A.R.J. v. Australia	60/D/	692/1996
Gi-Jeong Nam v. Republic of Korea	78/D/	693/1996
Arich Hollis Waldman v. Canada	67/D/	694/1996
Devon Simpson v. Jamaica	73/D/	695/1996
Peter Blaine v. Jamaica	60/D/	696/1996
Ali Maleki v. Italy	66/D/	699/1996
Cesario Gómez Vázquez v. Spain	69/D/	701/1996
Clifford McLawrence v. Jamaica	60/D/	702/1996
Steve Shaw v. Jamaica	62/D/	704/1996
Desmond Taylor v. Jamaica	62/D/	705/1996
T. v. Australia	61/D/	706/1996
Patrick Taylor v. Jamaica	60/D/	707/1996
Neville Lewis v. Jamaica	60/D/	708/1996
Everton Bailey v. Jamaica	66/D/	709/1996
Winston Hankle v. Jamaica	66/D/	710/1996
Carlos Dias and Carolina de Fatima da Silva Francisco v. Angola	68/D/	711/1996
A. Gerritsen v. The Netherlands	65/D/	714/1996
Dietmar Pauger v. Austria	65/D/	716/1996

NAME OF CASE	CCPR /C/	COMM. NO.
Conroy Levy v. Jamaica	64/D/	719/1996
Leroy Morgan and Samuel Williams v. Jamaica	64/D/	720/1996
Clement Boodoo v. Trinidad and Tobago	74/D/	721/1996
Alexander Zheludkov v. Ukraine	76/D/	726/1996
Dobroslav Paraga v. Croatia	71/D/	727/1996
Terrence Sahadeo v. Guyana	73/D/	728/1996
Clarence Marshall v. Jamaica	64/D/	730/1996
Michael Robinson v. Jamaica	68/D/	731/1996
Beresford Whyte v. Jamaica	63/D/	732/1997
Andrew Perkins v. Jamaica	63/D/	733/1997
Anthony McLeod v. Jamaica	62/D/	734/1997
Malcolm Ross v. Canada	70/D/	736/1997
Michelle Lamagna v. Australia	65/D/	737/1997
Ngoc Si Truong v. Canada	77/D/	743/1997
Dagmar Urbanetz Linderholm v. Croatia	66/D/	744/1997
Humberto Menanteau Aceituno and Mr. José Carrasco Vasquez v. Chile	66/D/	746/1997
Karel Des Fours Walderode, Johanna Kammerlander v. Czech Republic	73/D/	747/1997
Deon McTaggart v. Jamaica	62/D/	749/1997
Silbert Daley v. Jamaica	63/D/	750/1997
Allan Henry v. Trinidad and Tobago	65/D/	752/1997
A v. New Zealand	66/D/	754/1997
Clarence T. Maloney and his three children Benedikt, Malika and Konstantin v. Germany	60/D/	755/1997
Alzbeta Pezoldova v. Czech Republic	76/D/	757/1997
George Osbourne v. Jamaica	68/D/	759/1997
J.G.A. Diergaardt et al. v. Namibia	69/D/	760/1997
Ranjit Singh v. Canada	60/D/	761/1997
Michael Jensen v. Australia	71/D/	762/1997
Vladimir Albertovich Lantsova v. Russian Federation	74/D/	763/1997
Eliska Fábryová v. Czech Republic	73/D/	765/1997
Zouhair Ben Said v. Norway	68/D/	767/1997
Chisala Mukunto v. Zambia	66/D/	768/1997
Dimitry L. Gridin v. Russian Federation	69/D/	770/1997
Alexander Baulin v. Russian Federation	76/D/	771/1997
Mr. Y v. Australia	69/D/	772/1997

NAME OF CASE	CCPR /C/	COMM. NO.
Robert Brok (deceased) and his surviving spouse Dagmar Brokova v. Czech Republic	73/D/	774/1997
Christopher Brown v. Jamaica	65/D/	775/1997
Antonio Sánchez López v. Spain	67/D/	777/1997
Gustavo Coronel Navarro, Nahún Elías Sánchez Vega, Ramón Emilio Sánchez, Ramón Emilio Quintero Ropero, Luis Honorio Quintero Ropero, Ramón Villegas Tellez and Ernesto Ascanio Ascanio v. Colombia	76/D/	778/1997
Vladimir Petrovich Laptsevich v. Belarus	68/D/	780/1997
Azer Garyverdy ogly Aliev v. Ukraine	78/D/	781/1997
A.P. Johannes Vos. v. The Netherlands	66/D/	786/1997
Vishwadeo Gobin v. Mauritius	72/D/	787/1997
Geniuval M. Cagas, Wilson Butin and Julio Astillero v. The Philippines	73/D/	788/1997
Monica Bryhn v. Norway	67/D/	789/1997
Malcolm Higginson v. Jamaica	74/D/	792/1998
Samba Jalloh v. The Netherlands	74/D/	794/1998
Lloyd Reece v. Jamaica	78/D/	796/1998
Floyd Howell v. Jamaica	79/D/	798/1998
Damian Thomas v. Jamaica	65/D/	800/1998
Andrew Rogerson v. Australia	74/D/	802/1998
Eversley Thompson v. Saint Vincent and the Grenadines	70/D/	806/1998
Georg Rogl v. Germany	70/D/	808/1998
Mikhail Ivanovich Pastukhov v. Belarus	78/D/	814/1998
Grant Tadman et al. v. Canada	67/D/	816/1998
Sandy Sextus v. Trinidad and Tobago	72/D/	818/1998
Joseph Kavanagh v. Ireland	71/D/	819/1998
Keshva Rajan and Sashi Kantra Rajan and their minor children, Vicky Rajan and Ashnita Rajan v. New Zealand	78/D/	820/1998
Rodger Chongwe v. Zambia	70/D/	821/1998
Roger Judge v. Canada	78/D/	829/1998
Salah Karker v. France	70/D/	833/1998
Kestutis Gelazauskas v. Lithuania	77/D/	836/1998
Oral Hendricks v. Guyana	76/D/	838/1998

NAME OF CASE	CCPR /C/	COMM. NO.
Mr. Anthony B. Mansaraj et al.; Mr. Gborie Tamba et al.; Mr. Abdul Karim Sesay et al. v. Sierra Leone	72/D/	839, 840, 841/1998
Sergei Romanov v. Ukraine	79/D/	842/1998
Ivan Petkov v. Bulgaria	65/D/	844/1998
Rawle Kennedy v. Trinidad and Tobago	74/D/	845/1998
Gertruda Hubertina Jansen-Gielen v. The Netherlands	71/D/	846/1999
Miguel Ángel Rodríguez Orejuela v. Colombia	75/D/	848/1999
Rostislav Borisenko v. Hungary	76/D/	852/1999
Manuel Wackenheim v. France	75/D/	854/1999
M. Schmitz-de-Jong v. The Netherlands	72/D/	855/1999
Alex Soteli Chambala v. Zambia	78/D/	856/1999
Miroslav Blazek, George A. Hartman and George Krizek v. Czech Republic	72/D/	857/1999
Margaret Buckle v. New Zealand	70/D/	858/1999
Luis Asdrúbal Jiménez Vaca v. Colombia	74/D/	859/1999
Alain Lestourneaud v. France	67/D/	861/1999
Alfonso Ruiz Agudo v. Spain	76/D/	864/1999
Marina Torregrosa Lafuente et al. v. Spain	72/D/	866/1999
Albert Wilson v. The Philippines	79/D/	868/1999
Dante Piandiong, Jesus Morallos, Archie Bulan v. The Philippines	70/D/	869/1999
Eugeniusz Kurowski v. Poland	77/D/	872/1999
Jan Filpovich v. Lithuania	78/D/	875/1999
Yong-Joo Kang v. Republic of Korea	78/D/	878/1999
Antonina Ignatane v. Latvia	72/D/	884/1999
Natalia Schedko and Anton Bondarenko v. Belarus	77/D/	886/1999
Mariya Staselovich and Igor Lyashkevich v. Belarus	77/D/	887/1999
Vladimir Nikolayevich Telitsin v. Russian Federation	80/D/	888/1999
Emmerich Krausser and his mother v. Austria	76/D/	890/1999
David Wayne Tamihere v. New Zealand	68/D/	891/1999
Mohammed Sahid, his daughter amd his grandson v. New Zealand	77/D/	893/1999
Glenroy Francis et al. v. Trinidad and Tobago	75/D/	899/1999
C. v. Australia	76/D/	900/1999
Juliet Joslin et al. v. New Zealand	75/D/	902/1999
Félix Enrique Chira Vargas-Machuca v. Peru	75/D/	906/2000
Xavier Evans v. Trinidad and Tobago	77/D/	908/2000

NAME OF CASE	CCPR /C/	COMM. NO.
Ati Antoine Randolph v. Togo	79/D/	910/2000
Jayalath Jayawardena v. Sri Lanka	75/D/	916/2000
Michael Andreas Müller and Imke Engelhard v. Namibia	74/D/	919/2000
Alexandre Dergachev v. Belarus	74/D/	921/2000
Istvan Mátyus v. Slovakia	75/D/	923/2000
Wan Kuok Koi v. Portugal	73/D/	925/2000
Boodlal Sooklal v. Trinidad and Tobago	73/D/	928/2000
Mr. Hendrick Winata and Ms. So Lan Li, and their son, Barry Winata v. Australia	72/D/	930/2000
Marie-Hélène Gillot et al. v. France	75/D/	932/2000
Adrien Mundyo Busyo, Thomas Osthudi Wongodi, René Sibu Matubuka et al. v. Democratic Republic of the Congo	78/D/	933/2000
Ms. G. v. Canada	69/D/	934/2000
Zébié Aka Bi v. Cote d'Ivoire	75/D/	940/2000
Edward Young v. Australia	78/D/	941/2000
Jarle Jonassen and members of the Riast/Hylling reindeer herding district v. Norway	76/D/	942/2000
Mr. L.P. and his son v. Czech Republic	75/D/	946/2000
Ameer Keshavjee v. Canada	70/D/	949/2000
S. Jegatheeswara Sarma, his family and his son, J. Thevaraja Sarma v. Sri Lanka	78/D/	950/2000
Ernst Zündel v. Canada	78/D/	953/2000
Klaus Dieter Baumgarten v. Germany	78/D/	960/2000
Colin Uebergang v. Australia	71/D/	963/2001
Mümtaz Karakurt v. Austria	74/D/	965/2000
George Kazantzis v. Cyprus	78/D/	972/2001
Ricardo Ernesto Gómez Casafranca v. Peru	78/D/	981/2001
John K. Love, William L. Bone, William J. Craig, and Peter B. Ivanoff v. Australia	77/D/	983/2001
Joseph Semey v. Spain	78/D/	986/2001
Walter Kollar v. Austria	78/D/	989/2001
Rupert Althammer et al. v. Austria	78/D/	998/2001
Jacobus Gerardus Strik v. The Netherlands	76/D/	1001/2001
Franz Wallmann et al. v. Austria	80/D	1002/2001
P.L. v. Germany	79/D/	1003/2001

NAME OF CASE	CCPR /C/	COMM. NO.
Luis Pascual Estevill v. Spain	77/D/	1004/2001
Concepción Sánchez González v. Spain	74/D/	1005/2001
José Antonio Martínez Muñoz v.Spain	79/D/	1006/2001
Manuel Sineiro Fernández v. Spain	78/D/	1007/2001
Omar Sharif Baban and his son, Bawan Heman Babanet v. Australia	78/D/	1014/2001
Carlos Cabal and Marco Pasini Bertran v. Australia	78/D/	1020/2001
Rita Hiro Balani v. Spain	77/D/	1021/2001
Dáithi Ó Colchúin v. Ireland	77/D/	1038/2001
Alfredo Baroy v. The Philippines	79/D/	1045/2002
Kenneth Riley et al. v. Canada	74/D/	1048/2002
Mansour Ahani v. Canada	80/D/	1051/2002
Makram Asham Andrawos Mankarious v. Australia	74/D/	1065/2002
Ali Aqsar Bakhtiyari and Roqaiha Bakhtiyari and their five children, Almadar, Mentazer, Neqeina, Sameina and Amina Bakhtiyari v. Australia	79/D/	1069/2002
Jaime Carpo, Oscar Ibao, Warlito Ibao and Roche Ibao v. The Philippines	77/D/	1077/2002
Olivier de Clippele v. Belgium	77/D/	1082/2002
Sholam Weiss v. Austria	77/D/	1086/2002
Peter Hesse v. Australia	75/D/	1087/2002
Bernard Veriter v. France	78/D/	1088/2002
Tai Wairiki Rameka et al. v. New Zealand	79/D/	1090/2002
Abduali Ismatovich Kurbanov v. Tajikistan	79/D/	1096/2002
Joseph Kavanagh v. Ireland	76/D/	1114/2002
A.J. v. G. v. The Netherlands	77/D/	1142/2002
Antonio Hom v. The Philippines	78/D/	1169/2003
Fatima Benali v. The Netherlands	81/D/	1272/2004
John Wilson v. Australia	80/D/	1239/2004
Adrian Vlad v. Germany	80/D/	1214/2003
Elizabeth Hruska v. Czech Republic	79/D/	1191/2003
Benjamin Ngambi, Marie-Louise Nébol v. France	81/D/	1179/2003

INDEX: CASES

1

1/76 ... 145, 155
10/77 ... 39, 42, 45, 113, 145
11/77 ... 24, 39, 42, 95
16/77 ... 23, 35, 67, 145
103/81 ... 64
104/81 ... 81, 96, 141
106/81 ... 5, 50, 146
107/81 ... 27, 36, 143, 151
108/81 ... 5, 48, 50, 146
110/81 ... 5, 64
112/81 ... 57
115/82 ... 29, 64
117/81 ... 88, 99, 110, 149
118/82 ... 98
121/82 ... 152, 154
123/82 ... 44, 45
124/82 ... 28, 29, 39, 40, 89
125/82 ... 146
128/82 ... 145
132/82 ... 36, 37
137/83 ... 145
138/83 ... 36, 43, 50, 51, 89
139/83 ... 37, 38, 40, 42, 45, 150
146, 148-154/83 ... 20
147/83 ... 27, 45
155/83 ... 41, 54
156/83 ... 39, 40, 45, 66
157/83 ... 50, 51, 89, 112
158/83 ... 68
161/83 ... 20, 29, 150
162/83 ... 27
164/84 ... 7
167/84 ... 2, 125, 142
172/84 ... 122, 153
174/84 ... 147
176/84 ... 39, 45, 64
180/84 ... 125, 153
181/84 ... 20, 33
182/84 ... 121, 123, 125, 153
185/84 ... 85, 89
187/85 ... 140
188/84 ... 29, 36, 37
191/85 ... 124, 151
193/85 ... 54
194/85 ... 20, 27
195/85 ... 34, 84, 91, 115
197/85 ... 2, 126, 128, 142
198/85 ... 114, 117
1001/01 ... 76, 89, 148
1002/01 ... 98
1003/01 ... 155
1004/01 ... 148
1005/01 ... 122
1006/01 ... 66
1007/01 ... 74, 122, 147
1014/01 ... 35, 41, 90, 95, 106, 145
1020/01 ... 29, 45, 144
1021/01 ... 122
1038/01 ... 142
1045/02 ... 143
1048/02 ... 142
1051/02 ... 30
1065/02 ... 156
1069/02 ... 36, 81, 106, 140, 156
1077/02 ... 21
1082/02 ... 147
1086/02 ... 7, 59, 141, 153, 156, 176
1087/02 ... 122
1088/02 ... 147, 155
1090/02 ... 42, 62, 143, 147
1096/02 ... 22, 28, 37, 39, 64, 155
1114/02 ... 142, 147
1142/02 ... 62, 76
1169/03 ... 3, 147

1179/03 100
1191/03 122
1214/03 142
1239/04 .... 2, 58
1272/04 155

2

24/77 .... 51, 126
25/78 .... 8, 36, 41
27/77 .... 47, 65, 74, 81, 148
28/78 .... 29, 39, 40, 59, 64, 113, 156
201/85 104
202/86 .... 9, 57, 117
203/86 .... 56, 59
204/86 75
205/86 .... 2, 110
207/86 .... 56, 58, 59, 61
208/86 .... 87, 122
210/86 26
212/86 120
213/86 .... 8, 116
215/86 .... 56, 60
217/86 146
218/86 120
219/86 .... 71, 90
220/87 .... 15, 126
222/87 .... 15, 126
223/87 .... 59, 64, 68
225/87 26
226, 256/87 .... 56, 63, 179
229/87 56
230/87 .... 23, 56, 73, 74
232/87 .... 23, 67
236/87 .... 54, 58, 140
237/87 .... 70, 149, 150, 156
238/87 .... 36, 40, 42
240/87 28
248/87 .... 23, 36, 37, 39, 72
250/87 .... 23, 25, 69
253/87 .... 23, 37, 39, 63, 65, 68, 72
255/87 .... 29, 44
262/87 .... 91, 154
263/87 .... 51, 59, 60, 82
265/87 .... 30, 41
268/87 .... 7, 17
270, 271/88 .... 26, 29, 150
272/88 .... 58, 63
274/88 25
275/88 .... 4, 7, 8, 145
277/88 .... 29, 36, 39, 75
282/88 .... 23, 65
283/88 .... 23, 74
289/88 .... 39, 44, 47, 58, 65, 67, 149
291/88 41
295/88 .... 32, 120
296/88 54
297/88 120
298, 299/88 .... 124, 144

3

30/78 .... 30, 33, 151
32/78 .... 39, 42, 59, 64, 113
33/78 .... 29, 36, 38, 39, 42, 90
34/78 .... 11, 113
35/78 .... 9, 81, 102, 117
37/78 .... 36, 39, 42
305/88 35
307/88 .... 23, 59, 69
309/88 118
314/88 .... 34, 39, 50, 90, 110
316/88 .... 4, 71
317/88 .... 25, 26
318/88 .... 2, 141
319/88 .... 28, 36, 54
320/88 .... 23, 29, 65, 74
321/88 28
322/88 27
326/88 .... 37, 39, 44, 50, 90
327/88 71
328/88 .... 24, 36, 42, 142, 153

330/88 ....23, 39, 45, 47, 63, 72
333/88 ....23, 65
334/88 28
336/88 ....38, 40, 66, 145
338/88 ....33, 64, 67
341/88 ....68, 71
343 - 345/87 177
347/88 ....4, 15, 90
348/89 ....4, 15, 90
349/89 ....23, 56, 63, 149
352/ 1989 188
353/88 ....23, 59, 63, 69, 70, 156
355/89 ....65, 73
356/89 ....23, 65, 69
358/89 3
359, 385/89 ....91, 93, 125, 143
361/89 141
363/89 ....4, 15
366/89 ....27, 36, 37
367/89 148
373/89 ....26, 38, 39, 41
375/89 70
377/89 ....23, 57, 65, 74
379/89 148
380/89 83
381/89 154
383/89 69
385, 359/89 123
386/89 39
387/89 61
390/90 ....22, 65, 74
394/90 ....30, 32
395/90 ....122, 123
396/90 116
397/90 ....96, 99, 144
398/90 ....4, 17, 145

4

4/77 ....11, 27, 36, 42, 150, 155
40/78 88
43/79 ....37, 42, 45, 64
44/79 ... 11, 38, 40, 42, 45, 112, 145
45/79 20
46/79 ....11, 36, 40, 42, 58
49/79 29
400/90 ....78, 79, 107
401/90 ....19, 32
402/90 120
403/90 ....19, 32, 154
407/90 29
408/90 75
410/90 44
412/90 ....76, 90, 97
413/90 ....3, 141
414/90 ....37, 50, 90
415/90 119
417/90 ....100, 104, 144
418/90 ....6, 123
421/90 151
425/90 123
426, 406/90 124
428/90 ....66, 145
429/90 ....19, 142, 143
432/90 ....40, 42, 62
433/90 155
434/90 66
436/90 145
437/90 ....145, 154
438/90 145
439/90 15
440/90 ....29, 145
441/90 ....56, 58, 59, 153
445/91 ....23, 156
446/91 86
447/91 ....40, 66
448/91 ....147, 148
449/91 ....20, 27, 34, 145
450/91 ....56, 83
451/91 63
453/91 ....79, 87

454/91 123
455/91 91
456/91 ....49, 51
458/91 .....25, 28, 30, 35, 36, 90, 94
459/91 ....23, 64, 66, 68
460/91 82
461/91 ....23, 26, 67, 69
467/91 154
468/91 ...34, 37, 39, 50, 57, 60, 151
469/91 ....5, 21, 22, 27
470/91 ....5, 21, 22, 25, 27, 141
473/91 66
477/91 ....123, 143
478/91 ....6, 123, 143
480/91 ....65, 70, 74
483/91 86
488/92 ....6, 80, 119, 143
489/92 ....6, 141
491/92 58
492/92 51
493/92 ....45, 47

5

5/77 .....28, 36, 40, 42, 45, 113, 145
50/79 77
52/79 .....5, 36, 40, 67, 98, 146, 150
55/79 ....77, 143
56/79 ....5, 17, 36, 45, 146
57/79 ....5, 50, 146
58/79 54
500/92 ....111, 112
502/92 141
504/92 ....6, 141
505/92 ....49, 142
509/92 ....19, 30
511/92 ....111, 128, 155
512/92 45
514/92 ....56, 59, 79, 83, 104
518/92 ....90, 94
520/92 142
521/92 39
523/92 ....40, 44, 66
524/92 140
526/93 ...37, 40, 44, 63, 65, 74, 148
527/93 ....26, 44, 144
528/93 ....23, 40, 66, 69
529/93 ....29, 46
532/93 26
533/93 ....40, 45, 46, 66
534/93 73
535/93 ....23, 26
537/93 ....7, 23, 57, 64, 69
538/93 ....30, 53, 80, 101
539/93 ....21, 22, 27, 142
540/93 ....20, 29, 37, 107, 153
541/93 26
542/93 ....29, 34
546/93 ....20, 64, 145, 150
547/93 ....2, 128
549/93 ....80, 100
550/93 ....92, 93
552/93 115
554/93 ....26, 68, 74
555/93 26
558/93 ....30, 53, 80, 140
560/93 ....35, 36, 42, 155
561/93 ....62, 66
563/93 ....8, 20, 27, 37
564/93 ....66, 156
565/93 145
566/93 ....121, 122, 146
567/93 142
568/93 86
569/93 ....30, 44
570/93 ....85, 142, 148
571/94 ....40, 65, 144
572/94 ....23, 69
574/94 ....94, 146
577/94 ....29, 45, 61, 62, 153
578/94 116

579/94 ....78, 116
580/94 ....23, 65
583/94 39
585/94 ....26, 39, 45, 69
586/94 121
587/94 ....26, 28
588/94 ....23, 26, 66, 72
589/94 ....63, 70, 74
590/94 ....26, 38, 39, 44, 66
591/94 ....28, 30, 45
592/94 ....28, 68
594/92 ....23, 44, 69
596/94 ....26, 45, 68
597/94 ....26, 38, 39
598/94 150
599/94 26

6

6/77 ....40, 42
61/79 ....91, 95
63/79 ....40, 141
64/79 ....10, 73
66/80 ....33, 39, 46, 75
67/80 19
68/80 ....81, 100
600/94 26
602/94 ....79, 123, 142
606/94 29
607/94 ....26, 69, 70, 150
608/95 ....6, 118
609/95 29
610/95 ....26, 28, 44, 63, 69, 70
611/95 26
612/95 ....8, 20, 28, 30, 37, 156
613/95 ....26, 34, 39
614/95 ....26, 40, 65
616/95 ....40, 46, 66
617/95 ....40, 45, 66
618/95 ....26, 44, 69
619/95 44
623, 624, 626, 627/95 67
625/95 ....38, 39, 45
628/95 94
630/95 114
631/95 35
632/95 43
633/95 ....90, 92, 94, 98, 110
634/95 26
635/95 ....38, 41
639/95 ....26, 40, 45
640/95 26
641/95 ....8, 115
643/95 121
645/95 ....19, 140, 142
646/95 57
647/95 ....26, 28, 38, 39, 45
649/95 ....26, 39, 45
650/95 155
651/95 124
653/95 ....28, 45
658/95 121
662/95 73
663/95 ....23, 28, 38, 39, 65, 69
664/95 76
665/95 ....40, 65
666/95 120
668/95 ....29, 44, 69, 74
669/95 121
671/95 ....111, 128
672/95 ....26, 40, 66, 156
673/95 26
675/95 53
676/96 ....23, 44, 63, 66, 68
677/96 ....26, 40, 44, 45, 66, 68
678/96 61
680/96 ....28, 45, 58, 74
682/96 ....77, 86
683/96 ....26, 44, 66
684/96 ....27, 45
687/96 ....25, 82

688/96 .... 37, 61
689/96 .... 120, 155
692/96 .... 22, 30, 75
693/96 91
694/96 .... 88, 124
695/96 .... 26, 44, 68, 144
696/96 44
699/96 .... 58, 67, 142

7

70/81 45
73/81 40
74/80 .... 5, 29, 45, 59, 67, 81, 151
75/80 151
77/80 .... 5, 50, 146
701/96 .... 73, 122, 142, 144, 155
702/96 .... 23, 36, 39, 40, 58, 63, 66
704/96 .... 23, 29, 40, 44, 66
705/96 .... 23, 26, 40, 44, 57, 66, 69
706/96 .... 5, 34
707/96 .... 22, 38, 39, 40, 45, 66
708/96 .... 40, 46, 47, 65
709/96 .... 67, 74
710/96 64
711/96 34
714/96 143
716/96 .... 121, 152
719/96 .... 22, 45, 68, 148
720/96 45
721/96 .... 29, 40, 46, 66, 88
726/96 .... 39, 46
727/96 .... 42, 66
728/96 .... 40, 66, 147
730/96 .... 22, 39, 45, 64, 68
731/96 .... 28, 45
732/97 .... 29, 39, 40, 44, 66, 147
733/97 .... 24, 39, 40, 46, 65
734/97 .... 22, 45, 64, 69
736/97 .... 87, 92, 93, 95, 96
737/97 141
743/97 .... 34, 40, 101
744/97 152
746/97 146
747/97 121
749/97 .... 28, 44, 45
750/97 .... 22, 26, 39, 46, 64, 69
752/97 .... 28, 44, 57, 156
754/97 35
755/97 100
757/97 120
759/97 .... 30, 156
761/97 147
762/97 65
763/97 .... 21, 44
765/97 120
767/97 58
768/97 56
770/97 .... 37, 60, 61, 64
771/97 146
774/97 121
775/97 .... 22, 29, 64, 65, 68
777/97 .... 61, 72, 151
778/97 .... 20, 37, 82
780/97 .... 90, 91, 93, 94
781/97 .... 57, 64, 68
786/97 .... 121, 154
787/97 148
788/97 .... 40, 61, 62, 66
789/97 73
792/98 30
794/98 .... 35, 106
796/98 .... 35, 44, 64, 65
798/98 .... 28, 44, 46

8

8/77 .... 11, 36, 40, 42, 94, 145, 151
80/80 .... 30, 68
83/81 45
84/81 .... 21, 39, 145
85/81 .... 45, 145, 150

88/81 145
89/81 .... 75, 85
800/98 .... 47, 48, 104
802/98 .... 4, 66, 76
806/98 .... 23, 26, 45
808/98 .... 145, 152
814/98 .... 60, 115
816/98 .... 124, 142
818/98 .... 29, 41, 44, 65
819/98 .... 58, 62, 116, 122
820/98 .... 101, 107, 108, 147
821/98 .... 20, 34
829/98 .... 8, 21, 156
833/98 .... 51, 54
836/98 73
838/98 .... 23, 40, 66, 68
844/98 147
845/98 56
845/99 15
846/99 59
848/99 .... 59, 67, 70
852/99 .... 36, 39, 68
854/99 .... 123, 148, 154
855/99 119
856/99 .... 7, 36, 42
857/99 .... 118, 121
858/99 100
859/99 .... 21, 34, 52, 156
861/99 122
864/99 66
866/99 122
868/99 .... 27, 46, 155
869/99 .... 59, 141, 176
872/99 146
875/99 .... 66, 77
878/99 .... 46, 48, 86, 89, 118, 146
884/99 .... 112, 156
886/99 .... 27, 144
887/99 .... 27, 144
888/99 30
890/99 144
891/99 147
893/99 .... 101, 145
899/99 .... 41, 66

9

9/77 .... 30, 42
90/81 .... 7, 37, 39, 44
91/81 .... 35, 48, 77, 140
900/99 .... 27, 36
902/99 .... 78, 79, 102, 119, 147
906/00 .... 7, 114
908/00 .... 40, 46, 66
910/00 .... 153, 156
916/00 34
919/00 .... 117, 155
921/00 .... 90, 112
923/00 .... 113, 114
925/00 .... 147, 154
928/00 .... 30, 40, 66, 69
930/00 .... 80, 81, 101, 107, 156
932/00 .... 3, 112, 117
933/00 .... 11, 16, 61, 115
934/00 147
940/00 143
941/00 .... 119, 142, 155
942/00 154
946/00 .... 83, 156
949/00 144
950/00 .... 27, 33, 37, 156
953/00 91
960/00 78
963/01 42
965/00 .... 109, 119, 151
972/01 .... 7, 8, 155
981/01 .... 27, 36, 39, 60, 66, 77
983/01 .... 119, 148
986/01 .... 74, 152, 155
989/01 152
998/01 .... 119, 152

INDEX

A

abduction 33, 36
abortion.....................................19
actio popularis..........................142
administrative detention........33, 78
administrative remedy................20
affirmative action..........9, 116, 127
alien 51, 53, 54, 101, 119
appeal..................................23, 56
arbitrariness...............................34
arrest 33, 34, 37, 63
assembly 96, 97
association.........94, 96, 98, 99, 141
asylum..36

B

bail..61
banishment.................................43
belief..88
birth...107
bonded labour 32

C

cage-beds 43
capital punishment....31, 32, 35, 64
child 32
child-labour..............................105
compensation..20, 42, 75, 118, 121
compulsory labour 32
confession 72
confiscation..............................121
conscience..12, 14, 84, 85, 87, 102, 119
conscientious objection...32, 85, 89
contractual debt..........................48
contractual obligation 12
corporal punishment 30
correspondence....................45, 81
counsel.......................67, 122, 144
crime against humanity..............12
criminal charge 37, 62
criminal offence..........................76
cruel punishment 12
cruel treatment 14, 25, 27
culture.....................................128

D

death penalty............21, 24, 35, 67
death row 26
declaration 15
degrading punishment................12
degrading treatment........14, 25, 27
denunciation of the Covenant.....16
deportation8, 12, 21, 30, 49, 54, 80, 101, 117, 176
detention 33, 34, 106, 144
disciplinary punishment.............41
disciplinary remedy 20
discrimination......5, 9, 11, 81, 101, 103, 106, 116, 118, 125
divorce....................................104
domestic remedy.......154, 155, 156
domestic service 105
domestic violence 34

E

economic offence........................22
education 87, 88, 103, 124
effective remedy 7, 13, 15
election 112, 113
emergency 48
enforced disappearance..............27
enforcement of decisions 8
equality......5, 9, 52, 103, 114, 116, 117, 125

equality of arms 56, 59, 70
execution......................26, 27, 176
exhausten of remedy 147
exile 52
expression ..89, 90, 92, 93, 95, 103, 126
expulsion..12, 49, 54, 80, 101, 106, 107
extradition21, 54, 59, 141, 142, 149

F

faceless judge.............................60
fair trial 14, 22, 56, 58, 59
family......32, 80, 96, 100, 101, 105
family name 103
family planning...........................19
female warder 43
forced labour..............................32
forced recruitment....................105

G

genital mutilation 28
genocide.....................................12
guardian 32

H

hard labour.................................32
health 21, 87
home 81, 82
homosexual couple78, 79, 102, 119
honour.................................18, 82
human dignity 12, 24, 28, 29, 43, 44, 45, 82, 123

I

incitement to discrimination 13, 84, 95
incitement to hostility 13
incitement to violence 13
incommunicado....................29, 45
independence of judiciary...........60
indeterminate detention 34
infanticide..................................18
inhuman punishment..................12
inhuman treatment.........14, 25, 27
interim measures..........................6
interpreter 37, 71

J

juvenile person...............47, 59, 72

L

language..................................126
legal assistance 23, 57, 64
legal minimum age 105
life....................12, 14, 19, 22, 120
life imprisonment.......................35
limitation of rights 13

M

mandatory detention 36
marriage... 14, 32, 78, 79, 103, 119, 122
matrimonial property 9
mental health 46
mental integrity..........................24
military service 19, 86, 120
minority 12, 14, 24, 47, 51, 125, 126, 127
moral..............................87, 88, 95
most serious crime 22
movement 48, 49, 51

N

national security........51, 54, 87, 94
nationality 108
non-discrimination.....................52

O

opinion 89, 90
oral hearing 67
order...25
own defence 20

P

pardon 23, 75
parent 32, 87, 88
parole 35
petition 155
physical health 46
physical integrity 24
political offence 22
political opinion 46, 112
polygamy 123
presumption of innocence....13, 14, 22, 61, 76
pre-trial detention..........................40
preventive detention......42, 62, 143
principle of equality 57
principle of legality........................12
principle of non-discrimination 117, 119
privacy 78, 79, 81, 83, 100
procedural equality 56
propaganda for war ...13, 84, 95, 96
property..142
prostitution 32, 105
psychological torture......................27
public affairs 108
public emergency.....10, 16, 18, 24, 117
public funding................................88
public judgement 59
public life 93
public opinion 110
public order...................87, 94, 112
public safety 87
public security 42
public service........25, 86, 114, 115
publicity of hearing........................59

R

recognition as a person 12
rehabilitation 47, 77
religion........12, 14, 84, 87, 88, 102
religious schools 124
reparation..7
reputation 82
reservation 15, 139
reservation to the Covenant 14
reservation to the Protocol........154
residence 81, 103, 117
residence permit...........................107
restitution of property 120
restriction of rights 13

S

school...88
scientific experimentation............12
secrecy of the vote 113
security 34
self-defence....................................96
self-determination......2, 3, 96, 111, 117, 125, 141
separation.....................................103
serfdom 31
servitude 12
sexual orientation..................6, 119
slave trade 12, 31
slavery 12, 14, 31
social rehabilitation 48, 104
social security 119
solitary confinement 47
spouse 9, 102, 117
state of emergency 7, 11, 49, 87, 95
statement of policy 15
strike 90, 94, 98, 99

suit at law 57, 104

T

targeted killings 20
termination of the Covenant 16
thought 12, 14, 84, 87, 102
torture 12, 14, 25, 27, 28, 30, 150
trade union 98
trial in absentia 58, 67

U

unacknowledged detention 12
undue delay 59, 65

V

vocational guidance 47
vote 108, 111

W

withdrawal from the Covenant 16
women 112
work-council 109, 119

Bernd von Hoffmann (ed.)

Global Governance

Reports and Discussions of a Symposium held in Trier on October 9th and 10th, 2003

Frankfurt am Main, Berlin, Bern, Bruxelles, New York, Oxford, Wien, 2004.
199 pp., num. tab.
Legal Policy Symposium. Edited in the Institut for Legal Policy at the University of Trier by Bernd von Hoffmann and Gerhard Robbers. Vol. 2
ISBN 3-631-52770-5 / US-ISBN 0-8204-7325-1 · pb. € 39. *

While stopping globalisation no longer seems to be a valid option, the task of shaping it has gained priority. But who can effectuate good global governance? The ability of international institutions to provide reliable international structures seems challenged by the recent developments in international politics. What are the implications of the war in Iraq for international law and future global policy? How can governmental and non-governmental actors frame global governance? And what are the prospects of global development policy? These complex questions can only be addressed effectively in an interdisciplinary forum. On October 9th and 10th, 2003, the Institute for Legal Policy at the University of Trier invited notable experts from the disciplines of law, political and economic science to discuss and reflect on these issues. This volume embodies the results of that interdisciplinary workshop on global governance.

Contents: The Status of Public International Law seen from a European Perspective · The UN's Irrelevant Relevance · Globalisation, Politics and the State · The United Nations as an Actor of Globalization · The Role of NGOs in Global Governance: Controlling Corruption – The Example of Transparency International · International Business needs International Rules · The Role of the WTO in Global Development Policy · Findings from the World Bank Corporate Governance Country Assessments · Is Globalisation Detrimental for Developing Countries? · Conclusions